To a brilliant career,

Joe

April 10, 2019

Princeton

SUBVERSIONS
OF
INTERNATIONAL ORDER

SUNY series in
National Identities

Thomas M. Wilson, editor

SUBVERSIONS
OF
INTERNATIONAL ORDER

Studies in the Political Anthropology of Culture

John Borneman

STATE UNIVERSITY OF NEW YORK PRESS

Production by Ruth Fisher
Marketing by Fran Keneston

Published by
State University of New York Press, Albany

© 1998 State University of New York

For information, address the State University of New York Press, State University Plaza, Albany, NY 12246

Library of Congress Cataloging-in-Publication Data
Borneman, John, 1952–
    Subversions of international order : studies in the political anthropology of culture / John Borneman.
        p.   cm. — (SUNY series in national identities)
    Includes bibliographical references and index.
    ISBN 0-7914-3583-0 (hardcover : alk. paper). — ISBN 0-7914-3584-9 (pbk. : alk. paper)
    1. Political anthropology.   2. Political culture.   3. World politics.   4. International relations.   5. National characteristics.
6. Political socialization.   7. Homosexuality—Political aspects.
I. Title.   II. Series.
GN492.B674   1998
306.2—dc21   97-23444
                                                              CIP

10 9 8 7 6 5 4 3 2 1

CONTENTS

Acknowledgments

Grateful acknowledgment is made for permission granted to reprint essays that have appeared in previous publications, sometimes in an earlier form.

Chapter 2, 1995, "Anthropology as Foreign Policy," in *American Anthropologist* 97 (4): 663–671.

Chapter 3, 1988, "Race, Ethnicity, Species, Breed: Totemism and Horse Breed Classification in America," in *Comparative Studies in Society and History* 30 (1): 25–51.

Chapter 4, 1993, "Time-Space Compression and the Continental Divide in German Subjectivity," in *New Formations* (21) 1 (Winter 1994): 102–118; shorter version reprinted in *Oral History Review* 21/2 (Winter 1993): 41–57.

Chapter 5, 1996, "Narrative, Genealogy, and Historical Consciousness: Citizenship in a Disintegrating State," in *Culture/Contexture: Explorations in Anthropology and Literary Study*, eds. E. Valentine Daniel and Jeffrey M. Peck, pp. 214–235 (Berkeley: University of California Press).

Chapter 6, "Grenzregime (Border Regime): The Wall and Its Aftermath," in *1997 Border Cultures: Nation and State at International Boundaries,* eds. Hastings Donnan and Thomas M. Wilson (Cambridge: Cambridge University Press) revised and expanded version of 1995, "Heidi and the Wall," in *Canadian Woman Studies/ les cahiers de la femme* 16 (1): 15–22.

Chapter 7, 1993, "Trouble in the Kitchen: Totalitarianism, Love, and Resistance to Authority," in *Moralizing States and the Ethnography of the Present*, pp. 93–118, ed. Sally Falk Moore (Washington, D.C.: American Ethnological Society Monograph Series).

Chapter 9, 1986, "Emigrees as Bullets/ Immigration as Penetration: Perceptions of the Marielitos," in *Journal of Popular Culture* 20 (3): 73–92.

I owe special thanks to Stefan Senders and Jack Skarbinski who have helped at various stages of this manuscript.

1

Subversions of International Order: An Introduction

Anthropology and Political Order

The transcontinental chaos at the end of the twentieth century calls attention to political disorder and its representation, issues that had been relatively neglected during the Cold War. Established states, nations, and cultures seem to be dissolving and reappearing with an uncanny ease, unsettling belief in the adequacy of descriptive terms and in our ability to comprehend the present. We are witnessing the appearance of curious objects—retroviruses, quarks, and novel kinds of tribal and national identities—that resist facile objectification. I am not alone in noticing a radical sea change in Zeitgeist. Across the humanities and social sciences, we are learning to ask new questions, to develop new positions relative to truth and authority, to participate in what Clifford Geertz nearly twenty years ago dubbed a "blurring of genres." Most analysts agree that 1989 marked the definitive end of the Cold War regime, but they are at a loss as to how to represent the emergent world order. What are the most appropriate units of analysis and descriptive tools? From what framework or theoretical perspective can one best see the present and future contours of political order? The essays in this book present my attempt to develop an anthropological response to these questions. I have made only minor revisions, mostly

1

deleting repetitions in argument and in supporting evidence. Written over nine years, from 1986 to 1995, they also index my own intellectual development over a decade, its merits as well as its limitations.

To study culture as subversion of international order assumes that what we take to be particular cultures are both constitutive and subversive of international order, both alternative versions and subversions of large-scale global orders. In this assumption, I partake in a movement within the discipline of anthropology to contemporize our object and to engage ethnographic inquiry in formulating alternative political responses. Instead of identifying problems posed within simpler societies, we are concerned with forms of complexity; instead of traditional, stateless cultures or culture as resistance to the state, our accent is on identity conflicts imbricated in contemporary forms of state authority; instead of synchronic studies of ethnic solidarity in territorially bounded groups, our emphasis is on the historical dynamics of transnational or global processes such as migration, citizenship, war, and on the dissemination and effects of world ideologies. Critics within anthropology have stressed the need to refine techniques of participant observation (through increased reflexivity), to consider a wider variety of documentary forms (including poetry, film, legal texts, fieldnotes), and to reformulate the vocabulary used to conceptualize contemporary processes. My own response is to place the study of culture in a new thematic matrix that consists of globalization, nationalism, queer studies, and narrative theory, to mention a few key fields.

Describing and theorizing the place of local cultures or of culture-making within world order has always been an anthropological preoccupation, though most ethnologists have done so unsystematically and unselfconsciously. Fin-de-siècle anthropology had specialized on exotic peoples, or threatened and disappearing cultures. Most of these peoples and cultures were thought to be outside the "civilized world" from which the anthropologists themselves came. Nineteenth-century evolutionary schemes that placed peoples on a temporal and spatial developmental scale gradually gave way in the early twentieth century to functionalist accounts that assumed the autonomy and temporal stability of cultural sys-

2

tems. In some quarters, functionalist accounts were replaced, or at least supplemented, by a focus on the historical development of the local within a world system.

By the mid-twentieth century, most anthropologists had agreed to the view of a One World System composed of three interrelated parts: First World (developed, free, capitalist), Second World (developed, unfree, communist), and Third World (undeveloped). After World War II, anthropological research tended to follow the same exotic peoples who had been chosen at the end of the nineteenth century, peoples now placed in the Third World. In a neat academic division of labor, sociology and political science took for themselves the axis of Cold War power, the First and Second Worlds and relations between them. Hence relations between First and Third World peoples became a prominent focus of the discipline of anthropology. It was out of this extremely unequal relationship between observer and observed, and based on scholarly representations that frequently legitimated First World domination, that anthropological theory developed. Consequently, anthropologists tended to ignore the Second World, and to a large extent their own, but in particular they ignored relations between the First and the Second Worlds.

Given their concentration on peoples primarily located in the Third World, many anthropologists after World War II took up study of the decolonization processes in which their primary objects of research were involved. Because of this focus, anthropological contributions to understanding the making of the Cold War order have been minimal. Yet the two processes, of decolonization and Cold War ordering, though spatially distinct are temporally and thematically inseparable. For one, decolonization in places so disparate as India and Nigeria, for example, was always followed by a process of nation building, and the nation became the project of the former colony, deflecting its attention from both continued dependence on the former colonial power and new processes of internal stratification. For another, neither the loss of colonies nor the heat of the Cold War put a stop to nation building in First and Second World states; instead, these processes served to redirect and even consolidate older nations, such as France and Germany in the First, Poland and Bulgaria in the Second. In the First, and to a lesser extent Second, World, external decolonization was often followed by processes of internal colonization—the growth of the welfare state and in some places the movement of colonized peoples from their homes in the periphery to London, Paris, Brussels, and Moscow, the centers of the (former) empires.

Meanwhile, from 1945 to 1992 the number of internationally recognized sovereign states, each claiming its own nation, grew exponentially from 51 to 184. During the Cold War, newer nation-states, much as the older ones, had no choice but to choose sides, or to play the sides off against each other, notwithstanding the attempts of the Nonaligned Movement to find a position elsewhere. Hence, decolonization, whatever its local aims or goals, could never proceed independent of Cold War order. Group legitimacy depended on the ability to approximate national form. And nations could take form only within an inter-national order. Still, the process of nation formation was never as coherent in practice as it was in its representational forms. From the inevitable push and pull in different directions, national versions and their subversions were produced one after another.

My first attempt to deal with this complex of problems, in field research conducted from 1986 to 1989, resulted in *Belonging in the Two Berlins*, where I examined the project of kinship formation, nation building, and political authority during the Cold War in the two Germanys. At the same time, I edited and co-translated *Gay Voices from East Berlin*, a book articulating alternative sexual subjectivities at that time hidden from the eyes of the "free world." Even before these books were actually in print, however, my own project had shifted to an interest in the disintegration of identities and nations in the terminal stages of the Cold War order. In fact, I came to realize only in hindsight, while beginning a project on Berlin's repatriated German Jews in 1989, that the Cold War order I had been witnessing while living in East and West Berlin was already in an advanced stage of decomposition. "1989" only accelerated this dynamic, which I sought to explain in *After the Wall*, written between December 1989 and April 1990. Whereas ethnographers have long been interested in endangered and disappearing worlds, their regnant framework of cultural relativism and the listing of culture traits seemed inappropriate to my project, which

4

was to describe an unintended revolutionary transformation. And while anthropologists had long been active in constructing models of cultural continuity and change, they had not taken up the macro-themes which had occupied other scholars of the *Ostblock*: the totalitarian collective body, mass terror, Communist utopian revolutions. Above all, I could not imagine myself engaged in a nostalgic recovery of a particular tribal, ethnic, or national identity, which, regrettably, has become the project of not only many former socialist scholars and residents in those states but also of many of their counterparts in the First World. Situated at this intersection of the No Man's Land of a disappearing First–Second World and an academy that has largely not positioned itself to describe this world critically, my own work has necessarily been idiosyncratic, or, in the full sense of the word, "queer."

Making Culture and International Order

For several decades now, many anthropologists have been mourning for the "good old days" of representing cultures as totalistic, autonomous, self-reproducing wholes. This genre found its perhaps most elegant expression with the publication in 1934 of Ruth Benedict's *Patterns of Culture*, in which she represented cultures as unified Dionysian or Apollonian personalities. There has been a long history of critique of this particular form of representing peoples and cultures, with many contributors to the debates. But only in reaction to the critique of this form of representation in *Writing Culture*, edited by Jim Clifford and George Marcus and published in 1986, did the mourning sentiment begin to crystallize into a wave of nostalgia for the tried and true representational forms of the past.

Between 1934 and 1986 (my own rough dating for forms of Cold War representation), anthropologists in Britain, France, and the United States had come up with a standard formula for representing the world. Inspired by the geopolitics of Herder and the spirit of Rousseau, they agreed on a "cultural gardens" approach, as Johannes Fabian (1984) has characterized it. They chronicled indigenous (usually stateless) cultures as communities of customs,

5

habits, and traditions, and then equated these cultures with expressiveness, critique, even emancipation. In the postwar period, some anthropologists did indeed work with political authorities, but only an exceptional few thought they were working for the state. To the extent that they included interaction with states in fieldwork descriptions, they tended to situate political authorities in opposition to authentic "cultures," which they then proposed to represent. In fact, the norm among anthropologists continues to privilege distance from the state, as if spatial proximity is polluting and to be avoided at all costs. Such distancing from political authority has been based on a general suspicion that most governments are intent on either assimilating or annihilating authentic cultures, or on denying "indigenous peoples" rights and entitlements. However warranted, this suspicion does not justify representing folk cultures as authentic, organic, timeless, and apolitical. Of course there was no universal agreement about this folk model, as Peter Worsley, Eric Wolf, Eleanor Leacock, and Claude Meillasoux, to name but four major figures, proposed alternative representations involving Marxist-inspired world systems theory.

Today, faith and security in the culturalist form of representation has been so undermined within anthropology that only people in other disciplines and fields dare to employ it without some gesture to self-criticism. Many political scientists and sociologists, for example, have begun to embrace "culture" (or even its predecessor "civilization") as an independent variable, a (good) stabilizing factor or alternately the (evil) factor that stimulates change and exacerbates conflict. Culture, then, is either a "component," a set of symbols separable from measurable economic or political processes, or it is a whole used to explain the dynamic relations between the "nation," the "people," and the "state." These latter units are now too fluid and already too "deconstructed" to be convincing as a prior, empirical base that generates current international disorder. When influential analysts in other fields, such as the political scientist Sam Huntington (1993: 22–49) in "The Clash of Civilizations?" or the journalist Robert Kaplan (1994: 44–76) in "The Coming Anarchy," do employ the Cold War vision of the world as stable cultural gardens or ecological niches to understand political order, they seem to speak to contemporary needs to see the world in terms of Benedict's

6

1934 vision. They seek the security in a nostalgic view of coherent cultures in the Second and Third Worlds, but instead they are threatened by sights of fragmentation and lost order: tribalism, civilizational struggle, fundamentalism, anarchy. In a *New Yorker* review of Huntington and Kaplan, Philip Gourevitch (1996: 8) lumps them together with several other "misfortune tellers" (including Benjamin Barber (1995) and Hans Magnus Enzensberger (1994)), accusing them all of "proceeding from generality to generality without providing convincing access to the particular; . . . they are selling fear more than understanding."

An underlying assumption of these "misfortune tellers" is that expressive cultures are unified wholes in natural opposition to national states, although such cultures are now also frequently assumed to be self-interested political actors themselves actively in search of either collective citizenship rights and benefits or of their own states. This culturalist vision remains extremely powerful and convincing despite the fact that the world clearly never has been and never will be ordered accordingly. Analysts employing this vision inevitably reduce world tensions to fights between ahistorical cultures (Arab and Jew, Tamil and Sinhalese, Hutu and Tutsi, Serb and Muslim, American and Japanese), between cultures and states, or to clashes between civilizations (Europe and China, the West and the Orient) in a caricature of the actors involved.

What makes these new culturalists everybody's darlings? Their popularity rests, I suspect, on the easy-to-understand cartoonish nature of their cultural and political models. Their writing mimics Roy Liechtenstein's paintings: simple figures drawn in clear outline who speak everyday truths in short bubbles of discourse that float above the scenes portrayed. We are definitely outside these scenes, yet they are easy to "read." Such cartoon forms demand representation in sound bites of conversation or images for contemplation that television and radio journalists can use: much as Clark Kent turns Lois Lane down again, Saddam Hussein says "no" to U.N. negotiators. The work of such cartoonists would be innocent enough if it remained in museums or the academy, or even in the fantasy world of the culturalists—but it does not. These forms of representation enter public life quickly and reorder it. They are Xeroxed, faxed, wired, picked up by the world's media networks and advertising

7

artists and put into international circulation where they ineluctably lead to the stabilization of prejudices and to the proposal of false solutions to problems of inter- and intra-cultural tensions, genocide, economic crises, and political authority.

I am not here trying to exculpate anthropologists for their responsibility in creating cleaner, more classical, more elegant representations of culture. The fact is, however, that an entire generation of young American anthropologists has now deserted this mode of image production, leaving in its wake a contemporary void into which other disciplines have stepped by simply appropriating this older version of anthropological representation. Since it is impossible to do away with this archetypical form of cultural representation, with all its allure and power, the question for anthropology becomes how to subvert it. Is it possible to fill the need for understanding cultural complexity and political order without reducing peoples to stereotypes and caricatures? How can one make convincing pictures that explain and account for self-understandings without reproducing them and without resorting to cartoons?

One response to the critique of culturalism has been to focus on the relation of the global to the local. Even here, though, the "condition of postmodernity" (Harvey 1989; Jameson 1983) has made the positing of separate local and global spaces less than useful. If the global now consistently penetrates local space, just as quickly and readily the local seems to become global. Ulf Hannerz (1992), for one, has characterized this process as "creolization," part of a new "global ecumene." At the end of the twentieth century, most Coca Cola is produced and drunk outside the United States, and it makes little sense to dismiss calls for free speech in China as the imposition of Western ideals. Both Coca Cola and free speech are categories of things that not only shuttle between local and global but are located simultaneously at both levels. They are categories of things as transnational and controversial as are "the family," "mother's brother's uncle," and phallic authority. The same can be said for Andean music, United Nations peacekeepers, nationalism, tourism, gay identity, Marielito refugees, horse breeds, and the Greenhouse Effect. To be sure, anthropologists can always find isolated examples of localisms that resist appropriation outside the contexts of their production,

8

and of globalisms that leave little imprint on the local. Still, it no longer makes much sense to set global and local in opposition to each other when describing most of what we see. As Arjun Appadurai (1990: 15) suggests, local primordia, "sentiments whose greatest force is in their ability to ignite intimacy into a political sentiment," have now become a global force.

Nor does it make sense, however, to collapse global and local processes into vectors, flows, and imaginary scapes. People everywhere continue to invest in objects that appear to have their own integrity; they continue to understand meaning in terms of parochial definitions of kin, color, and property—and this very specificity of objects in a field of power is the precondition for any vector or flow to take place. The so-called modular effect, the copying of things like the nation or rock music or territorial sovereignty in places far removed in time and space from the original situation of production, often confuses social scientists into thinking that they have identified the same thing everywhere. Marshall McLuhan's (1964) seductive vision of the medium controlling the message, of a global village where people's local differences would become negligible due to media standardization, has proven to be an extremely misleading conceptualization of the emergent world order. Experience may be globally inflected through the use of identical technologies, but it is always lived locally, in concrete surroundings, regardless of how convinced some people are of their own otherworldly, extraterrestrial, virtual reality, or of their cosmopolitan sensibilities. At least this is what most ethnographic studies consistently tell us.

Hence, we are left with the task of situating the local and global in relation to one another without either assuming an opposition between levels or collapsing the two into one, or ignoring the political field in which they generate meaning. Ethnographers are uniquely positioned to locate the global in the local, and vice versa. Most anthropological research is framed and conducted in a way that mirrors the dialectical process whereby objects, persons, and things shuttle between local and global spaces. Although there has always been a movement within anthropology encouraging certain categories of people (primarily "indigenous," "minority," or "Third World") to study themselves, most anthropological knowledge has

9

focused around a foreign-identified researcher generating knowledge about self-identified natives. It is this aspect of culture making that I address in "Anthropology as Foreign Policy," first delivered in abbreviated form as a talk, titled "Rethinking Anthropological Coherence," on a circus-like panel intended to present an inter-generational and inter-national dialogue at the American Anthropological Association Meetings in Washington, D.C., November 1993.

What distinguishes anthropology from other disciplines is its direct and unavoidable confrontation with the distinction between foreign and native. Anthropologists consistently produce not merely particular but privileged knowledge, meaning knowledge distinct from that in other disciplines, through a singular, accidentally discovered method and because of the challenge to construct a particular object. That *method* is fieldwork: face-to-face interactions requiring some kind of sensory experience, in time at a particular place, of the person or peoples one seeks to describe. That *object* is the "human" or "humanness," formerly called "man." In the Enlightenment tradition, anthropology's challenge has been to adumbrate humans in a continuous process of unmaking and remaking man. We do this, I suggest, by distinguishing the native (or us) from the foreign (or them).

Anthropologists happened onto this experiential and participatory method accidentally as they took up the task of describing and documenting people who had no written texts. Our ethnographic pioneers, such as Bronislaw Malinowski, whom everyone credits as the father of modern fieldwork, were forced to interact with the natives. With no alternative but to use themselves as instruments of research in intensive fieldwork, they were constantly confronted with the impossibility of the Enlightenment goal of methodological objectivity through distance from the object of study. The discipline has come a long way in developing and critiquing this method. In the process, anthropologists have largely rejected Alfred C. Haddon's Torres Straits method (1888–1899) of interviewing natives by having them brought to his tent, Ruth Benedict's wartime culture-from-a-distance reading of texts, and Robert Murdoch's postwar Human Area Relations File of systematized comparison of the world's distribution of culture traits. But these rejections have not led to a unified method of fieldwork, and the discipline remains in this sense experimental.

10

One of the responses to the contemporary critique of participant observation has been to embrace textual analysis and to prioritize "representations" over practices. Such a return to textual authority often marks a parallel movement away from face-to-face interaction. It also ends up fudging the distinction between representations and discursive practices. Documenting practices requires dealing with the problematic but ethnographically indispensable categories of "experience," "being there," "participation," and "observation." My response has been not to see texts and representations as an alternative to participant observation but to seek ways of incorporating them into the interactive fieldwork setting. Given the proliferation of new, powerful forms of non–face-to-face interaction, the kinds of ethnographic methods today must necessarily vary as widely as the types of processes and peoples which ethnographers try to describe. Anthropology toward the end of the twentieth century is characterized by eclecticism in methodological approach and problem selection. At the same time, it coheres around a reflexive project that is just as important now as it was at the end of the nineteenth century: adumbrating the human.

"Race, Ethnicity, Species, Breed" is an early attempt of mine to relate the local and global in the way suggested above. Written originally in 1985 as an attempt to theorize part of my own history, it is simultaneously an ethnographically-informed reflexive history, a comparative sociology, and a critique of anthropological theory. I begin with native categories and local practices of horse breeding and performance, a field in which I worked professionally for eight years before becoming an anthropologist. I examine these practices in light of anthropological theories of totemism and demonstrate that animal and human classifications (of race and ethnicity) in the United States cannot be understood independent of the history of nation-state formation. When U.S. American horse breeding practices are compared to those in France and Germany, it becomes clear that all three cases are interrelated yet each nation has its own peculiarities. The specificity of each case is explained in terms of the dynamic processes by which three unstable units—"state," "nation," "horse breeding and performance"—take on durable form over time.

Ethnographic work that deals with larger world systems risks losing the feeling for concreteness, for the evocation of experience of particular people at a particular time. To avoid this risk, I situate the historical development of national orders in the actual experience of horse breeds, in the categories of breeding and performance as they are practiced in everyday life and in ritual. The local experience of breeds is then related to the categorization of peoples in the United States, which in turn is illuminated by comparing this relation to a different though interrelated set of experiences of breeds and peoples in Europe. Even the category European ("Continental" in U.S. American jargon) has different local inflections, which I specify at the French and German national levels. Further, accounts of the various national categories and experiences required an explanation of state-building processes.

This essay reformulates the relation of culture to international order with several postulates. First, that anthropological concepts such as "totemism" are equally appropriate and enlightening when applied to complex "Western" societies, and perhaps only in this reflexive application can one understand their full utility and limitations. Second, that the utility of anthropological concepts is best illustrated not in the synchronic study of isolated societies but when informed by a comparative historical sociology. Third, by using this mundane example of the relation between horse breeding and performance and racial/ethnic classification, I demonstrate that international order does not exist as a practice outside of local categories. Rather, local practices generate national and international political orders, which in turn work to refashion the local into a simulacrum of the international. In this refashioning, the national of course fails measured by its own goals, for local variations are never fully uniformized through the discursive practices of the nation or the international; yet one cannot deny the singular influence of the national on local category formation.

National Identities in a Disintegrating Political Order

Increasingly dissatisfied with the old binaries of culture/individual, modern/traditional, global/local, public/private, and state/society, many anthropologists have begun to talk of subjectivities, flows, polyvocality, and multiple identities. This shift is particularly wel-

12

come with reference to the study of nations and national identifications. Most anthropologists no longer consider the nation form the sole property of the state, since both states and local societies claim its loyalties and insist the nation belongs to them. Traditional state-centric studies tended to assume that national pomp replaced local ritual, modernity replaced tradition, and public replaced private. With respect to the states and societies of East-Central Europe during the Cold War, such a perspective led to the belief that "civil society"—intermediate institutions between state and individual will—was either weakened or had virtually disappeared, and therefore all that was left to observe was the state (meaning pomp, modernity, and public routine). Because a sudden dissolution or radical transformation of these states marked the end of the Cold War, analysts with state-centric perspectives were left attributing change either to pressures from foreign (capitalist and socialist) states or to internal contradictions within (socialist) states. While both external pressures and internal contradictions certainly entered into the dynamic collapse of Central-Eastern European states, it is singularly absurd to assume that Cold War states existed in social vacuums, responsive only to themselves and other states.

It is true that *Ostblock* states had very little independent "civil society," as the term is conventionally applied to Western Europe and the United States. Parent-teacher associations were usually run by Party members, Boy Scouts were organized around a Young Pioneer model of socialist brotherhood rather than a Horatio Alger self-help story, religious groups were regularly harassed and infiltrated by the state, oppositional political groups were outright banned. But it is just plain wrong to claim that the organizations of civil society that are independent of the state are somehow more civil and friendly to society than those influenced or controlled by the state. Hitler's Storm Troopers, an intermediate uncivil organization that sought to undermine the democratic Weimar state, particularly its civil society, differs negligibly from Mao's Red Guard, a state-directed group that sought to intimidate civil society. The relevant question is not who controls social groups in public life but for whom, for what purposes, with what results. The current proliferation of uncivil, anti-state organizations in many parts of the

13

world, including the United States, should make us doubt both the utility of assuming a cross-cultural state/society antagonism and the cross-cultural civility of civil societies.

It is also true that First and Second World states during the Cold War regularly exaggerated their self-importance, often convinced themselves (and scholars who studied them) of this illusion, and accordingly ignored the lived realities of the people whom they supposedly represented. Hence the legacy of environmental catastrophes, bloated governments, and peoples extremely suspicious of governmental legitimacy. But because "the people" in the *Ostblock* had never disappeared during the Cold War (but were only represented that way), they are not today readily amenable to re-creation in the heralded U.S. American model of weak state-civil society—private life and culture. Rather, there exists a plurality of forms of individual and group identification with states, old and new, and these forms are now in rapid flux. Today the readily observable subjectivities of peoples in the First and Second World—irrespective of which collective form they take, such as families, clans, tribes, classes, ethnicities, races—are the result of reciprocal influences of individuals with state structures in the reproduction of the nation form.

The three essays in this section analyze the attempt to define national identities in Berlin at a time of disintegrating political order. If the national form of belonging is the result of reciprocal influences of state doctrine and individual experience, then how does this form coalesce and change at a time of competition for and rapid disintegration of state loyalties? How do the resulting national identifications themselves function as political processes to reconstitute, in turn, states, local societies, national and international orders? In this I have not followed Ernest Gellner's top-down focus on centralized education, industrialization, and the creation of national homogeneity, nor Benedict Anderson's emphasis on print-capitalism, territorial mapping, museums, and census taking, nor Katherine Verdery's concentration on intellectual discourse and ideology, to refer readers to three alternative approaches that have much to offer. Additionally, while other analysts see national identities as fixed in semiological systems, which then can be analyzed in terms of a self-contained cognitive or cultural system separate

14

from political order, or a habitus that encloses the national, I have insisted on studying the nation as a set of public practices that are generated and made sense of in the so-called private life of the domestic sphere. Moreover, each nation is a non-autochthonous unit, always forming as part of an international order.

"Time-Space Compression and the Continental Divide in German Subjectivity" analyzes the sequences in East and West German experience of "time-space compression"—the quickening of time, the collapse of spatial barriers—in the first three years following the opening of the Wall. Here I do not restrict myself to single individuals but consider elaborate collective identity formations that continue to work within Cold War processes, despite the formal end of the Cold War. Above all, these processes include East-West mirror-imaging and a dialectic of asymmetrical recognition. I examine the way in which the occasion of the opening as well as events in the year following it—primarily the currency reform and political elections—affected a reordering of temporal and spatial categories in both East and West Berlin. During the Cold War, the East and West created the effect of being outside and external, whereas they were in fact inside and internal, to each other: the other was always already there. In the push for formal unity, East and West Germans began representing themselves as kin reuniting, denying or misconstruing the differences that had been created in the forty years of political division and cultural demarcation. Two separate peoples, internally marked with each other's differences yet each with its own set of dispositions, were suddenly assumed to be equal parts of a national whole. Unification between East and West unfolded in a process similar to a "first encounter," as a sequence of eroticization, striptease, and an incomplete funeral/burial of the East.

"Narrative, Genealogy, and Historical Consciousness" examines a single autobiographical account of East Berliner Susan R. as she attempts to narrate her life in September 1989. At this moment the state and society in which she lives are disintegrating and her citizenship and nationality are rapidly losing coherence. I focus not so much on the ethnographer and text produced as on the processes of narrativization during the telling, that is, on the act of authorship or inscription of identity. This analysis is used to make an argument about method and interdisciplinary: that the relationship between

15

anthropology and literary studies is not merely one of convenience but necessary and indispensable. The two disciplines are interrelated through the process of narrativity, the method of genealogy, and the condition of historical consciousness, all of which presuppose one another in a mutual practice centered around the production and interpretation of narrative texts. Susan R.'s telling demonstrates that the ethnographic encounter is extremely revealing precisely at the moment of inscription of experience, when Susan R. struggles for self-articulation and definition, in other words, before her story obtains coherence. I conclude from this analysis that the inescapable embeddedness of the fieldwork situation in the present should not be seen as a problem to overcome. Instead, the moment of inscription in a fieldwork situation is a fundamental and specifically anthropological source of knowledge. Today, when national and international political orders are unstable and disintegrating, or, to paraphrase Marx, when all that is solid melts into thin air, anthropological knowledge produced through fieldwork is limited only if one seeks fixed, self-reproducing cultures and unchanging traditions. Alternatively, if anthropologists pay attention to struggles for articulation, the moment of inscription itself, then they are positioned to observe or document firsthand the processes of disintegration and reconstruction of order.

"Grenzregime (Border Regime): The Wall and Its Aftermath" traces the experience of the collapse of the "dual organization" of Germany in the life of one woman and her three daughters. Born in 1944 in Cottbus, Heidi is one of those women on whose labor the socialist state had staked its future. This essay analyzes the changes in her relation to the state as it loses its Utopian vision. Raised with cradle-to-grave security, she eventually decides to move to an insecure life in the West but only manages to obtain an exit visa for November 11, 1989. The Wall is opened three days before. I fashion Heidi's story to address the peculiarities of balancing liberty and security while living along the border in a "border regime" during the Cold War and its aftermath. Borders, I conclude, are the products of ambivalent and multiple inputs; they are fortuitously constructed and dismantled because of contradictory processes that simultaneously support and undermine their continued existence.

16

Resistance and Opposition to Authority

In this section, I ask not only what it means to construct a subjectivity within a state, or to reformulate one in a disintegrating state, but what it means to attempt to construct one in opposition to the state. The first essay takes up modes of critical leftist resistance to authority in East Germany during the Cold War, the second traces this resistance generationally in an attempt to understand the generation of contemporary forms of radical-right wing resistance to authority in the unified Germany. Both essays situate forms of resistance in their particular times and places, and in their relation to the key ideologies of this century (totalitarianism, fascism, communism, and democracy) and to institutions of legitimate authority (e.g., states, the media, supranational organizations).

"Trouble in the Kitchen" examines the efficacy of forms of resistance to genres of state authority in East and West Germany during the Cold War. It compares two sets of relationships in East and West: that between citizens and the state generally, and that between self-proclaimed dissidents or resisters and the state. In East Germany, the dominant genre in which authority was represented and legitimated in relations between state and citizen was romance, in contrast to West Germany, where satire was the dominant genre. Use of one or the other genre by the state in law and public policy created different generational dynamics and therefore different modes of identification and resistance. Satire has proven to be a more effective form of authority in dealing with resistance than romance because of its particularism, with roots in the local, in contrast to romanticism, which is abstract and universalistic. As a consequence, satire must first recognize or acknowledge difference before undermining it, whereas romance, due to its basically monologic and narcissistic idealism, is rooted in a denial of reality.

The final part of the essay focuses on resistance to romantic forms of authority and examines the relative efficacy of the responses of three self-proclaimed dissidents in the East German state. The first response was what I call a "hetero sex withdrawal into a private niche," the second a satiric response of modernist resistance, the third a postmodernist response. I argue that the most important criterion for efficacy is whether actions provoked reactions and repressions by the state. In the latter two cases, both kinds of dissidents forced the state to show that it relied on coercion for its legitimacy, which, in turn, revealed dangerous knowledge about the limitations of its control—and, I would argue, accelerated its loss of legitimacy. Moreover, the "dissident" was neither an emic nor etic invention, neither merely a result of some autonomous free will nor merely a reaction to the dominant authority, but a complicitous category, a supranational product of Cold War competition between states and their nationals over the legitimacy of political representation. I conclude that the end of the Cold War is likely to mean a universalization of forms of satiric authority, as well as an end to romantic authority and to forms of resistance tied to it, such as those of revolutionary action.

"Education after the Cold War" asks how to explain the right-wing violence following unification of the two Germanys. In particular, does this violence illustrate a repetition compulsion, and if not, what is it a result of? Intellectuals in the two Cold War Germanys had developed different positions with regard to eliminating the preconditions for Nazi crimes, with the Federal Republic arguing for more democracy, and the German Democratic Republic (GDR) maintaining a position that the proper response to fascism entailed the elimination of capitalism and anti-fascist education, especially in the schools. This essay depicts the relation to authority of three generations of East German intellectuals as part of an inquiry into the conditions that made possible a Cold War and how to educate to prevent its repetition. I argue that both "more democracy" and the "elimination of capitalism and anti-fascism" were examples of successful education after World War II, but that successful education after the Cold War must begin by acknowledging a different set of historical problems. Hence, the violence in Germany today should not be seen as a repetition of old antagonisms suddenly allowed to resurface, the "eruption of the past," as it is often put, but as a new phenomenon, a product not of fascism, nationalism, and World War II but of the Cold War. Postunification violence in the East and the West must be understood not as a repetition of repressed aggression and traditions rooted in "Auschwitz" but as generated by the disintegration of mechanisms that structured Cold War order. Violence is being "regenerated" because of post-unity problems: lost orientation, fear of the future, economic and status insecurities growing out of present concerns. Today, I argue, intellectuals, especially those in the West, have a special responsibility to take insecurities—regardless of their "real" status or origin—seriously instead of demonizing or humiliating people in the East, or trivializing the concerns of disenchanted youths.

Territorial Sovereignty and Its Violation

The final set of essays examines the effects of the principle of territorial sovereignty on European and American order, respectively. They take sexual practices and movement of peoples as objects of analysis, specifically male rape of men and ethnic cleansing in Europe and responses to an international border crossing of homosexually identified men in the United States. Both essays investigate border sites where the principle of territorial sovereignty is most vulnerable, therefore frequently violated and at the same time most transparently asserted as necessary.

Many contemporary ethnographers are studying the state from the Weberian perspective that focuses on increasing technical rationality, power and control, and interactions with bureaucracies. Another Weberian question, that of state legitimacy and violence, is of equal if not more importance. A focus on legitimacy redirects us from top-down or bottom-up models to the reciprocal effects of the state and citizen on the formation of national practices in everyday life. In both essays, I begin with sexuality—sexual fantasies, practices, and identities—not because I consider it prior to other social identifications or relations but because it is the one set of discursive practices that is constantly evoked to speak about and legitimate relations of domination in particular social orders. It never fails to be there. And it doesn't speak "mere gibberish either" but screams, as Maurice Godelier (1986: 232–233) argues in his analysis of the New Guinea Baruya. Indeed, Godelier concludes, "sexuality is an indiscreet screaming chamber for relations of oppression and exploitation. " I wish to ask how sexuality functions as the "screaming chamber" through which the practices of genocide and illegal movements of people are both represented and constituted. How does sexuality function to legitimate "the social order to which it is obliged to submit" (Godelier 1986: 232)? In events such as genocide and immigration, one can observe the state reasserting the principle of territorial sovereignty, which the international system represents as its generative principle of legitimate order. Because territorial sovereignty is intricately tied to sexuality, both the state and social groups involved speak, or scream, through the discursive practices of sexuality. In doing so, the state reveals its strategies for constructing particular people and, because some sexuality always escapes attempts to control it, these events also indicate the limits of the state's ability to control sex. Exploring these limits might direct anthropological analysis to alternative categories and practices where change is possible or even likely.

"Emigrees as Bullets/Immigration as Penetration" takes as its object the Marielitos, a group of Cuban refugees from a 1980 boatlift, and it examines how three groups of Americans perceived these emigrees. In contrast to the extremely generous welcome U.S. Americans had given to former groups of Cubans who had escaped to the United States, the Marielitos were received with ambivalence. The key to this ambivalent perception was that approximately 10,000 of the 120,000 emigrees were self-described homosexuals. Whereas the generic "Cuban refugee" had always been welcome in the United States, the category "Cuban homosexual" prompted an open conflict between U.S. American positive valorization of Cuban escapees and negative valoration of homosexuals. A heretofore political event—reception of Cuban refugees—was interpreted in a psychosexual idiom, which in turn created the possibility for shifts in the semantic content of both categories, of emigrees and homosexuals.

"Toward a Theory of Ethnic Cleansing" begins a genealogy of the historical and local expressions and effects of two pan-European institutions: territorial sovereignty and heterosexuality. If ethnic cleansing is an old European practice that grew out of the state's vision of a homogeneous nation, then what specific institutions continue to motivate it? And under what circumstances might these institutions be influenced to change? The first part of the essay asks about the influence of international or European principles and structures on Yugoslavia's dissolution, and vice versa, the significance of Yugoslavia's dissolution to Europe. Here I argue that the peoples in the former Yugoslavia, specifically in the Bosnian war, were motivated by reproductive heterosexuality and a principle of territoriality. They then employed ethnic cleansing as a method to organize themselves according to the principles of territorial sovereignty and national homogeneity in order to become properly European. Therefore, the post-1990 division of Yugoslavia into separate states with peoples imagined as culturally distinct—Bosnia's ethnic cleansing being merely the means—is a necessary (though not sufficient) condition for admittance of these peoples into the European order as presently conceived.

The second part of the essay examines the way anthropologists in the past have constituted Europe as an object, and, given this history of a relationship, it sketches a possible anthropological response to "Yugoslavia." Via comparison of contemporary violence in Bosnia with parallel forms in pre-1945 Germany, I demonstrate that the institutions of territorial sovereignty and European heterosexuality generate the categories and inter-national forms that both motivate and make sense of ethnic cleansing, including rape as its most violent expression. The German example illustrates that these institutions are historical, hence under certain conditions subject to change.

Reception

Finally, I wish to address the general reception of my work, so as to situate it in the fields of knowledge it addresses. Every article in this volume, as well as my books, was already reviewed by at least two anonymous reviewers before initial publication. Let me emphasize that despite the shortcomings of the standard American review process, which I will go into below, I find no superior alternative to the practice of anonymous reviewing. Nonetheless, how my work has been reviewed may illustrate some of the peculiarities of this practice at a time when genres and disciplinary boundaries are blurred. Let me deal with two of these peculiarities. First, because few anthropologists work in northern Europe, and even fewer on Germans in Germany, journal and book editors have sent

most of my work either to non-area specialists or to advanced graduate students doing research on things German in other fields such
as sociology, political science, and literature. Unlike most anthropologists, I do not, then, belong to a circle of acquaintances—methodological, theoretical, or area-based—who reciprocally review each
other's work. In other words, at least to 1995, most of my work has
been reviewed anonymously by non-anthropologists.

The most unusual review process was perhaps of *Belonging in
the Two Berlins* for Cambridge University Press. The editor, Jes-
sica Kuper, sent the manuscript to three anthropologists: a senior
American-based British editor (who specializes in Greece) and two
German-based Germans (who work in Italy and Pakistan, respectively). The two Germans were quite clearly being asked for a judg-
ment not merely as anthropologists but also, and perhaps primarily,
as natives. I applaud the boldness of Kuper's choice and would
hope that natives in other places might be given more opportunity
to critique anthropological work about them. As "area specialists,"
few if any anthropologists can obtain the depth of knowledge that
academic natives have. Certainly, I have benefitted from reviews
by German natives of this book and of articles. The more intriguing
question is: to what extent did the natives feel confident that they
could rely on their personal knowledge to challenge an academic
work? Or alternately, did they feel compelled to give their authority
an academic cover? In his book review, one native explictly situated
himself within one of the generational narratives of my manuscript, the other did not use his personal knowledge but instead
criticized from a more distanced, scholarly position. Only after I
had met the latter person several years later did I begin to realize
what I had missed, because he did not feel it appropriate in a
review to situate himself within my description.

Questions about my ethnographic authority to describe things
German go well beyond the nativeness of the reviewer, for there
remains—notwithstanding a recurrent romance with ethnographic
accounts—a great deal of skepticism among non-anthropologists
about the value of participant observation. This leads me to the
second peculiarity: reviewers tend to ignore evidence I use that is
ethnographically based and instead focus nearly entirely on the
authority of cited or uncited written texts. Although ethnographic

inquiry still enjoys a relatively unquestioned authority in describing (primarily oral) practices in Melanesia and Polynesia, it has never attained such an authority in northern Europe. In the past, this may have been all for the good in protecting Europeans from their own totalizing and circular forms of description, but, at least for the last decade, anthropologists have preferred partial and situated knowledge to more totalistic claims, regardless of where they worked. Moreover, scholars employ a different kind of uncritical authority in describing Europe, one based on a politics of citation. As Edward Said (1978) convincingly argued in *Orientalism,* for Europeans the location of the written source carries more authority than the nature of the argument advanced, in particular if that argument is based on native utterances. Nowhere is the importance of a priori written documentation more fetishized than in Germany. A joke often repeated among foreign students in Germany, when they talk about what is needed for documentation to enroll in a university, always ends with asserting "and they'll only accept my transcripts if they come "mit Stempel" (with an official stamp)." Representations of reality can be trusted only when they have already been inscribed in authoritative texts.

Not only in Germany, though, but elsewhere too the stamp of authority is attached to official conduits and channels of information. One should cite "good scholarly accounts," in the words of one reviewer. Hence, a British reviewer chided me for citing "work written by an undergraduate under [my] supervision," as well as an article by a feminist novelist who interviewed rape victims in Bosnia—rather than Amnesty International or official international commissions. Although these commission reports were not yet published when I initially wrote the essay, even if they had been, the question remains why students and novelists writing non-fiction accounts are considered unreliable. Granted, all sources are not of equal credibility. But it seems that few scholars are willing to credit their students—or, let's say, non-established authors— with arguments or evidence (and are only too eager to cite their accredited peers) for fear that it will discredit what they write. Scholarly accounts of contemporary events that rely only on established, academic sources to describe objects and processes in this "age of information" are likely to miss what is new about these objects and processes. It seems as if all the fuss about authority and sources frequently serves as a retreat into scholasticism and an excuse not to take seriously the substance of arguments. Anthropology, after all, has not distinguished itself historically by "proving" statements through systematic testing and offering answers to pre-formulated questions. As a discipline, anthropology's greatest contributions to science have been in presenting thick descriptions of experiences and hypotheses to account for them, in specifying appropriate questions and descriptive units. Often our descriptions are novel only when they do not rely on citational authority, when they take into account perspectives and experiences usually excluded from scholarly accounts.

Ultimately, the critical comments of my peers are much more original and revealing about the historical reception of my work than are words of praise. Some of the individual comments about particular essays include criticisms for trying to "cram too much in," for leaving "me (temporarily) speechless," for making it difficult to "write a calm review," for arguments that are "bizarre (to put it no more strongly)," for making statements that "leave me feeling uncomfortable . . . [though they] are not in themselves objectionable," for a "lack of seriousness," for making him "*think* the paper is brilliant," for being "too quick, but I am not sure," for "not considering England," "for not citing John Davis." One reviewer, angered by yet another example of what he characterized as "socialist gobbledygook," asked "What is it with these people? Don't they know when they've had it?" Some editors consistently struck out words in my earliest efforts, such as "alterity" and "structuration," that today, ten years later, are considered perfectly acceptable and reappear in many works of my colleagues.

One of my favorite comments was in a review that suggested my "overall tone is fear of the (effete) text." I was, said the critic, engaged in a "sort of reaction formation—defending the essence of anthropology." For a while I puzzled over what it could mean for me to "fear a text," and in particular an "(effete) text." I suspect that his objection was to my unqualified support of fieldwork as central to anthropological knowledge. He likened this support with defense of an "essence," characteristic of a "reaction formation." What I found particularly revealing here was his assumption that textual analysis is effete whereas fieldwork is masculine. In my own experience, others have never identified fieldwork as particularly masculine. In fact, most social scientists have historically identified anthropology's method of participant observation as a soft practice opposed to the hard sciences where real data (statistics, tables, quantitative information) is produced. But this reviewer (for a leading anthropology journal) was suggesting that what was formerly soft or effete (fieldwork) in contrast to the hard sciences had been reclassified as hard in contrast to a kind of cultural studies' textual analysis which had become the new effete or soft practice. He could be right, of course. Is he describing the sea change in Zeitgeist that I intended to analyze but which instead, because of my reaction formation and fears of the (effete) text, I am merely acting out?

REFERENCES

Appadurai, Arjun
    1990. "Disjuncture and Difference in the Global Economy," Public Culture 2 (2): 1–24
Barber, Benjamin
    1995. *Jihad vs. McWorld.* New York: Times Book
Benedict, Ruth
    1934. *Patterns of Culture.* New York: New American Library
Clifford, James and George Marcus
    1984. *Writing Culture: The Poetics and Politics of Ethnography.* Berkeley: University of California Press
Enzensberger, Hans-Magnus
    1994. *Civil Wars: From L.A. to Bosnia.* New York: New Press
Fabian, Johannes
    1983. *Time and the Other: How Anthropology Makes Its Object.* New York: Columbia University Press
Godelier, Maurice
    1986. *The Making of Great Men.* Cambridge: Cambridge University Press
Gourevitch, Philip
    1996. "Misfortune Tellers," *The New Yorker* (April 8, 1996): 96–100

Hannerz, Ulf
     1992. *Cultural Complexity*. New York: Columbia University Press
Harvey, David
     1989. *The Condition of Postmodernity*. London: Oxford University Press
Huntington, Samuel
     1993. "The Clash of Civilizations?" *Foreign Affairs* 73 (3) (Summer 1993): 22–49
Jameson, Fredric
     1983. Postmodernism and Consumer Society. In *The Anti-Aesthetic: Essays on Postmodern Culture*. Hal Foster, ed. Port Townsend, Wash.: Bay Press, 111–125
Kaplan, Robert D.
     1994. "The Coming Anarchy," *Atlantic Monthly* (February 1994): 44–76
McLuhan, Marshall
     1964. *Understanding Media*. New York: McGraw-Hill
Said, Edward
     1978. *Orientalism*. New York: Pantheon

PART I

Making Culture and International Order

2

American Anthropology as Foreign Policy

In the late nineteenth century, philology, the study of the word, gave way to two disciplines: anthropology, which initially focused on "primitive society" or "primitive mentality" as a site of origins, and also the study of language, which later developed into both "linguistics" and "language and literature," as in the contemporary disciplines of, for example, German, English, Romance Studies, or East Asian Studies (Ackerman 1983: 423–447). Today we are witnessing an analogous disciplinary shift, as many English departments have come to embrace "cultural studies," a textualist-based movement that takes politicized culture(s) as its object. As proponents of "multiculturalism," many English departments are displacing their traditional objects (language and high-culture literary products), and circling back, so to speak, to recover that other child of philology, "the cultural," which, in the last eighty years, has become the cherished and central object of anthropology. In recent years, anthropologists, too, have taken an interest in texts and literary criticism and even in high-culture literary products, but that interest has not been oriented toward the reincorporation of language and high culture literary products (except perhaps at Rice University, and there the project is a future-oriented experiment and not a lapsarian recovery). American anthropology now appears to have yielded to English departments and cultural studies programs the disciplinary high ground—the right to name, define, and explain the subject—in debates and definitions of the cultural. Anthropologists often seem to resent this fact, assuming that their work already defines what cultural studies should be (see the illuminating discussion by Keesing 1994: 301–310).

While many anthropologists fear that scholars in literary and cultural studies are encroaching on their intellectual territory, their fears are misplaced. This territory was never ours. Since their respective institutionalizations around the turn of this century in the United States, the function of ethnology and of anthropology as well as their understanding of "culture" is profoundly and fundamentally different from the function of English literary studies.[1] English has been engaged in *modelling domestic policy,* whereas anthropology has engaged in *modelling foreign policy.* While I am overdrawing the distinctions between the disciplines and their discursive fields, I deploy this formalized contrast in order to make visible the ideological and political functioning of this division of labor over time. This contrast suggests an alternative outline for a history, necessitating an expanded and self-conscious (re)vision of anthropology's role in constituting international order. Because the international order is continually reconstituted by processes of group formation, it is never merely a context in which the "human condition" unfolds and anthropologists do research but also a set of mechanisms that structure human lives and scholarly work about them.

Recently, in the pages of the *Anthropology Newsletter,* anthropologists engaged in an exhortatory debate about what anthropology is and whether or not a traditional "four fields approach" is needed in order to provide coherence in anthropological study in the United States. This debate was oddly framed because it posited a past coherence around a four fields approach that anthropology has never in fact enjoyed. A reframing of this past coherence in terms of *what anthropologists do* instead of *what we are* would enable us to quit lamenting the dissolution of our subject and come to accept and work through the conditions in which we now find ourselves. Perhaps by doing so we might not only come to understand our work better but also gain more institutional power—in the face of a shrinking employment market for anthropology

Ph.D.s—and provide an argument for employing more anthropologists in the making of foreign policy.[2]

Domestic Policy: English Literature and Language

Consider domestic policy and its relation to the evolution of the discipline of English literature and language. English departments, as we now know them, came into existence only after the Civil War. Before then, American colleges did not teach literature. They employed individual professors of either Greek and Roman classics or rhetoric and oratory to teach the boys "golden passages in Shakespeare and the poets" (Graff and Warner 1989: 4). Such study was to produce gentlemen with good manners and taste, who could be counted upon to distinguish intuitively good from bad poems or literary works and to understand what they meant. In the words of Gerald Graff, who has written a superb history of the discipline, the idea "that literature could or should be taught—rather than simply enjoyed or absorbed as part of the normal upbringing of gentlefolk—was a novel one" (1987: 1; see also Graff 1979: 103–127). No model for organizing literature into a canon was proposed until the last quarter of the nineteenth century, and its proposal and institutionalization at that time were part of a move away from socializing a particular elite class to a "democratizing", "humanizing," civilizing, in the Renaissance sense, of the masses who were perceived as a new threat as they moved to the city, and began entering schools and voting in large numbers.

Immediately following the Civil War, the extreme divisions were not only between North and South, but also between industrial laborers and privileged elites, new immigrants and more established Americans, employers and employees, city and country. Some pedagogues proposed the teaching of English language and literature as a way to overcome social divisions and to create national unity. Even at that time, however, there were countervoices arguing that literary education should remain "an instrument of political education, ... a means of keeping the lower orders in check" (Graff and Warner 1989: 5). The institutionalization of literature in the 1870s and 1880s took place amid ideological fights and class

31

realignments that were generally kept out of public view. Gerald Graff and Michael Warner have recently published the evidence of these fights in the form of summaries of faculty meetings and autobiographies of the professionals involved. Despite post–Civil War reforms, humanities education in English departments, while espousing democracy, remained nondemocratic, as is evident in the development of a literary canon at that time precisely for the purposes of distinguishing the elite from the vulgar.

The canon was not opposed to equality and democracy as such but to the grounds used to measure equality—to which any assimilation-minded American could theoretically aspire. That "canon" (at the time it was called simply "literature") created and reaffirmed essential exclusions, not only of black, female, and gay-inflected voices—among groups now challenging the canon—but even the study of white male American authors, such as Emerson. Not until 1909 did a professor in an American college teach a course on Emerson (Perry cited in Graff and Warner 1989: 142).[3] Moreover, it is ironic that current fights about the canon often focus on fiction, or the novel, which, for the first twenty years of the discipline, was not considered proper reading for undergraduates (Graff 1987: 124–126).

What I want to stress here is that American English departments were always political fields where models for domestic social relations were proposed, debated, and ultimately institutionalized in the academy—models for relations between the native and the alien, rich and poor, law and order, labor and capital, correct speech and slang, relevance and irrelevance. This political field changed in the twentieth century, and with it the content of "general education," especially after the rise of the United States as a world power and the creation of a large middle class after World War II. As Michael Geyer has shown, American monocultural general education came to define "the West" in the process of excluding "non Western traditions, ideals, and values by designating them as specialized knowledge for experts rather than general knowledge for the American citizen" (1993: 507). At the same time, the American institutional arrangement differed from European systems in that U.S. higher education emerged in a "mediating position between corporate and state executives on the one hand and society on the other" (Geyer 1993: 505). The current embrace of multiculturalism, and of a "discourse model" as opposed to a narrow focus on literature (Todorov 1990: 1–12) by many English departments is a reaction to demands posed by changes in American demography, collective power and sources of cultural capital, and stratification patterns. It should be seen as an opening up "to [new] voices whose heterogeneity approximates that of American culture itself" (Graff and Warner 1989: 13). It is also a recognition that "the canon" is a false issue. The question for English is not which canon—which social structure—to teach, but how to situate oneself with regard to any canon in such a way that the reasons for inclusion and exclusion become more transparent and therefore open to critique.

Repositioning Anthropology to Its History

It is not only the discipline of English that has had to grapple with the dissolution of its authoritative objects—"literature" and "the canon." American anthropology has also actively participated in dissolving both its initial object of study, "the primitive," as well as its subject, a coherent and comprehensive (four-fields) understanding of "the human." I want to read this dissolution as an opportunity for repositioning and renewal. The definition of anthropology as a four-fields discipline—biology, archaeology, ethnology, and linguistics—has always been disputed, and much like the canon for English, it is a false and divisive issue. The idea of a coherent human subject with four dimensions, or, as George Stocking (1983: 5) puts it, "the systematic study of human unity-in-diversity," has provided little more than justification for an institutional alliance within the academy. However important that alliance may have been or may be for academic reasons, intellectually anthropology has cohered less around the "systematic study" of its subject than a challenge to construct it: distinguishing the native (or us) from the foreign (or them) as part of an Enlightenment project of adumbrating "humanness."

American anthropology, much like English literature, has also been involved in domestic debates. From 1880 to 1920, what Margaret Mead and Ruth Bunzel (1960) coined "the golden age of

33

American anthropology," most ethnologists were concerned with salvage operations within the United States and Canada: recovering Indian culture assumed on the verge of extinction. After the institutionalization of the discipline, especially under the leadership of Franz Boaz, American anthropology made significant contributions to the discourses of race, poverty, and cultural integrity. Practitioners have also often taken up global issues with local significance, such as immigration, urbanization, and the organization of labor. Nonetheless, these particular domestic debates have always been part of a supranational discourse, often written by foreign-born anthropologists and provoked by the geographic movement of peoples and world economic crises. The internal or intra-national mediating function performed by academic "general education" (allocated above all to humanities departments) to which Geyer (1993: 499–533) referred was paralleled by an external or inter-national mediating function performed by anthropology.

Anthropology has defined itself less in terms of mapping national social structure than in terms of mapping global categories of otherness.[4] Each subfield of the discipline has been involved in a separate project of distinguishing the foreign from the native, and throughout the history of the discipline, each has been making these distinctions as part of a project adumbrating—foreclosing, constituting, delimiting—the category "human." Chroniclers have proclaimed widely variant beginnings for the field of anthropology: Edward Bourne (1906), for example, insisted that Christopher Columbus was the founder; T. K. Penniman (1935) traced the "Science of Man" back to the ancient Greeks. But regardless of where one dates the origin, anthropologists have consistently been concerned with the distinction native/foreign. Each subfield delineated a different domain of the foreign across space. For linguistics it has been language and migration, for archaeology it has been prehistory or a quest for spatial origins, for biological anthropology it has been racial difference and origin, and for ethnology, or sociocultural anthropology, it has been contemporary customs or habits and their diffusion from an originary "primitive" state.[5] Through its institutionalized focus on defining the foreign, anthropology may best be thought of as a form of foreign policy.

In the American context, the constructed category "Indian"—an amalgamation of different native groups—occupied the space of the

34

quintessential "foreign." It is not that Indians were the only foreigners, for, as we all know, continuous waves of "foreign" immigrants settled or were resettled in the New World. At first they were primarily light-skinned Europeans and dark-skinned African slaves, but soon other peoples from all parts of the globe came. Yet, as much as certain groups of resettled peoples, especially African Americans, have been central to the definition of the American, often by the very nature of their radical exclusion, I want to insist on the centrality of the Indian for the category "foreign" in the formation of the American national Imaginary, at least through 1870. The formidable cognitive and emotional task for white Americans was to (re)create oneself as and to occupy the category "American," though fully "foreign" oneself, through the expropriation of native lands and the liquidation of those natives. (On "Indian hating and empire building" see Drinnon 1980.)

The mapping of this space of the foreign predates the academic institutionalization of anthropology as a discipline. European settlers' initial relations with the natives revolved around two primary interactions, war and trade, not coincidentally the arenas in which the political is formed and foreign policy made. Notwithstanding Thomas Jefferson's admonition in 1804 to avoid "entangling alliances" in war or trade, and notwithstanding the myth that the United States remained isolationist up to the First or even the Second World War, the United States has always had an activist foreign policy. Its "foreign" during this so-called period of isolation was primarily the Indian. Within the government, the War Department took charge of Indian affairs, and it was concerned first and foremost with controlling trade and commerce between the Indians and the British. Indeed, one can trace a continuous and uncanny history from prerevolutionary treaties with the Indians to the present North American Free Trade Agreement that illustrates how conceptualizations of foreignness grow out of debates on commercial relations. Moreover, such commercial relations have always been a concern of both domestic and foreign policy, meaning that at least in this discursive field English literature and language and anthropology were continually deploying the same set of concepts.

The foreign was demarcated in a series of asymmetrical counterconcepts (Koselleck 1985: 159–167), each of which successively reveals a shift in the historical and political conceptualization, and therefore constitution, of the foreign in the United States. To oversimply for heuristic purposes, one can map two discursive fields: political-economic and racial.

Political Economy

After a brief period in which Indians were viewed as sovereign nations to be protected against crimes by whites, a century of hostility and war followed (Horsman 1967: 32–65). From approximately 1796 to the mid–nineteenth century, non-Indians characterized their commercial and political relations with Indians in terms of a "civilizing" process opposed to "savage" or "tribal" states. As is well known, this entailed buying, stealing, trading, and outright expropriation of land, most of which was then sold or given to whites and turned into private property.

By the mid–nineteenth century, the European concept of a "polity" organized by a sovereign, territorial state was juxtaposed to the Indian's lack of territorial organization, which, in turn, made Indians, in the words of Chief Justice Marshall in 1831, into a "domestic dependent nation" as opposed to a "foreign state" (cited in Baca 1988: 231). Indians were thus sovereign in some respects, wards of the state in others. But this sovereignty, both in domestic and foreign affairs, remained contested, and even with the movement of the Office of Indian Affairs from the War Department to the Department of the Interior in 1849, the military continued to play a major role in Indian policy. Throughout the nineteenth century, many Indians became American citizens through marriage to whites, military service, or treaties, but their new status supplanted and did not eliminate their identity as members of Indian tribes with limited sovereignty. Not until June 2, 1924, were all Indians made into American citizens, though this legal act also did not limit the sovereignty of Indians engaged in what were called "tribal relations," nor did it extend state jurisdiction into Indian country.

Toward the end of the nineteenth century, with the pacification of Indians and their confinement on reservations, the division between the Departments of the Interior and War became final. The

36

Spanish-American War of 1898, justified by moralistic rationale (against the harsh Spanish treatment of Cubans), prefigured a shift in foreign policy from intra- to extra-territorial concerns (McCormick 1992: 28). American Indians remained symbolically important in demarcating the foreign, but after this war they were considered fully outside the scope of the foreign policy establishment. In fact, the growth of "applied anthropology" after 1935, initiated by New Deal Indian Commissioner John Collier, was a direct response to the needs of Indian communities and at that time considered solely part of a clearly demarcated domestic policy.

Following World War II, the United States began a period of global involvement as a recognized superpower, and anthropologists accompanied this global reach, especially to the Pacific (Luria 1988: 553). However, as Mead and Bunzel point out, anthropology departments had already begun reorganizing after World War I, with anthropologists engaging in "new kinds of research . . . far afield in the South Seas and in Africa" (1960: Editor's Note). The disputed categories of political sovereignty that had so bedevilled dealings with Indians in the nineteenth century were supplanted by asymmetrical economic concepts in the context of interventionist policy after 1945[6]: "modernizing" was opposed to "underdeveloped," and "capitalism" to "communism." "Modernization theory" became part of a global strategy for relating to all "third world" peoples, including American Indians. Sometime around 1960, sovereignty again became an issue; "self-realization" and "democratizing" became universal concepts that stood for the human potential of Indians and non-Indians alike. Many of the issues with which North American Indians are most concerned—for example, fishing and water rights, land claims, education policy—revolve around "Who is an Indian?" and the politics of identity claims, seen today as relevant simultaneously to issues of the domestic domain, cultural studies, and foreign policy (see Clifford 1988: 277–348; Taylor 1984: 135–156). After 1989, a renewed emphasis on a universal or global human teleology, with the assumption of liberal-democratic government and market-based economics as core framing institutions, has been accompanied by an immediate practical failure of these institutions to perform as expected in many parts of the world. In this new political economy, "foreign affairs" appears to be a field adrift.

37

Race

After the first encounters, non-Indians employed a set of proto-race categories that defined "the Indian" or "the tribe" as the counter of "the Pilgrim," "the Teutonic," "the Aryan," "the Saxon," "the American Citizen," or "the White." As the power to define and administer the Indian gradually shifted, after 1849, from the War Department to the Department of the Interior, policy vacillated between removal, isolation, and integration, followed by a long period in which "assimilation" was the dominant goal—although that concept was first clearly articulated in theoretical terms as "acculturation" more than eighty years later, in an article by anthropologists Robert Redfield, Ralph Linton, and M. J. Herskovits (1936: 149–152). Within a decade after World War II, this "story of acculturation and assimilation" was rapidly renarrated, as Edward Bruner (1985:140) has shown, as a story of "ethnic resurgence." By the 1960s, the themes of identity recovery and resistance had become global in scale, with black, ethnic, feminist, and gay movements proliferating within the First World, with anti-colonial and nationalist liberation movements proliferating in the Third World. As American Indian protest and resistance to assimilation tactics became more widespread and more visible in the late 1960s, Indians lost their counterconceptual value as opposed to whites. By the 1980s, however, among many people, including Indians themselves, the category "Indian" had been reaffirmed in asymmetrical opposition to "government" itself, as either pre- or outside of government. Consequently, the question of sovereignty (land disputes, nuclear waste disposals, control over education, "wild man" rites, the rights to control gambling and casinos) has again become central.

Because Indians were both the first natives and the ultimate foreigners, American governments and ethnographers vacillated ambivalently in their conceptualization of Indian otherness, for any assertion of one term would be haunted by the specter of its opposite whose possible return threatened to expose the limits of the representation. The Indian's paradoxical status as simultaneously domestic and foreign has been expressed, for example, in captivity narratives and hunting myths where the Indian, as a beast of the wilderness, served as "symbol for the secret, darkened soul within each man," a "lost half" or anima that, failing exorcism, was hunted and "transformed into an object of love, a woman . . . to whom the hero is wedded in symbolic sexual violence" (Slotkin 1973: 156–157). This dual status was also acted out in the policy of the Bureau of Indian Affairs (BIA), created in 1824 within the War Department. The BIA functioned alternately as a military body for aggression and defense, an international trust, a property development agency, a social welfare agency, and a nationalizing agency (Taylor 1984: 33–106). Its role always depended on how the foreign and the native were defined and demarcated.

As anthropology developed into a discipline in the latter part of the nineteenth century, it found a place in a foreign policy that had already been shaped by early ethnographers, the Monroe Doctrine, Social Darwinism, and by ideas of an American missionary purpose to civilize and democratize the world (Hinsley 1981; Tenbruck 1990: 193–206). While understandings of the Indians shifted, and American imaginings of the foreign grew to include many other peoples, one thing did not change: the Indian's radical alterity remained the continuous object of anthropology (cf. Keesing 1994). After the Civil War, Americans became increasingly conscious of their ethnic and racial heterogeneity, of what were identified as its "foreign elements": aboriginal peoples, immigrants, and former slaves. Deep concern "about the quality of the 'American stock' and the effects of mixing with Indians, Blacks, Orientals, and others" even led in 1904 to a proposal by the Bureau of American Ethnology (despite the reluctance of the Smithsonian Institution's secretary to be involved in projects involving "social questions") for a study in "applied anthropology" titled "Biological Study of the People of the United States" (C. Hinsley 1981: 274). The model for conceptualizing radical alterity was the American Indian, initially constituted by use of the concept of "culture" and the documentation of "culture traits"—especially, at the Smithsonian and elsewhere, documenting Indian languages and material artifacts. Such a project in "culture" made possible "the transformation of the aborigine from historical actor to aesthetic object. [Native Americans became an] artistic abstraction [that] served to deflect a painful history of violence and injustice" (G. Hinsley 1983: 53). Despite the antiracist intent of many individual anthropologists, Indian policy relegated

39

Native Americans' own alternative definitions of Indianness to secondary statuses and instituted a "blood quantum mechanism" or "degree of Indian blood" standard for Indian identity (Jaimes 1992: 123–138).

The history of these counterconcepts in relations with American Indians is already well known, in general outline if not in detail. Therefore, I will only briefly sketch the relation of anthropological models to foreign policy through the period of so-called isolation, after which both American anthropology and American foreign policy employed the conceptual apparatus created in Indian policy as part of a global strategy in dealing with foreignness outside the territorial boundaries of the United States. It is important to emphasize that a conceptual framework or model is a perceptual orientation for political action; it is intellectual labor and distinct from the labors of anthropologists who themselves worked as administrators in the carrying out of foreign or domestic policy. Such administrators are much smaller in number than academicians, and they necessarily rely on the work of the former, or do such intellectual labor themselves, in order to orient policy. My focus will be restricted to the nature of the models themselves without distinguishing between these two sorts of laborers.

Cultural Difference and Political Boundaries: Whites and Indians

Immediately following the defeat of the British in the Revolutionary War, George Washington wrote in a letter on September 7, 1783, that the "Savages" were a "deluded People" in "taking up the Hatchet against us," but that Americans were a "generous People" resolved to pursue friendship and to "draw a veil over what is past and establish a boundary line between them and us." He was convinced of "the propriety of purchasing their Lands in preference to attempting to drive them by force of arms out of their Country; which as we have already experienced is like driving the Wild Beasts of the Forest which will return as soon as the pursuit is at an end" (Prucha 1975: 1–2). Based on this assessment, Washington outlined the initial terms of foreign policy: the regulation of trade,

40

a moralistic self-representation of the American as "generous" and a "friend," the removal of Indians from land needed for settlement, and the establishment of "a boundary line between them and us." In 1818, Secretary of War John C. Calhoun made this foreign policy more precise—trade was to be licensed only to "American Citizens," and not to "foreigners who are odious to our citizens, on account of their activity or cruelty in the late war." The foreigners cited by Calhoun who engaged in trade and needed to be controlled included "the Indians, foreign boatmen, & interpreters" (Prucha 1975: 29).

In 1824, Calhoun set up a Bureau of Indian Affairs (BIA) within his department and charged it with the dual functions of "regulating the intercourse with the Indian tribes" and of administering "a fund for the civilization of the Indians" (Prucha 1975: 38)—functions it retains to this day. "Regulating the intercourse" meant not merely controlling the fur trade but also preparing for the advance of white settlers as they flooded west by resettling and remaking Indians. The civilization fund, as it was called, had already been appropriated in 1819 "for the purpose of providing against the further decline and final extinction of the Indian tribes" by instructing Indians "in the mode of agriculture suited to their situation; and for teaching their children in reading, writing, and arithmetic" (Civilization Fund Act in Prucha 1975: 33). Approximately a century before "assimilation" had entered the vernacular, much less become a scholarly concept, its semantic reach had been sketched.

Most of the BIA agents employed to study, control, and interact with Indians shared the goal of preventing "final extinction" of the Indians, but they also uniformly doubted that this would be possible. The "Red Race" was doomed, according to the naturalist Henry Rowe Schoolcraft, because "civilization had more of the principles of endurance and progress than barbarism; because Christianity was superior to paganism; industry to idleness; agriculture to hunting; letters to hieroglyphics; truth to error" (1848: 369). As an enthusiastic ethnographer, folklorist, linguist, and archaeologist, Schoolcraft worked as an agent for the BIA from 1822 to 1841. "It is impossible," he wrote, "to incorporate them, in such masses, in any form whatever, into our system" (1848: 375). Schoolcraft himself did not make policy, but ethnographies like his provided the counterconcepts that were later employed in a (foreign) policy that proposed as a solution territorial sovereignty for the Indian outside jurisdiction of the Union's states.

Writing for the journal "Democratic Review," Schoolcraft argued that "it was impossible that . . . the Indian and the American should co-exist on the same territory." Hence he supported "the sovereignty of Indian races," to be realized by "remov[ing] them, with their own consent, to a position entirely without the boundaries of the State jurisdiction, where they might assert their political sovereignty, and live their national character, under their own laws" (1848: 373). Particularly worrisome for Schoolcraft was the geographical movement and mixing of Indian tribes. "The Kickapoos," he wrote, "an erratic race, who, under various names . . . have . . . skipped over half the continent, to the manifest discomfort of both German and American philologists and ethnographers, who in searching for the so-called 'Mascotins,' have followed, so far as their results are concerned, an *ignis fatuus*" (1848: 386).

In 1849, the BIA moved from the War Department into the Department of the Interior and began a policy of "removal" of Indians from the Union and, after the Civil War, of creating reservations. Even in the Department of the Interior, however, Indian policy was never totally divorced from its earlier placement in the War Department. As Indian commissioner Walker stated in his Annual Report of 1872, "Indians should be made as comfortable on, and as uncomfortable off, their reservations as it was in the power of Government to make them. . . . [U]se of the strong arm of the Government is not war, but discipline. . . . They must yield or perish, [for they cannot] stay this tide, whose depth and strength can hardly be measured. [It is] to snatch the remnants of the Indian race from destruction before it, that the friends of humanity should exert themselves at this juncture" Prucha 1975: 137–141). As a "friend of humanity," Walker found his voice, enabling him to confidently divorce "war" from "discipline," the former defining a political act, the latter a humanitarian one.

Following the Civil War and the end of the so-called Indian wars came a period of intense and disruptive fighting between various secular and religious authorities, along with open hostility between the Senate and the House of Representatives, for the control of Indian policy (Berthrong 1988: 255–263; Prucha 1979). In this context Henry Lewis Morgan's (1851, 1871, 1877) seminal ethnographic work was initially received. Morgan pioneered a kind of study that was soon followed by a generation of talented ethnographers, including Frank Hamilton Cushing, Francis La Flesche, Alice Fletcher, James Mooney, and, in the academy, Franz Boas. All of these researchers assumed the integrity of Indian cultures and fought for Indian rights; they also ignored the foreign policy implications of their work. In particular, Morgan's books *Ancient Society* (1877) and *Systems of Consanguinity and Affinity* (1871) are less significant as documents about American social structure than as treatises on international order. They were attempts to deal with all peoples in a single, evolutionary framework—civilization measured by culture and state of polity. Even his early *League of the Ho-Dé-No-Sau-Nee or Iroquois* (1851) was preoccupied with setting up democracy as a universal equivalent by which to measure other governments and societies, and then to ask how the Iroquois could be assimilated as American citizens and enjoy true democracy. In the United States, Morgan's writings were not taken up to offer alternative models of society, but to provide a set of measures—democracy, territorial statehood, consanguinity, and affinity—that could be the conceptual grounds for modelling foreignness. These measures had other uses and meanings in England, France, and Germany, countries that had no "Indians" within.[7]

Perhaps the provision that best symbolizes the United States Indian policy of this period was the 1887 Dawes Act, which "assumed that by making Indians owners of private property they would be forced to become farmers, to acquire an education, and to accept Christianity" (Berthrong 1988: 263). The means employed to accomplish this end included the following: allocating land to individuals instead of tribes, replacing communal with private property schemes, expanding schools and compulsory education, making Indians American citizens, encouraging self-determination and democratization, and, from 1947 to 1973, terminating reservation status (Nash 1988: 264–275).

Making Indians into Americans around the turn of the century was not an example of an extension or universalization of rights but an elimination of difference in the name of a universal value. Behind this elimination was the assumption of the inevitability of becoming "American." Admission to citizenship was part of a ritual, with a prepared script, informing Indians that they were to live as "White men and women." Each activity in the ritual was an act of self-abnegation: "men used their Indian name for the final time and shot their last arrow; men took a plow and, addressed by their White name, were admonished about the importance of work for a White man; a purse was given as a symbol of thrift; an oath was made while touching the American flag; and finally, a badge of citizenship, adorned with an eagle, was pinned on their breasts. The ritual for women, somewhat shorter, began with a presentation of a work bag and a purse, accompanied by a speech regarding the nature of the White woman's role in the home and the importance of thrift; an oath was then pledged on the flag; a pin, also adorned by an eagle, awarded. The woman's Indian name was not used in the ritual (Baca 1988: 233). As native names and signs were replaced by a white semiotic system, one cannot miss the irony in the fact that the eagle, the totemic representation of "the American" to which the Indian supposedly aspires, is a symbol for surveillance and stupidity in much native American mythology.

As the Indians became more of a domestic issue, around the turn of the century, American anthropological interest accompanied United States foreign policy to the Philippines to the West and Panama to the South, and soon thereafter to other parts of Asia and South America (on the Smithsonian interest in Asia, see C. Hinsley 1981: 114–115). During and after World War II, United States anthropologists became more intensely involved in imperial policies. Some aspects of these relationships are documented in Stocking's edited volume, *Colonial Situations* (1991) (see also, Asad 1973; Huizer and Mannheim 1979; Kuklick 1991, 1978; LeClerc 1972). In particular, Ira Bashkow's fascinating explication of the context of David Schneider's fieldwork in Micronesia illustrates how the cooperation of the Departments of the Interior, State, and Navy articulated with anthropological research on governmental depopulation policies. Bashkow concludes, these "liberal, assimilative policies emphasiz[ed] the opening of Micronesia to economic

44

'development' and the prompt organization of self-government on a Western, democratic model" (1991: 179).

In this case, George Murdock's vision and his Yale Cross-Cultural Survey File were integral in "establish[ing] the postwar framework of colonial rule in Micronesia" (Bashkow 1991: 180). A 1943 memorandum primarily authored by Murdoch is written in language that recalls Schoolcraft's of approximately a century earlier: "Most of the islands [have a] scanty native population possessed of a very primitive social organization, and with only a primitive political tradition. Autogenous government has always been limited to feudalistic family, clan, and village systems. Attempts to impose government systems based on representations which cut family and village lines are, for the time being, doomed to failure." This memo argued for "full and undivided" naval control "on a permanent or at least a semi-permanent basis" (cited in Bashkow 1990: 181). The antidote to what Bashkow dubs the "scientific progressivism" of Murdoch and others is not a withdrawal from involvement in policy, but, as Clyde Kluckholhn argued at the time, not to lose sight of "actual people," and for more "humility as to what may be predicted with present instruments for observation and conceptualization" (cited in Bashkow 1990: 189). Combined efforts of anthropologists and other social scientists resulted in establishing postwar academic "area studies."

Shortly before this particular "assimilative" foreign policy, grounded on an implicit understanding of "the typical" American, reached its ultimate test, and failure, in Vietnam, the U.S. Senate Committee on Foreign Relations succinctly concluded that "the American interest [is] in furthering a process of modernization which will enable the transitional societies to develop their own versions of responsible government" (Millikan 1961: 6). To make the world safe for democracy was both in "the American interest" and part of "a process of modernization," which would be realized by identifying "transitional societies" and helping them "develop their own versions of responsible government." Except in the title of the powerful committee, the word *foreign* is omitted, for American national interest had become synonymous with global humanism as a domestic project. During the Vietnam War, anthropological models of humanness were very much congruent with, if not themselves employed as, the conceptual tools that enabled an envisioning of the Vietnamese as radical cultural Others, yet domesticable, in transition much like American Indians, and integrable into the institutions of electoral democracy and free market capitalism (see Drinnon 1980: 355-442).

Conclusion

How might we bring this history to bear on an understanding of anthropology's role in the post–Cold War world? The four fields approach debate in anthropology resembles only superficially the canon debate in English. Whereas literature and language as a particular model for domestic social relations did at one time provide English with its coherence, it was radical alterity as a model for the foreign, not the four fields approach, that provided anthropology with a coherent subject. The idea that anthropologists united around the study of "human unity-in-diversity" was never more than an academic conceit. It was always a point of contention, for the discipline was fully implicated in international political processes largely outside its control. Anthropology's object has been the foreign, the other in another space who is different from oneself, and this foreign always functions in a political field as an asymmetrical counterconcept. The universalism implicit in humanistic stances, as in anthropological appeals to the "psychic unity of mankind," was predicated not only on overcoming specific divisions, such as that between primitive and civilized, but also on constituting the ever-changing boundaries, the inside and outside, of the category human. The asymmetry between the terms and the directionality inferred by "human unity" was always clear: it was the primitive or the foreign other who would eventually be negated, overcoming him/herself in a process of becoming "man"— civilized, white, properly gendered, heterosexual, married, private property owner. This directionality was pointedly captured by Richard H. Pratt, founder of the Carlisle Indian Industrial School in 1879, the foremost model for Indian education, who was fond of saying that he "hoped to destroy the 'Indian' with the 'race' in favor of the 'man'"(cited in Berkhofer 1978: 171; see Garmhausen 1988).

46

That anthropology has not circled back to reclaim the literary model (as English has reclaimed the cultural) should be of no concern to us, for our primary contribution has not been to a narrowly conceived domestic policy. In fact, such a provincial view of the discipline has often served to mask the highly political and global nature of anthropological research, even of that done within the United States. It has reinforced a kind of protective self-marginalization of anthropologists in and outside the academy. Fieldwork among the foreign, not the reading of texts, and not the salvage or preservation of vanishing ethnic identities, remains anthropology's unique location from which it makes continued contributions to knowledge. Fieldwork offers privileged insights not into already constructed cultural "texts" but into the conditions of possibility of such texts and the processes by which they take on form and meaning. During the course of fieldwork, anthropologists experience the foreign and inter-group relations directly, in an empirical fashion not comparable to experiences in the archives (on the function of hospitality in fieldwork, see Herzfeld 1987). Study of written texts and participant-observation are distinct practices that offer different insights. They should not be collapsed together in a trendy cultural studies, where they are often used as an alibi by bourgeois academics to avoid the discomforts and uncertainties inherent in face-to-face interaction with strangers.[8]

To avoid misunderstanding, let me make clear that this is not an argument that anthropologists should become State Department employees—though that also might be one way in which an anthropological position could be articulated. Nor is this an argument for reifying divisions between anthropology and literary studies, or between the foreign and the domestic. I would hope to have demonstrated that the line between these domains is not necessary but contingent. It shifts over time. And since the study of historical contingencies is what most anthropologists do, we will unavoidably be crossing back and forth between these domains. The foreign is not something that has meaning in and of itself, nor is it territorially fixed. It is an unstable counterconcept, which, for anthropology, has been opposed to the native and constitutive of the human. Our task is to situate ourselves more clearly in relation to the foreign and to justify our positions more rigorously. Such positions, with or without the assent of anthropologists, provide the grounds on which foreign policy is made and on which distinctions between us and them are drawn.

Today, spatial and temporal differences between groups are simultaneously rapidly dissolving and being radically reasserted, with the consequence that the foreign/native distinction is perceived alternately as more necessary or as entirely impossible to draw. This places anthropologists working in inter-group relations in the difficult position of having to choose between two versions of multiculturalism: a vision of the world as made up of plural cultures organized as autonomous, settled units or a vision of the world as a process of unsettling and resettling syncretic, interdependent, and global units. Roger Keesing, in arguing for a broadening of the discipline to include the issues of this latter version of multiculturalism, pointed to the dilemmas provoked by this vision and "the ironies that emerge when a conception of culture, indirectly borrowed from anthropology, is used to denounce foreign researchers, with anthropologists as the quintessential villains" (1994: 307). Whether villains or heroes, anthropologists must begin by historicizing their present location, meaning acknowledging that our work is already in the domain of foreign policy and international order. During fieldwork, foreigners are never merely tropes or mythical figures in a text but tangible people whom we confront in their bodily integrity. Given the insights to be gained from this location, we should engage more self-consciously in the post–Cold War debates on foreign policy, including reconceptualizing national security and defense, citizenship and immigration, exile and home, human rights and world order (cf. Hymes 1972). Many, if not most, anthropologists are already engaged in such work, although they may not have represented it this way.

NOTES

This essay was initially given as a talk titled "Rethinking Anthropological Coherence," for a panel organized by Robert Borofsky at the American Anthropological Association Meetings, Washington, D.C., November

1993; it was also presented at Humboldt University in Berlin and the University of Tübingen. My special thanks to Jack Skarbinski for assistance in research on American Indian policy, to Liisa Malkki and Stefan Senders for clarifying many of my arguments, to Joe Masco and Bernd Lambert for insights and references.

1. By and large, Social Anthropology originated in Britain, with a focus on social structure and political organization, while Cultural Anthropology originated in the United States, with a focus on cultural wholes and symbolism. Neither French nor German anthropology was marked by this sort of division (cf. Augé 1982). The history that I am sketching regarding anthropology's definitions of the foreign and relation to conceptualizing foreign policy (and literature's relation to national domestic policy) can be made for other national traditions also. I am merely suggesting a framework in which such a history might be written for American anthropology. Needless to say, while each nation is situated uniquely to a foreign, national traditions are not discrete. Along these lines, see the exemplary historical study by Henrika Kuklick (1991) of British anthropology's relation to both domestic debates and the changes in the Empire.

2. To quote the *Anthropology Newsletter*: Anthropology jobs in academia have declined steadily since 1989. Positions advertised at the AAA Annual Meeting have decreased from 154 in 1989 to 95 in 1992. Positions-open listed in the *AN* also have decreased, from 473 in 1989 to 310 in 1992. Thus, the market for academic positions is shrinking, while the total number of anthropology PhDs produced has remained constant at around 400 per year since 1974. [Givens and Tucker 1993: 50].

3. Perry remarks ironically in this section of his autobiography that the course on Emerson was accepted "perhaps [because] they were afraid that I might offer a course on Walt Whitman!" (cited in Graff and Warner 1989: 142).

4. In a different context, Lévi-Strauss (1966: 256) rightly made this point (though drawing different conclusions) for the discipline internationally, arguing that while history was concerned primarily with temporal contiguity, anthropology was concerned primarily with spatial distribution.

5. From this perspective, one can explain the uneasy distancing of both anthropology and English to the study of folklore. Being text-based and domestic, yet often concerned with the foreign in time, folklore studies was, and remains, an impure category. Further, it was explicitly and consciously

tied to a nationalist project, whereas anthropology and English saw themselves as more or less autonomous (and often critical) intellectual pursuits.

6. Blecher and Kaplan identified 215 incidents from 1946 to 1975 where the United States engaged in "political use of the armed forces . . . as part of a deliberate attempt . . . to influence, or to be prepared to influence . . . another nation without engaging in a continuing contest of violence" (cited in McCormick 1992: 81). These interventions were in addition to numerous direct invasions in e.g., South Korea, Guatemala, Iran, Vietnam, Lebanon, the Dominican Republic, and Panama.

7. It is a commonplace now to state that anthropologists were implicated in the colonial policies in all three countries. Unlike anthropologists in the United States, however, Europeans did not have the ambiguous situation of the foreign being within instead of without, the first native instead of the immigrant or the colonial. Following World War I, Germany lost its colonies, and following World War II, German anthropologists had a difficult time reestablishing the discipline, and therefore have had marginal input into debates on foreigners and immigration and citizenship policy. This speechlessness is also due to the fact that the two Cold War Germanys had no independent foreign policies, and therefore were not in the same position as England and France, which had to deal with the breakup of colonial empires and articulate new classifications of peoples, or the United States, which was trying to build a new world empire.

In German anthropology (Ethnologie, Völkerkunde, and biological anthropology) up to World War I, for example, research on Hottentots, on *Mischlinge* (mixed races), on "South African bastards," as they were called, served as the "scientific" model to construct radical, racial Otherness. Germany's loss of its colonies following this war in no way slowed race research, for anthropology's tools were soon supplemented by the growing field of eugenics and eventually turned inward and to the East; Nazi race policy employed anthropological terms to create the foreign within—the Jew, the Slavic body and mentality, the Gypsy, the homosexual.

Unlike historians and psychologists, for example, German ethnologists have engaged in little research into the history of their discipline, specifically avoiding the relation of the Nazi period to pre- and post-war anthropology. In a new volume dedicated to this topic, edited by Thomas Hauschild (1995), Ute Michel (1995) shows how German Völkerkunde made itself relevant and politically useful during the Third Reich by taking its research methods and concepts from African work, what it already then called a "socio-biological perspective," and applying them to the study of

"Osteuropa" or "Eurasien." Hauschild lists three effects of this absent history: first, since anthropologists sympathetic to some Nazi policies continued working uninterruptedly after 1945 in West Germany, they controlled research agenda and the allocation of positions, with the intent to dissolve the memory of ethnology's relation to race theory; second, the institutional and intellectually untenable division between Volks- and Völkerkunde, studying oneself in terms of folklore and history, studying the other through participant observation, was never critically examined and therefore perpetuated itself in the academy (as was not the case among Scandinavians, who also had previously shared this division but created social anthropology departments after the war), keeping German ethnology outside of most debates in modern sociocultural anthropology; and third, since unification of the two Germanies in 1989, new departments are being organized (social anthropology, cultural studies, the empirical science of culture) that have no relation (or avoid drawing a relation) to the history of German Völkerkunde/Ethnologie and therefore reinforce historical amnesia in the old disciplines, from which they distance themselves and are thereby exculpated from having to reform.

8. The recent spate of books and articles on the technologies of fieldnotes and writing and on the experience of fieldwork is not, in my opinion, an indication of diminished support for fieldwork but an expression of its continued significance and extreme relevance to disciplinary practice. It illustrates the necessary adjustments being made to doing fieldwork at a time when the nature of information and images, and therefore experience, is changing in substantial ways. At the same time, the knowledge obtained in fieldwork is valuable not because one overcomes travel impediments to get to faraway cites, where the access is extremely difficult and the natives are likely to expose the ethnographer to illnesses (e.g., malaria, typhoid). This kind of "hard" initiation rite, provides no privileged insight into alterity. However, neither does a cultural studies practice of reading texts or watching television, or a political science version of fieldwork that involves interviews with the political leaders of six different countries in between hotel stops, that is not accompanied by the researcher leaving the book, computer screen, or hotel to "interact" over an extended period of time with the people. Even anthropologists (certainly myself included) may engage in all these pleasures and find them useful to their work, but the discipline has little to gain by ecclectically conflating them with fieldwork, which I as well as many others have argued obtains special insights from the temporal qualities inherent in face-to-face interactions with strangers (Borneman 1992: 1–56).

REFERENCES

Ackerman, Robert

1983. From Philology to Anthropology—The Case of J.G. Frazer. In *Philologie und Hermeneutik im 19. Jahrhundert*, Vol. 2. Mayotte Bollack and Heinz Wismann, eds., Pp. 423-447. Göttingen: Vandenhoeck and Ruprecht

Asad, Talal, ed.

1973. *Anthropology and the Colonial Encounter.* London: Ithaca Press

Augé, Marc

1982. *The Anthropological Circle: Symbol, Function, History.* Cambridge: University of Cambridge Press

Baca, Lawrence

1988. The Legal Status of American Indians. In *History of Indian-White Relations.* Wilcomb E. Washburn, ed. Vol. 4 of *Handbook of American Indians.* William C. Sturtevant, ed. Pp. 230–237. Washington D.C.: Smithsonian Institution Press

Bashkow, Ira

1991. The Dynamics of Rapport in a Colonial Situation: David Schneider's Fieldwork on the Islands of Yap. In *Colonial Situations: Essays on the Contextualization of Ethnographic Knowledge.* George Stocking, ed. Pp. 170-243. Madison: University of Wisconsin Press

Berkofer, Robert

1978. *The White Man's Indian: Images of the American Indian from Columbus to the Present.* New York: Knopf.

Berthrong, Donald J.

1988. Nineteenth-Century United States Government Agencies. In *History of Indian-White Relations.* Wilcomb E. Washburn, ed. Vol. 4 of *Handbook of American Indians.* William C. Sturtevant, ed. Pp. 255–263. Washington D.C.: Smithsonian Institution Press

Borneman, John

1992. *Belonging in the Two Berlins: Kin, State, Nation.* Cambridge: Cambridge University Press

Bourne, Edward

1960 [1906]. Columbus, Ramon Pane and the Beginnings of American Anthropology. In *The Golden Age of American Anthropology.* Margaret Mead and Ruth Bunzel, eds. Pp. 18-21. New York: George Braziller

Bruner, Edward
    1985. Ethnography as Narrative. In *The Anthropology of Experience*. Victor Turner and Edward Bruner, eds. Pp. 139–155. Urbana: University of Illinois Press

Clifford, James
    1988. Identity in Mashpee. In *The Predicament of Culture: Twentieth-Century Ethnography, Literature, and Art.* Pp. 277–348. Cambridge: Harvard University Press

Diamond, Stanley, ed.
    1980. *Anthropology: Ancestors and Heirs.* The Hague: Mouton

Drinnon, Richard
    1980. *Facing West: The Metaphysics of Indian Hating and Empire Building.* New York: Schocken Books

Garmhausen, Winona
    1988. *History of Indian Arts Education in Santa Fe.* Santa Fe: Sunstone Press

Geyer, Michael
    1993. "Multiculturalism and the Politics of General Education." *Critical Inquiry* 19 (3): 499-533

Givens, David and Rosalind Tucker
    1993. "Survey of Underemployed and Unemployed Anthropologists." *Anthropology Newsletter,* Vol. 6 (6): 49–50.

Graff, Gerald
    1979. *Literature Against Itself: Literary Ideas in Modern Society.* Chicago: University of Chicago Press
    1987. *Professing Literature: An Institutional History.* Chicago: University of Chicago Press

Graff, Gerald, and Michael Warner, eds.
    1989. *The Origins of Literary Studies in America: A Documentary Anthology.* New York: Routledge

Hauschild, Thomas
    1995. "Dem Lebendigen Geist": Warum die Geschichte der Völkerkunde im "Dritten Reich" auch für Nichtethnologen von Interesse sein kann. In *Lebenslust und Fremdenfurcht. Völkerkunde im Dritten Reich.* Thomas Hauschild, ed. Berlin: Suhrkamp

Herzfeld, Michael
    1987. "As in Your Own House": Hospitality, Ethnography, and the Stereotype of Mediterranean Society. In *Honor and Shame and the Unity of the Mediterranean.* David Gilmore, ed. Pp. 75-89. Washington, D.C.: American Anthropological Association

Hinsley, Curtis M., Jr.
> 1981. *Savages and Scientists: the Smithsonian Institution and the Development of American Anthropology 1846–1910.* Washington, D.C.: Smithsonian Institution Press

Hinsley, George
> 1983. Ethnographic Charisma and Scientific Routine: Cushing and Fewkes in the American Southwest, 1879–1893. In *Observers Observed: Essays on Ethnograhic Fieldwork.* George Stocking, ed. Pp. 53–69. Madison: University of Wisconsin Press

Horsman, Reginald
> 1967. *Expansion and American Indian Policy, 1783–1812.* Ann Arbor: Michigan State University Press

Huizer, G., and Bruce Mannheim, eds.
> 1979. *The Politics of Anthropology: From Colonialism and Sexism Toward a View from Below.* The Hague

Hymes, Dell, ed.
> 1972. *Reinventing Anthropology.* New York: Vintage Press

Jaimes, M. Annette
> 1992. Federal Indian Identification Policy: A Usurpation of Indigenous Sovereignty in North America. In *The State of Native Americans: Genocide, Colonization, and Resistance.* M. Annette Jaimes, ed. Pp. 123–138. Boston: South End Press

Keesing, Roger
> 1994. Theories of Culture Revisited. In *Assessing Cultural Anthropology.* Robert Borofsky, ed. Pp. 301–310. New York: McGraw Hill

Koselleck, Reinhard
> 1985. The Historical-Political Semantics of Asymmetric Counterconcepts. In *Futures Past: On the Semantics of Historical Time.* Pp. 157–197. Cambridge: MIT Press

Kuklick, Henrika
> 1978. "The Sins of the Fathers: British Anthropology and African Colonial Administration." *Research in the Sociology of Knowledge, Science, and Art* 1: 93–119
> 1991. *The Savage Within: The Social History of British Anthropology, 1885–1945.* Cambridge: Cambridge University Press

LeClerc, G.
> 1972. *Anthropologie et colonialism: Essai sur l'histoire de l'africanisme.* Paris: Gallimard

Lévi-Strauss, Claude
> 1966. *The Savage Mind.* Chicago: University of Chicago Press

Lurie, Nancy Oestreich
    1988. Relations Between Indians and Anthropologists. In *History of Indian-White Relations*. Wilcomb E. Washburn, ed. Vol. 4 of *Handbook of American Indians*. William C. Sturtevant, ed. Pp. 548–556. Washington D.C.: Smithsonian Institution Press
McCormick, James M.
    1992. *American Foreign Policy and Process*. Itasca, Ill.: F. E. Peacock Publishers
Mead, Margaret, and Ruth Bunzel, eds.
    1960. *The Golden Age of American Anthropology*. New York: George Braziller
Michel, Ute
    1995. Neue ethnologische Forschungsansätze im Nationalsozialismus? Aus der Biographie von Wilhelm Emil Mühlmann (1904–1988). In *Lebenslust und Fremdenfurcht. Völkerkunde im Dritten Reich*. Thomas Hauschild, ed. Frankfurt A.M.: Suhrkamp
Millikan, Max F., F. M. Bator, D. L. M. Blackner, R. Eckhaus, E. Hagen, D. Lerner, I. de Sola Pool, L. Pye, P. Rodan, and W. Rostow
    1961. U.S. Senate Committee on Foreign Relations Study No. 12, "Economic, Social and Political Change in the Underdeveloped Countries and Its Implications for United States Policy." In *U.S. Foreign Policy: Compilation of Studies*, 87th Cong., 1st session, Senate Document 24 (March 15)
Morgan, Lewis Henry
    1871. Systems of Consanguinity and Affinity of the Human Family. In *Smithsonian Contributions to Knowledge*, 218. Washington D.C.: Smithsonian Institution
    1877. *Ancient Society; or, Researches in the Lines of Human Progress from Savagery, through Barbarism to Civilization*. Chicago: Charles H. Kerr & Co.
    1901 [1851]. *League of the Ho-De´-No-Sau-Nee or Iroquois*. New York: Burt Franklin.
Nash, Philleo
    1988. Twentieth-Century United States Government Agencies. In Wilcomb E. Washburn, ed. Vol. 4 of, *Handbook of American Indians*. William C. Sturtevant, ed. Pp. 264–275. Washington D.C.: Smithsonian Institution Press
Penniman, T. K.
    1935. *A Hundred Years of Anthropology*. London: Gerald Duckworth

Prucha, Francis Paul

1975. *Documents of United States Indian Policy.* Lincoln: University of Nebraska Press

1979. *The Churches and the Indian Schools, 1888–1912.* Lincoln: University of Nebraska Press

Redfield, Robert, Ralph Linton, and M. J. Herskovits

1936. "A Memorandum for the Study of Acculturation." *American Anthropologist* 38: 149–152

Schoolcraft, Henry Rowe

1848. *The Indian in His Wigwam.* New York: AMS Press

Slotkin, Richard

1973. *Regeneration Through Violence: The Mythology of the American Frontier, 1600–1860.* Middletown: Wesleyan University Press

Stocking, George

1983. History of Anthropology. In *Observers Observed: Essays on Ethnograhic Fieldwork.* George Stocking, ed. Pp. 3–12. Madison: University of Wisconsin Press

Colonial Situations: Essays on the Contextualizaton of Ethnographic Knowledge. Madison: University of Wisconsin Press

Taylor, Theodore W.

1984. *The Bureau of Indian Affairs.* Boulder: Westview Press

Tenbruck, Friedrich

1990. The Dream of a Secular Ecumene: The Meaning and Limits of Development. In *Global Culture.* Mike Featherstone, ed. Pp. 193-206. Newbury Park, Cal.: Sage

Todorov, Tzvetan

1990. The Notion of Literature. In *Genres of Discourse.* Pp. 1–12. Cambridge: Cambridge University Press

3

Race, Ethnicity, Species, Breed: Totemism and Horse Breed Classification in America

Totem: the iconic representation of a specific ordering of plant and animal species. Clan: the representation of a group identity. Totemism: the relationship between totem and clan. From Emile Durkheim and his nineteenth-century antecedents to Claude Lévi-Strauss, the discussion of totemism has addressed the way in which people classify themselves with reference to the animal and plant world. This discussion began with the observation among different exotic peoples of the widespread practice of arranging certain animal and plant species into a pattern that, while differing from culture to culture in content, seemed to indicate a consistent formal relationship between totem and clan. The iconic representation of so-called nature—the totem—seemed invariably the model for the representation of intra- or intergroup identity—for the clan.

This article examines the historical development of the American system of light-horse breed classification[1]—a striking instance in which the animal world is classified according to the categories used for persons, a case of "reverse totemism." The lay understanding of horse breeds is that they are particularly successful experiments in genetic engineering. Whereas voluntaristic explanations

57

of horse-breed categories, as based on the appreciation objective and identifiable biological differentiation, are considered quite acceptable, the same kind of explanations for people groupings, such as "race" and "ethnicity," are now generally rejected. When it comes to explaining their horse pets, most Americans—lay and scientific—will maintain that horse-breed distinctions are by and large objective issues of taste that bear little relation to concurrent developments in social structure, national identity, or state formation. In spite of the common knowledge that horse breeds differ from nation-state to nation-state, this fact of historical cultural contingency does not seem to enter into the consciousness of those who breed, own, and ride horses.

In explaining the American system of breed classification this essay will be organized around the following comparative observation: that the many light-horse breeds in the United States are organized into distinct caste-like species, with an exclusivist set of allegiances to each, whereas in continental Europe light-horse breeds are not seen as so separate and distinct. Furthermore, Europeans tend to be agreed upon a single performance standard for all such light-horse breeds, whereas Americans subscribe to a multitude of standards, some having nothing to do with, or having even an adverse relation to, performance.

The concepts of breed, species, and lineage, and the regulation of these differ markedly between America and the Continent, even though the animals involved in the classification are often of the same "stock" (consanguinity), or are put to the same use (function), or share similar morphological characteristics ("conformation"). While social scientists and historians in this century have been intensively engaged in formal structural analysis of category systems, only recently have they begun to deal with the origin, historical development, and transformation of the categories themselves (e.g., Todorov 1984; Sahlins 1981). I will examine the working of these three primary (often-used) principles of classification in the structuring of particular breeds and their relationship to the evolution of a people, a national identity, and a state. This involves an explication of both the patterning of the underlying generative structure and the historically specific content. I will proceed via a discussion of the debate on totemism and myth within anthropology.

58

What Is Totemic Classification?

> Let us be careful not to imagine that totemism has vanished like
> a cloud at the tap of the fairy wand—slight enough, in both senses
> of the word—of Malinowski.
>
> —Claude Lévi-Strauss, *The Savage Mind*

Totemism, after dominating much of the anthropological debate
centered around "primitive thought" in the early part of this century, was defused as an intellectual issue by the early 1960s.
Already in 1929 A. R. Radcliffe-Brown suggested a shift in the
debate, away from a question about the nature of primitive thought
to one about universal thought patterns: He asked, "Can we show
that totemism is a special form of a phenomenon which is universal in human society and is therefore present in different forms
in all cultures?" (1952:123). In the case of Australian systems, he
explained, "The only thing that these totemic systems have in
common is the general tendency to characterize the segments into
which society is divided by an association between each segment
and some natural species or some portion of nature. This association may take any one of a number of forms" (1952:122). In 1951
Radcliffe-Brown gave us a succinct working definition of totemism,
the full import of which was not further developed until Lévi-
Strauss wrote *The Savage Mind* in 1962. The Radcliffe-Brown
definition reads: "The resemblances and differences of animal
species are translated into terms of friendship and conflict, solidarity and opposition. In other words the world of animal life is
represented in terms of social relations similar to those of human
society" (1952:116). Working with and expanding upon this general definition, Lévi-Strauss articulated precisely how particularities and generalizations about systems of difference can be
fashioned out of homologies made between different levels of categories, and how metaphorical and metonymical relations constitute the socio-logic of different cultural classificatory schemes.[2]
Moreover, Lévi-Strauss suggested redirecting study to "the

59

ritualization of relations between man and animal" (emphasis added), which, he said, "supplies a wider and more general frame than totemism, and within which toemism must have developed" (1963:61).

While mindful of the critical contribution of Lévi-Strauss to this debate, the simple tap of his wand—metaphorical and metonymical operations of the mind—does not complete the task of explicating totemism. The formal ordering mechanisms of cognitive categories will reveal neither the origins nor the development of the structured and structuring practices, which are, after all, the raison d'être of both the categories and the totems. Lévi-Strauss also acknowledged the historicity of any specific application of totemism; he concluded that in "[so -called primitive societies] there is a constantly repeated battle between synchrony and diachrony from which it seems that diachrony must emerge victorious every time" (1966:75, 155). Yet in his own work he ignored the implications of this statement, namely, that any account of a system of classification that focuses solely on the semiological aspects will not be able to explain the significance of the conditions of its production. Without a historical account, the most significant aspects of any system of classification—the limits of its ability to generate structures—will remain unintelligible.

We can radicalize Lévi-Strauss's contribution to *le totémisme aujourd'hui* with three further observations. First, the postulation of homologies between so-called natural and cultural distinctions is not something reserved to the "primitive" mind. While Lévi-Strauss, like Radcliffe-Brown, admitted the theoretical universality of totemic devices, he drew most of his examples from "cold societies." Nor can the use of a totemic device be reduced to "pure thought," whose contemporary manifestation is a genetic inheritance from past times. Where it exists, it does so as a motivated action with mechanisms causing its present production. Second, all totemism is initially a kind of reverse totemism. The animal and plant world does not order itself in a way that is immediately recognizable from a pan-cultural or universal-human perspective. The ordering that humans perceive to exist in the animal world is not initially an inference, it is a projection (Foucault 1973). Third, through an examination of a specific "totemic mythology," we can complete the

60

task that Lévi-Strauss set aside, of explaining "how and why it exists" (1957:8). Lévi-Strauss stated that the "operative value" of totemic classifications derives from their formal character: "they are codes suitable for conveying messages which can be transposed into other codes, and for expressing messages received by means of different codes in terms of their own system" (1966:75, 76). As for mythology, he argued that it "has no obvious practical function: . . . it is not directly linked with a different kind of reality" (1975:10). Here he is absolutely wrong. What I will argue in this essay is that the semiotic codes that make up the patterning of totemism are brought into being by ideological factors, which subsequently also determine the content of the codes. The resulting myths are never innocent, never merely a product where "the mind is left to commune with itself" (1975:10).

The Wide World of Horses in America:
Criteria of Classification

The horse has three gaits—walk, trot, and canter—that are generic to the horse as a species. These three gaits are not in every horse manifested as "pure gaits," meaning that the gait can lose its regularity. For example, the *walk,* a four-beat gait, becomes a *pace* (an impure gait) when the horse moves the legs diagonally instead of laterally. The two-beat *trot,* a diagonal gait, becomes impure when the horse simultaneously moves a front and hind leg laterally (that is, on the same side). At that point the trot loses its moment of suspension. The three-beat *canter* becomes impure when the horse lapses into a four-beat gait. International performance horses, which compete in the three Olympic sports of dressage,[3] show jumping, and combined training, are bred according to the conformational specifications that relate to the purity of the three gaits. This single *performance* criterion is also the basic generative structuring principle of the continental European horse world. The American horse world, however, is structured upon various *breed-specific* criteria, of which the performance criterion is but one among many principles.

Most northern European horse breeding is rigidly (by American standards) regulated by the state, which tests and designates approved stallions and mares considered qualified for breeding stock. This has resulted, over the course of the last two centuries, in the production of superior warm-blood performance horses (crosses between light breeds, such as Thoroughbreds, and local carriage horses and draft horses), some of which have been imported to America, where they are now also being bred. While the international sports performance horse is the focus of European horse categories, it still constitutes but a small percentage (less than five percent) of American horse breeding, pleasure riding, and competition. The categorization of the other ninety-five percent of the light-horse breeds in the United States, which serve purely national or local purposes, is the subject of this essay.

Unlike the Europeans, Americans have more than twenty-six kinds of breed recognized nationally by the American Horse Show Association (ASHA), yet either esoteric or unknown internationally, that are deemed functional and/or meaningful for ends other than international performance sports. These ends include breed criteria of, for example, *color* (Apaloosa, Pinto, Paint, Palomino), *endurance and trail* (Morgan, Peruvian Paso Fino), *sprinting and cattle herding* (Quarter Horse), *elegant, high-stepping action* (Saddlebred, Tennessee Walking Horse). While European breeds are evaluated not only on multiple scales of performance, but also on arbitrary breed standards other than performance, such as temperament, conformation, and coloring (Haynes 1976:61).

Whereas the European breeds, focused upon a single performance criterion, will readily take superior animals from other breeds into their registries in order to improve the stock, Americans place great importance on breed "purity" and invest a great amount of energy in keeping the breeds pure and separate. At times the criteria will even be redefined in order to demarcate more clearly one breed from another. While the strategies used to maintain breed distinctions are multifarious, one strategy held in common among the various breeders involves the use of polythetic classificatory devices, such as versions of unilineal or cognatic descent categories, where no single significant feature is to be found in every member of the breed, but each member is assumed to share a common ancestor. Thus mythologies are constructed around a particular prepotent foundation sire who is said to have originated the breed.

Thereafter, all horses included within that breed registry, while perhaps not sharing any "substance" such as temperament, looks, or ability, are traced back to the same ancestor.

Within and across breed standards Americans have developed distinctive styles of riding, which have their correlates both in the ritually demarcated show arena and in everyday riding practices. At the most general level, Western and English styles are the major categories, but both are further subdivided in the horse-show world. For example, the "Western pleasure" (a stylized performance, aesthetically judged) and the "Western gaming" (timed competition) divisions of Western riding have their English riding counterparts in "dressage" and "hunt seat" (both aesthetically judged) and "show jumping" (timed competitions). The breed and performance standards are open to constant reformulation, depending upon changes in the state of the art for performance, and in the state of the science for breeding, and thus constitute a social field of overt struggle over classificatory schemes. Since the knowledge of the making and unmaking of the system of categories is in the public domain, it can be acquired, thus empowering individuals with various forms of ritual expertise. For example, certain performance classes for nearly all breeds are structured male/female and professional/amateur. These classes include, for example, "men's English pleasure" and "ladies English pleasure," or Western riding, open" and "Western riding, amateurs only." Other riding domains, such as "dressage" or "combined training," require such an extensive investment in training, equipment, and time, that they become, in fact, limited to select classes of individuals. Many of these breed and performance standards conform to the major cleavages in American society and serve as indices of gender, color code, and class.

Yet, the democratic ideal in America has it that everyone has or should have equal opportunity to pursue pleasure, although this does not include a guarantee nor provide the mechanism whereby everyone will in fact have this equal opportunity. And the American myth correspondingly goes that anyone can own a horse. Anyone can also breed a horse, as there is no effective regulation of breeding by the state or by other regulatory agencies, as exists in Europe. Anyone can also show a horse. And, in fact, many people of disparate cultural groups and socioeconomic categories do own, breed, and show horses. Rather than make uniform the standards for owning, breeding, or showing horses, as in continental Europe, the American practice assumes that there is a horse to fit every pocketbook, to match every color preference, every temperament, every personal body-type, and so on and so forth. The horse in America is a democratic ideal.

To illustrate the development of specific American breeds and the distinctive strategies involved in their construction, I will offer an ethnography of four exemplary American breeds that are constituted according to the criteria of function and temperament (the Morgan), conformation (the Quarter Horse and the Arabian), and color (the Paint). These examples are intended to give the reader, on the one hand, a sense of the lack of functional necessity in breed categorization, and, on the other, a sense of the detailed elaboration of symbolic differences.

Function and Temperament: The Morgan Horse

In the case of the first American breed, the Morgan, the origin is traced to Justine Morgan, a horse received by a Vermont school-teacher in payment for a bad debt. Conceived in 1789 in Springfield, Massachusetts, this horse possessed excessive strength for his size and a temperament characterized as industrious, docile, kind, commonsensical, versatile, and independent (*Horse Identifier* 1980:96).[4] A biography of this foundation sire reads:

> the small bay stallion entered a life of hard labor—and, at first, little recognition. Although standing only 14.0 hands and weighing scarcely 950 pounds at maturity, Figure (his original name) was put to any task which required horse power, from skidding heavy logs to racing the local talent at day's end. However the spunky little stud proved he not only had the mettle to attempt anything asked of him, but invariably left the competition eating his dust as well (Mellin 1973:5).

According to one widely held myth, the Morgan had been a necessity in the past: How could America have been settled without him? The founding of breed registries, of which the Morgan in 1894 was the first, is accompanied by an extensive list of rules, based on morphological criteria, to determine what the breed is and what it is not. In the words of one expert, "acknowledging that of course there are always likely to be found some variations on type within so versatile a breed, those people who are dedicated to the Morgan *per se* realize their obligation to perpetuate, in fact, his basic character and disposition" (Mellin 1973:47). Once a breed is established, morphophological criteria and a particular expression—the Morgan "look"—are used to distinguish it from other breeds: "It is a bright, proud expression, at once intelligent, mischievous, a bit defiant and—totally irresistible! It is usually coupled with a snorty attitude, a tossing mane and an abundance of nervous animation" (Mellin 1973:47). Can it be mere coincidence that the Morgan look matches the characteristics ascribed to the archetypical Jeffersonian yeoman farmer? This Jeffersonian ideal-typical construction of The American is the sum total of perceived American virtues.

It is appropriate that the Morgan, as the first official American breed to serve as a marker of distinction, simultaneously claims to incorporate the essence of Americanism. The development of a distinctively American way of life was accompanied by what the historian John Higham, in a definitive account of this phenomenon, calls racial nativism: "intense opposition to an internal minority on the ground of its foreign (i.e., 'un-American') connections" (1967:4). Higham points to popular movements in the 1790s and 1850s in which nativistic agitation to define the American was particularly widespread. It was assumed, in both the popular and "scientific" literature of the nineteenth century, that there were at least three distinct European and many "non-Western" races. Yet it wasn't until the end of the nineteenth century that political and literary speculation on "racial difference" received its "scientific" legitimation from biologists, anthropologists, and genealogists (Higham 1967:149–157). In a parallel manner, the initial political and social origin of the Morgan horse of 1789 was only later, in 1894, legitimated by "science." Not until the end of the nineteenth century did the Morgan become a separate and distinct breed, based on scientifically verifiable "natural" biological distinctions.

While the notion of breed purity is common to most American breed registry associations, European warm-blood breeders seem unconcerned with purity, often using other breeds in order to improve their own, and switching identities freely. For example, a superior horse in the Hannoverian registry may be purchased by the Westphalian registry (or vice versa) and offspring will be registered without qualification. It is worth noting, then, what happens when Americans import these European "unprotected" breeds. To keep the imported bloodlines pure, Americans have created separate registries for each European warm-blood, reproducing the breed-exclusive registry that exists within more established American breeds. In some cases, separate registries are even kept for those bred in Europe and for those bred in America, as if the geographical locus of conception made a difference. The justification given is that the change in climatic conditions results in a loss of breed purity. The cross-breeding of imported European warmbloods with American breeds (such as Thoroughbred and Quarter Horse) has resulted in the recent creation of many half-breed registries. There have also been attempts in the past ten years in America to create single performance horse registries that would incorporate qualified "performance" horses from different breeds. But, significantly, these registries do not intend to challenge the breed-exclusive categories, for they allow and even encourage listing in both the specific breed and the performance registry. In other words, dual identities are created.

Conformation: Arab Breeders and Quarter-Horse People

The construction of breed criteria based on morphological characteristics can be clearly illustrated by comparing two well-known and popular American breeds, the Quarter Horse and the Arabian. Although it has been an official breed only since 1940, the Quarter Horse embodies more than any other breed the American West, and its origin is often expressed in a folksy Western manner. L. N. Sikes writes, "The history of the Quarter Horse goes back a long way—back before the time when anybody kept good accounts of what stock horses in this country even looked like" (1958:13). Of course, Sikes is not unaware of the part he plays in myth building, for he appropriates other myths of the Quarter Horse as myths, such as a virility myth told of Steel Dust, a foundation sire of the breed: "So much of

66

a reputation did Steel Dust get that, pretty soon, he began siring colts in places he's never been. In fact, up until recent years, lots of cowmen would refer to a Quarter-type horse as a 'steel dust'" (1958:13). One chronicler of the Western horse, Robert Denhardt, comments that "every horse trader who has not recently joined a church will modestly admit that his horses are direct descendants of Steel Dust" (1967:17). While the Morgan represents a particular east-coast-derived American archetype, the Quarter Horse appeals to a more general Western myth. Says Denhardt, "The Quarter Horse is a scion of the oldest and most aristocratic of American equine families, a race which can trace one side of the family to the May-flower and the other to the Conquistadors of Spain" (1967:178).

Arab breeders, as they are called by other horse people, are among the most eccentric horse owners in America. This is attrib-uted to many factors: They often fear riding their own spirited horses, they usually prize beauty and sentiment over function, and they commonly display an extreme fetishization of the parts of the horse. When asked to identify what makes an Arabian an Arabian to an Arab breeder, one man replied, "They have lots of mane. Lots of head with big eyes. And they are surrounded by fog." Arab breed-ers have made a fetish of the head, so that regardless of how the body of the horse is put together, or of how the horse moves (how it carries its rider), a proper Arab head—bulging eyes and nostrils, dished forehead, wild and flowing mane—is the most prized and determinative characteristic of the breed. Most pictorial represen-tations of the Arab show only the head and at times part of the neck. Sometimes it is surrounded by mist.

This contrasts with realist representations of the Quarter Horse, which often focus on the rear. At times the horse's head is turned so that it is staring back at the camera, though many photos in Quarter Horse advertisements show only the rear end. The history of the Quarter Horse parallels that of the territorial expansion of the United States. It originated in the southern United States, and was bred to run a sprint, a quarter of a mile. The thrusting power of a horse is to be found in a powerful rear end: a long hip with a muscular loin and well-developed gaskin muscles. The Quarter Horse was bred for this powerful rear end. Because of its special stopping and starting ability, it is particularly suited for use in cattle herding on the open range. With the western expansion and the growth of the open range, Americans, not surprisingly, found Quarter Horses to be most suited to their needs. Thus, this American sport horse was developed for purely local ends—for short-distance racing and cattle herding. Yet a third use of the Quarter Horse arose, that of a docile and tractable show horse. The number of horses devoted to this third use presently far exceeds that in the racing and cattle-herding oriented uses for which the horse was initially bred.

Paradoxically, as the initial functions of the Quarter Horse became less important, the prime symbol of those functions—the distinctive rear end—took on increased significance. The fetish surrounding this body part has resulted in the breeding of some horses that are uncomfortable to ride, for often the rear end is out of proportion to the front, creating not a more powerful engine but an unbalanced, downhill-moving horse. This kind of horse, known as the Bull-Dog type, "hits the ground hard" when it moves, jarring the teeth of its riders and decreasing the longevity of the horse, as its legs and feet have difficulty withstanding the pounding. One admirer of the leaner type of Quarter Horse refers to the Bull Dog as a "muscle-bound weight lifter trying to be a boxer" (Davis 1962:9).

During the 1960s the popularity of showing horses greatly increased and show classes proliferated.[5] Halter classes, where the horses are led into the ring and judged purely on conformation with no concurrent attempt to link this to a performance aspect (like a swimsuit beauty competition, where the contestants need not swim), expanded greatly in number and took on increased status and significance. This was accompanied by increased specialization within each breed, so that a racing Quarter Horse was of a type different from a Quarter Horse used for show. And the show-horse category was further subdivided into horses that could win "at halter" and those that could win "in performance." With the increased importance of the showhorse aspects to the majority of breeders, who prized (with money and status) competitive wins in the halter classes over those in performance classes, less attention was paid to those aspects that keep the horses sound, that is, physically healthy. Put simply, beauty became divorced from function. In order to accentuate the bulk (thus, the beauty) of the body, Quarter-Horse breeders during the 1960s and 1970s also selected horses with refined bones and

68

feet, and they introduced some Thoroughbred blood—Thoroughbreds have slighter bodies and more refined limbs—into the registry. Many breeders today acknowledge that these particular conceptions of beauty, having an attenuated and even adverse relationship to function, have resulted in a physical weakening of the breed.[6]

A particularly distinctive and popular class at Arabian horse shows is the "Arabian costume class," for which owners dress their horses and themselves in what they think of as typical Arabian costumes. The horse's head is appropriately highlighted, with plumes on the top. The horse's body is covered (who wants to see the body?) by sequined silk multicolored blankets with small white or blue pompons sewed around the edges. While most of the body is cloth covered, the head and neck are further accentuated with silver-plated bridles on which are inscribed the names of the horse, names of Arabic origin that none of the participants can pronounce. After all the performers are gathered in the arena, they circle the judge, each at a pace the individual prefers. They are then asked by the judge, usually a male, to perform individually. From a line-up in the middle of the arena, the performers individually circle the judge and the other riders, displaying their costumes to best advantage. Most often this is done at a hand gallop—a very fast canter—so that the rider's long silk robe and the pompons on the horse's blanket will billow in the wind, creating the feeling of speed and light movement. In several classes that I have watched, the female performers played upon Western ideas of the sexuality of the Arab world by going braless under their light silk robes. A Wisconsin woman, Fanny O'Brien, who had imported an Egyptian Arabian stallion, would also, after her gallop, race up to the male judge, stopping within inches of him, and lean forward so that he could smell her perfume and see her form under her Arab silks. She was always the talk of the show, and never lost a costume class during the four years (of the 1960s) in which I knew her.

Color: The Paint

The color breeds—for example, Paint, Appaloosa, Pinto, Albino, Palomino—while incorporating all three breed-classificatory criteria (function, conformation, and color) in both their mythology and

69

their current registry standards, single out color as the necessary and sufficient condition of incorporation. A color breed such as the Paint, in order to constitute itself as a separate and distinct breed that is understood as a biological (that is, genetic) category, must assert that certain criteria, either singly or in combination, are uniquely Paint. In the effort to maintain and justify the distinctiveness of the color category, Paint owners and breeders engage in ceaseless semiotic and ideological maneuvering. In an article on the social uses of color codes, Marshall Sahlins provides an initial framework for explaining the semiotic aspect of the construction of the Paint breed: "Colors are in practice semiotic codes. Everywhere, both as terms and concrete properties, colors are engaged as signs in vast schemes of social relations, meaningful structures by which persons and groups, objects and occasions, are differentiated and combined in cultural orders" (1977:166)

The Paint provides a specific example of the development of a color code, and can be used to extend Sahlin's insight. Two related questions should be kept in mind: First, can one isolate the various strategies used to produce this cultural order, and, second, what is the relationship between the ideological motivations and the semiotics of color coding?

Even though the founding of the Paint-Horse registry, with which its legitimation as a breed begins, did not occur until February 1962, much importance is placed upon its ancestry, that it has existed forever, or nearly so. Its beginnings are traced back to 20,000 B.C. in Spain, southern France, Arabia, and North Africa. There is some confusion in the early records (that is, prior to 1519, when the Paint is definitively dated as reaching America), as it is "impossible to trace the movements of each breed" because no distinction was usually made between the different kinds of spotted horses (Haynes 1976:3).

After the fifteenth century, the record supposedly becomes clearer, and we are told that, for instance, the Indians in America domesticated the Paint Horse "because they had an eye for anything bright or colorful," and that they apparently thought Paint Horses were better camouflaged than solid colored ones (Haynes 1976:24, 25). "Paints" continue to be associated with the domesticated Other, which in this case is the American Indian. Popular forms of representation, from such diverse media as films and horse-show costume class performances, index the Paint as "colored." From the television serial

70

"The Lone Ranger" in the 1950s, where the Ranger (white) rides a Palomino but Tonto (Indian) a Paint, to the film *Silverado* in the 1980s, where the hero rides a white horse and the buffoon a Paint, the mythical history of the breed is reconfirmed. Today the Paint Horse and the other color breeds can be found in all parts of the United States, although they tend to be more concentrated in the West.

Since 1962, the criteria of classification have changed several times because it has been difficult to decide, as one breeder put it, "How much color is a Paint Horse?" (Haynes 1976:54). Initially, it was required that the Paint be recognizable as such from both sides, but this has been changed so that now only one side need be so recognizable. At present the other requirements for inclusion are height (fifty-six inches at age two years), gaitedness, and conformation approval (in the case of a stallion). For those that fulfill these requirements but are not offspring of registered parents, patrilateral descent, that is, paternity from a stallion in another approved registry (for example, Quarter Horse or Thoroughbred), is an added requirement. Apparently, the dam's lineage can be considered inconsequential for the purposes of breed inclusion. This American oversight—denial of the genetic importance of the mother—is not peculiar to the Paint breed; it is a quite common practice in the origin of most breeds.[7]

The requirements for participation in show classes for the Paint Horse are similar to those of the Quarter Horse, which the Paint Horse closely approximates in function and performance.[8] The one characteristic that all Paints are supposed to share—color—is also the only characteristic that is ruled out as a consideration when judging halter classes. The only class in which color is to be considered a factor is in a color class, a nonpoint (no cumulative year-end award) class judged solely on color. For show purposes, any Paint Horse, once accepted in the registry, has sufficient color.

What is most significant about the Paint Horse breed is that the criterion on which it bases its claim to a breed status is not and never can be genetically isolated, for "noncolor breeds" will at times produce horses that theoretically qualify as ideal Paints, and Paint Horses will often produce full-colored offspring. Many color patterns are carried by recessive genes.[9] Some horses unpredictably change color patterns several times during their lives. Nevertheless, given the social importance in America of the horse breeds as

71

a form of distinction making, each breed must necessarily be conceptualized as distinct, and invested with an ideal type. Horses not adequately measuring up to this ideal will be rejected as impure. Thus, the Quarter-Horse registry will refuse to register full-blood Quarter Horses with impeccable lineages but that have too much white or have color in the "wrong" place (that can, in other words, qualify as Paints) and will demand that the animals be withdrawn as breeding stock (by gelding the stallions and spaying the mares). The rules for inclusion as Paint are the same as the rules for exclusion as a Quarter Horse, namely, that color markings as decided by "body contrasts" must or must not be of a particular type and in a specific location (Haynes 1976:70).

The use of color as a "primordial classifier" illustrates the social embeddedness of semiotic codes and the consistency of ideological motivations within any particular cultural order. The resort to mythical histories, to genealogies based on shared blood or patrilateral descent, and to functional claims (conduct codes) parallels the kind of strategies most often used to constitute the kinship systems of human groups. The consistent breakdown of the category-use does not result in a denial of their naturalness, but rather in a reformulation of the color combinations that signify the breed. Color use never merely names objective differences in the visible spectrum of *signified* color patterns; it also, as Sahlins has argued, arbitrarily *signifies* and communicates culturally constituted social relationships.

The Production of Distinction: Good Horse Flesh

As we have just seen, the practico-theoretical logics governing the life and thought of so-called primitive societies are shaped by the insistence on differentiation.

—Claude Lévi-Strauss, *The Savage Mind*

The practice of sports ... owes part of its "interests," just as much nowadays as at the beginning, to its distinguishing function, and more precisely, to the gains in distinction which it brings.

—Pierre Bourdieu, "Sport and Social Class"

72

It should now be clear how American horse breeds, based on arbitrary distinctions of function, conformation, and color, are constantly manufactured. Furthermore, these distinctions and significations are not derived from some natural pan-cultural ordering of the animal kingdom, but are peculiarly American social distinctions that are in turn mapped onto differences found within a given species. The differences are indeed arbitrary: fetishes of parts (nostrils, eyes, and necks for the Arabian, rear ends for the Quarter Horse), priorities of color (for the Paint Horse or the Palomino), mythologies of origin and temperament (for the Morgan). By *arbitrary* I do not mean that these significations are unmotivated signs, but simply that the motivation chosen is one among other possibilities. There are, indeed, limits to the arbitrariness of a signification, but these limits are ideological constraints, not semiological ones. For the example of horse breeds, the meaning attached to function, conformation, and color is possible precisely because it is motivated by similar divisions in the social world of people.[10]

In the remainder of this essay the question to be addressed, then, is how and why this particular set of ideological constraints motivates the semiotics of horse-breed distinctions. Why do Americans set up new rules for each breed rather than, like the Europeans, agree to one set of performance rules for all breeds? A passage from Lévi-Strauss, explicating the relation of totem to caste and the "conceptual transformations marking the passage from exogamy to endogamy," suggests an answer to this question:

> But if social groups are considered not so much from the point of view of their reciprocal relations in social life as each on their own account, in relation to something other than sociological reality, then the idea of diversity is likely to prevail over that of unity. Each social group will tend to form a system no longer with other social groups but with particular differentiating properties regarded as hereditary, and these characteristics exclusive to each group will weaken the framework of their solidarity within the society. The more each group tries to define itself by the image which it draws from a natural model, the more difficult will it become for it to maintain its links with other social groups and, in particular

73

to exchange its sisters and daughters with them since it will tend to think of them as being of a particular "species" (1966:177–78).

If Lévi-Strauss's conceptualization is correct, then the movement from exogamous to endogamous horse breeding would involve specific formative steps. How did the American horse breeds become species-like (or, one might ask, are endogamy and caste-status preconditions for constituting a breed)? This can be illustrated by examining the three processes involved in the creation of "good horse flesh": Breeds are conceptualized, registries are created, and breed divisions are enforced.

While the definition of breed varies from writer to writer, certain themes are held in common. Wayne Dinsmore says a breed exists when a "substantial number of animals within a species . . . differentiat[e] them[selves] from others of the same species" (1978:103). J. W. Evans relies on an argument of human or abstract needs to explain breeds: "Breeds were developed according to the needs of horsepeople in each locality, or they developed naturally" (1977:101). Along with these two basic assumptions, many writers date the official origin (other than that offered in their mythologies) to the foundation of a registry. The importance placed on the official codification is often so great that, in his history of the Appaloosa (1975) for example, Jan Haddle dates the breed to the opening of its official registry in 1949, even though this is a year after the first full-Appaloosa horse show.

Haynes makes the above connections explicit: A breed is "a variety or stock of animals related by descent with certain inherited characteristics and capable of reproducing those chracteristics," but has also come to mean "animals registered in some association or club" (1976:61). This emphasis upon being recorded in the stud register or the registry of a particular breed is also regarded as the distinguishing characteristic of breed by the *Manual of Horsemanship,* which is published by the British Horse Society and The Pony Club, and is the most authoritative text on horse basics in all the Western English-speaking countries. The registry—that is, the concept consanguinity—has now taken on an institutional raison d'être, so that superior animals fitting the breed specifications will be rejected if their progenitors are not already members of the registry.[11] This needs to be so, says Haynes, because "it takes several generations of recorded and scientific breeding to establish a family or strain" (1976:62). Horse breeders themselves recognize the creative and constitutive nature of their endeavor. "There is no reason," says John Gorman, "why a group of horse breeders of a certain type and color cannot preserve the purity of the horses' breeding and eventually establish a breed" (1958:229).

In order to establish "pure breeds," most breed associations at some point established extensive inspection programs through which individual animals were (or are) initially approved for a breed registry. Haynes points out that the desire to "ensure uniformity in the breed" led to "rigid stallion inspections" as one of many necessary "police actions" (1976:52). The Quarter-Horse inspection program (no longer active because the breed registry is closed) can serve as an example of how these actions were carried out. If a horse's progenitors were not both registered, or if the progenitors were unknown, an owner could petition for inspection. After an initial inspection by an officially approved inspector, who was most often flown to the site where the petitioned animal was kept, the animal would be either rejected or accepted into the registry as an appendix-registered horse. The horse would then be required to compete and win in several different divisions (for example, racing, halter, performance) at official Quarter-Horse shows in order to accumulate the required number of points. Thereafter, animals that fulfilled these requirements were automatically admitted into the full registry, with the possibility that they could be used as breeding stock.[12]

The State, Social Structure, Cultural Categories

Just as there are many distinct, mutually exclusive—that is, castelike—American horse breeds, there are also many styles of riding. On the Continent[13] not only is there a single standard—performance—for breeding, but also a uniform set of presuppositions concerning how training and riding the horse should progress.[14] These continental presuppositions are formalized and systematized in the art of "dressage." I will briefly sketch how this codification pro-

75

gressed, concentrating on the post-Medieval period, as it allows us to bring together the interactions among cultural categories, social structures, and the nascent states of Europe.[15] This comparative discussion of the sociopolitical context in which breed categorization developed is intended to illuminate the American situation, and not to provide an exhaustive account of European state and horse-breed development.

The first written texts on the different aspects of horsemanship in the West are attributed to Xenophon in 500 B.C. For the next twenty centuries, however, there was very little written on breeding type and riding style. According to the current literature on horses and horsemanship, there were also no appreciable improvements in understanding, training, or breeding of the animals (at least in the West)[16] until the fifteenth century. After the fall of the Roman Empire, the use of infantry declined and that of cavalry increased, although this does not appear to have had any immediate effect on improving the caliber of horsemanship. Yet between 1500 and 500 B.C. the domesticated horse, arriving from the East, became common to much of Western Europe. This "noble beast . . . was associated with a new social distinction," comments Emmanuel Le Roi Ladurie, "[and] in its way it marked the appearance of a group of aristocrats, living off contributions levied from the peasants" (1979:80). In addition to its function in changing agricultural techniques, the horse was simultaneously appropriated as an indexical symbol, associated with the growing nobility and with knighthood.

The formalization of riding and the development of *haute école* began again during the Renaissance in the fifteenth century. It reached a fountainhead at the riding School of Naples, which served as a source for subsequent developments among the Hapsburgs (and the Spanish Riding School) in Austria, the French, and the British. A student from that school, de Pluvinel, is thought to be the originator of the French school. Antoine de Pluvinel's book, *The Instruction of the King in the Art of Riding,* printed in 1626, was written as a dialogue between the author and his pupil, Louis XIII. Following upon these beginnings, Louis XIV, from the splendor of his court, created a French riding school—the School of Versailles— in the Tuileries. In 1733, the Frenchman Robichon de La Guérnière, who conducted this school, wrote what is still considered the classic text on dressage. His teachings formed the basis for all subsequent cavalry schools, the most famous of which is the Cavalry School of Saumur, founded in 1771, a direct descendant of the School of Versailles. Advances in horse breeding and training in France subsequently emanated from contacts with the Saumur school, which to this day retains its role in licensing instructors, trainers, and judges.

What one can conclude from this account is that horse riding in France is marked by the reliance of a particular cultural standard upon the court culture and upon the development of a military elite situated in and near Paris. The growth of the performance standard in France is inextricably linked both to the process of formalization of rules of etiquette among French nobility and to the utilization of the horse in the military-political centralization of France.[17] One is reminded of Alexis de Tocqueville's account of the demise of the *ancien régime,* his central thesis being that "in France, more than in any other European country, the provinces had come under the thrall of the metropolis, which attracted to itself all that was most vital in the nation" (1955:72). Despite the fact that Louis XIV "tried to check the growth of Paris" six times, administrative centralization was the marked tendency of the French territory from the beginning of the seventeenth century, where the "true owner" of the landed estates in the kingdom "was the State and the State alone" (Tocqueville 1955:189). Tocqueville illustrates the tendency of the provinces to look toward Paris for leadership in all aspects of cultural and political life with a comment from a provincial: "We are only a provincial town; we must wait till Paris gives us a lead." He infers from this that the provinces seemed "not to dare to form an opinion until they knew what was being thought in Paris" (1955:74). The German historian Otto Hintze is in accord that "the transition occurred only in the seventeenth and eighteenth centuries, the period of absolutism and administrative centralization; it was finally completed by Napoleon. As a unified state, moreover, France became the model of development for the entire continent" (1973:168).[18]

Whereas the development of "France" is marked by political centralization, that of "Germany" is by bureaucratization. The most common explanation for the bureaucratic centralization of Prussia in the eighteenth century is that external, chiefly military, threats from the new states in the West forced internal developments toward increasing centralization (*Cf.* Hintze 1973:168–169; Craig 1978:1–34; Wehler 1973).[19] Thus, in the Prussian case, military needs, initially tied to cavalry effectiveness, necessitated breeding of animals that correspond somewhat to our present light-horse category.[20] This effort followed upon, and was modeled after, the successful school at Saumur in France, for monarchs and nobility commonly borrowed from each other. Since the purpose here is not to explain differences on the Continent,[21] but the differences between the American model and the continental one, it is important to emphasize that the Germans and French are much alike in holding a particular pan-national breed standard (although the manner in which and reasons for which these standards were propagated differ), whereas in America, with a weak state formed on pluralist (federalist) premises, there occurred a proliferation of breed standards.

For Americans, nation building—the creation of shared cultural-identity markers—took precedence over state building. In marked contrast to Europe, America had neither a court culture, nor large, threatening states on its borders. The classic formulation as to why political centralization never occurred to the same extent in America as in Europe was put forth by Louis Hartz, who argued that the absence of feudal social institutions, including an aristocratic *cultural* elite, made unnecessary the centralization of power required to dislodge it (1955:43–46). Samuel Huntington concludes from this initial premise that, while the American state, in its subsequent development, "often helped to promote economic development, . . . it played only a minor role in changing social customs and social structure" (1973:193). Furthermore, without "external enemies" as a backdrop against which a national identity is imagined,[22] American *national* identity was (and is) imagined as an internal affair. This has meant both a nativist universalism, as Higham has articulated, and a pluralist melting-pot folk ideology concerning the nature and expression of cultural difference.

In France and Germany, centralization—political in the French case and bureaucratic in the German one—played the key role in establishing a universalistic cultural standard, which for horse breeding is expressed in a single performance criterion. In the United States, diverse cultural standards and social strata were never subject to strong political or bureaucratic structures capable of or in need of bringing about a uniform performance standard. Consequently, particularistic cultural standards, as in the domain of horse breeds, were generated as "separate but equal" social-identity markers. Where state building precedes nation building on the Continent, centralized administration and hierarchical modelling leads to uniform breed standards. Where nation building precedes state building in the United States, the denial of social difference and of hierarchy leads to heterogeneous and separate but formally "equal" cultural breed standard.

Race, Ethnicity, Species, Breed

Totemism, as Lévi-Strauss argues, is the postulation of a homology between two systems of differences. It is a way of thinking that has no intrinsic content. Lévi-Strauss makes it clear that totemism is the establishment of homologies not between the terms themselves, but only between the *differences* "which manifest themselves on the level of groups on the one hand and that of species on the other" (1966:115). He represents this as follows:

Nature: species 1 ≠ species 2 ≠ species 3 ≠ .... species n

Culture: group 1 ≠ group 2 ≠ group 3 ≠ .... group n

It is the same "pure totemic structure" that I am suggesting exists in the creation of breed categories in America. The relationships suggested are not between particular breed and particular ethnic or racial categories but between a *system of human differentiation* and a *system of breed differentiation*. It can be represented as follows:

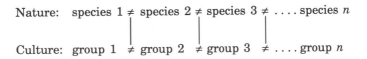

Breeds: Quarter Horse ≠ Morgan ≠ Paint ≠ Arabian ≠ .... breed n

Humans: Anglo Saxon   ≠ German ≠ Black ≠ Italian   ≠ .... ethnic/racial group n

The melting-pot ideology notwithstanding, American social groups increasingly tend to be in practice statistically endogamous, occupationally differentiated, and residentially separated from one another (Thurow 1980, 1975; Harrington 1984, 1980).

The term *ethnicity,* which has traditionally been used to refer to forms of regional identity based upon customs and influences from outside the society in which the groups now live, is increasingly recognized as indicating relationships based upon differences used to demarcate indigenous groups from one another (Glazer and Moynihan 1975). Michael Hechter has postulated that a common form of ethnicity is a reactive group formation, where groups adopt historically established distinctions to demarcate themselves from other groups, rather than adopting these identities in an interactive, closed group (1978). Sociolinguistic work by John Gumperz (1982a, 1982b) indicating the persistence of linguistic and discourse differentiations has forced reevaluation of the logic behind and reasons for the use of diverse discourse conventions.

There is no need to go into detail on the significance and persistence of collective descent and race as distinction-making categories in American history (Gossett 1963; on the relationship of race to ethnicity and class, see Altschuler 1982). Many writers have argued that race is the most significant category for Americans. A 1937 study of etiquette and race in the American South begins with the assertion that "the American people seem to exhibit a perennial interest in problems pertaining to contact and association of the many races which constitute the general population" (Doyle 1937:viii). The logic of racial differentiation is often explained in a manner similar to Hechter's reactive-group-formation thesis. L. Copeland states, "Wherever the groups and classes are set in sharp juxtaposition, the values and mores of each are juxtaposed. Out of group opposition there arises an intense opposition of values, which comes to be projected through the social order and serves to solidify social stratification" (1959:171).

Conclusion

That is why myth is experienced as innocent speech: not because its intentions are hidden—if they were hidden, they could not be efficacious—but because they are naturalized.

[M]ythology harmonizes with the world, not as it is, but as it wants to create itself.

—Roland Barthes, "Myth Today"

80

Horse breeders and riders experience their breed classifications innocently. The myths they spin about their cultural performances, while not maliciously motivated, are also not harmless. These classifications do not arise from virginal minds. Rather, at the point of their origin and in their reproduction they serve as perpetual alibis, by naturalizing and legitimating the social order about which they speak. Unlike "the primitive," the century-old creation of anthropological study, who is said to deny nature and to reify culture, Americans seek to reify certain parts of their culture which they falsely identify as nature. Americans forget that "nature," in as far as it is experienced and becomes part of a human life-world, is also a cultural construct.

It is no accident that American notions and usage of horse breeds—where the concepts of race and ethnicity, blood and breeding, have all become reified into biological naturalisms—are first taken from human categories and then projected onto animal classifications. In the American case, Durkheim's basic insight about the relation of totem to clan can be confirmed. The concept of horse breeds is, in fact, a stolen language, stolen from our practice of social structure. This is a specific instance of a general phenomenon that can only be explained as a reverse totemism. Horse breeds are thus an example of what Sahlins has called scientific totemism (1976:106).

The creation, in our image, of a world of differentiated animal species is also inextricably linked to the reciprocal influences of cultural categories, social-structural practices, and the formation of nation-state identities. Although in everyday speech the terms *breed* and *species,* or *race, ethnicity,* and *species* may not be confused, in practice the different horse breeds are treated as if they were separate species. Since breed, like race, is confused with and often considered a matter of genetics and biology, and not culture, and since biology is considered the ultimate arbiter of phenomenological disputes, the naturalness of this social order is never questioned. In this case, the post-Mendelian scientific discourse on genetics enters the history of horse breeding after the forms of classification and their motivations have already been culturally cast. Today, the relationship of the science of genetics to popular representations and practices, when not serving a merely legitimating role for what is already there, remains tenuous.

81

Though this essay focuses on the analysis of the totemic nature of horsebreed categorization in America, the theoretical implications of the argument are broader. As Roland Barthes so perspicaciously argued, and as the specific examples here illustrate, the mythical systems produced through classificatory devices, while experienced as innocent speech, are in fact constructed, first, by a plagiarism of the social world, and second, by a harmonization of that plagiarism with its dominant discourse. This kind of myth is neither simply a charter for reality nor is it an invention of pure thought. It is both a language for analogically representing and reconstituting another reality—a hierarchical system of human differentiation—and a means by which that reality can be validated.

NOTES

I would like to thank Sally F. Moore for several critical readings of this essay. Thanks are also owed to Charles Lindholm, Chris Waters, Peter Sahlins, Daniel Goldhagen, and Carlos Forment for their suggestions.

1. When dealing with horse breed classification, one encounters several coexisting category systems. In the words of one authority, "now nearly every country has its own national, as opposed to native, breeds. . . . In each case, these breeds have been developed to meet the interest, demands and requirements of the individual country" (Skelton 1978:10–11). The cultural differences at the linguistic level alone can be the subject of an entire book. For example, *breed* and *race* have separate, though overlapping, semantic usages in English. Yet, the words *race* in French and *Rasse* in German are used for both people and animal classifications.

There are three categories of horse generally recognized throughout the world among people who domesticate horses. The *cold-blooded* horses, which are not dealt with in this paper, are those functional draft breeds used for pulling heavy loads but generally not ridden. *Cold-blooded* can also mean phlegmatic and tractable. The term *hot-blooded* is most generally limited to horses of the Thoroughbred and Arabian breeds. Three Arabians, imported to England in 1689, 1705, and 1730, are the foundation sires of the English Thoroughbred. These two breeds are also considered *full-bloods* because they have engaged in endogamous breeding programs over a long period of time. *Full-blood* and hot-blood are often used, many maintain incorrectly, interchangeably. *Hot-blooded* can also mean excitable and sensitive. The third category of horse, the subject of this essay, are termed *light-horse* breeds, often a cross between the other two types and used for domestic riding and competitive performance. In the United States they are not simply animals for "ritually-demarcated" use, and the theoretical distinction between ritual and everyday is not useful in explaining their categorization.

The term *warm-blood* refers to those European breeds established specifically for show purposes. They are a cross between Thoroughbreds or Arabians and locals draft horses, and are the primary light-horse category in Europe. Each European country has at least several different warm-bloods, which tend to be named after their geographical origins. While draft-horse and Arab breed categories have been constant over several centuries, light-horse breeds (which also includes the English Thorough-bred) are relatively recent in origin (eighteenth and nineteenth centuries), and in the United States new ones continue to be created. The point being elaborated in this essay is that the continental European and American breeds are constituted by different generative principles. The American breeds discussed here are uniformly recognized within the American horse world (see, e.g., AHSA 1982–83; Kays 1982; Skelton 1978; Davis 1962, Evans 1977; Gorman 1958; Haddle 1975; Haynes 1976; *Horse Identifier* 1980).

2. Lévi-Strauss has often been accused of reifying cognitive struc-tures. Although he does not deal with the social relations out of which the ideological transformations he outlines are drawn, he recognizes their theoretical significance: "It is of course only for purposes of exposition and because they form the subject of this book that I am apparently giving a sort of priority to ideology and superstructures. I do not at all mean to suggest that ideological transformations give rise to social ones. Only the reverse is in fact true. Men's conceptions of the relations between nature and culture is a function of modifications of their own social relations. But, since my aim here is to outline a theory of superstructures, reasons of method require that they should be singled out for attention and that major phenomena which have no place in this programme should seem to be left in brackets or given second place. We are however merely studying the shadows on the wall of the Cave without forgetting that it is only the attention we give them which lends them a semblance or reality" (1966:117).

3. *Dressage,* meaning to school or train, provides the basic principles for all hippology, but is today often narrowed to what is in the vernacular called classical riding. Classical, or "high school," riding takes many years of training and supervision, for both the horse and rider, to achieve a moderate level of accomplishment. While in most other riding sports horses

can be trained to their maximum capacity in from six months (racing) to two years (show jumping), a horse generally requires seven years of methodical ballet-like training under the guidance of an expert trainer to achieve the ability to perform at the Grand Prix level of dressage.

4. Authors differ in accounting for the nature of Justine Morgan's death. Jeanne Mellin, in her idealistic biography of the horse, claims he "died of an injury" (1973:10). Charles Trench maintains that after the death of the original owner, Justine Morgan was turned out to pasture in the harsh northeast winter, like any other horse, "where he was eaten by wolves" (1972:28).

5. The entire "industry" of horse-breed production and showing is in fact growing rapidly. The following table listing the growth of several major breeds is taken from Dinsmore (1978).

REGISTRY	YEAR FORMED	HORSES IN 1960	HORSES IN 1977
AQHA	1914	37,000	1,350,000
Thoroughbred	1894	12,901	760,000
Appaloosa	1938	4,052	760,000
Morgan	1894	1,069	275,000
Paint	1962	2,390	30,000
Palomino	1936	657	9,013
Half-Arab	1955	2,200	178,400
Arabian	1908	1,160	125,000

6. The Arabian horse, incidentally, has always been known as an endurance horse rather than a quick stopper and starter; it has a weakly muscled rear end and often crooked hind legs (cow-hocked or sickle-hocked). Consequently, there is no fetishization of the rear. Yet, as in the case of the Quarter Horse, halter classes have increased in importance for the Arabians. Although this shift was based upon different sets of morphological criteria, in both cases less attention was paid to how the horse performed. Many Arabs, bred for heads and necks that blend gently with the rest of the body, for "smooth toplines," lack an adequate withers to hold the saddle in place. Consequently, not only the saddle, but also the rider is continually sliding forward. Such fetishization of parts and "dysfunctional developments" have not, to my knowledge, occurred in Europe, perhaps because of the close ties of function to performance in the European sport horse.

7. An old aphorism says: The mare contributes the disposition, the stallion the conformation. Then, again, there are commonly recognized

84

stallions in each breed that are called prepotent because they pass on their characteristics to their offspring. In America, these particular stallions are said to have a lot of "type" and to be "true to their breed."

8. The exact description of the Ideal-type and conformation is given as follows: "The Paint Horse is a stock-type horse. Head relatively short and wide with small muzzle and shallow, firm mouth; nostrils full and sensitive; ears short and active, set wide apart; large eyes, set wide; well-developed jaws with width between lower edges; neck of sufficient length, with a trim throatlatch and not too much thickness or depth joining the head at a 45-degree angle and blending into sloping shoulders which are long and relatively heavy muscled; medium-high and well-defined withers the same height as croup; deep and broad chest with wide-set forelegs and well-muscled forearm; back short, close-coupled and powerful across loin; deep girth with well-sprung ribs; broad, deep, heavy, well-muscled quarters that are full through the thigh, stifle, and gaskin; cannon bones short with broad, flat, clean, strong, low-set knees and hocks; firm ankles and medium length, sloping pasterns; tough, textured feet with wide open heel" ASHA 1982–83:235).

9. For a useful discussion of the genetic component in breed reproduction, see Warwick and Legates (1979:553–585). They conclude that although the horse appears to be a "genetically plastic species," we are still ignorant of the "genetic parameters of quantitative traits in horses" (1979:567).

10. In an extensive discussion concerning the names given to animals, Lévi-Strauss classifies racehorses as metaphorical inhuman beings (1966:207). He first narrows his discussion of names to racehorses, for "ordinary horses whose place approximates more or less closely to that of cattle or that of dogs according to the class and occupation of their owner . . . is made even more uncertain by the rapid technological changes of recent times" (1966:206). Reflecting upon English names, Edmund Leach agrees with him concerning racehorses, but disagrees as to cattle and dogs (1974:100–102). With regard to the American case, I would emphasize Lévi-Strauss's caveat concerning the historical nature of naming "ordinary horses," which, as he uses the term, are the subject of this essay. I would also extend the caveat to racehorses, dogs, and cattle. While naming always involves political power in that it never merely describes but also constitutes the object, there are serious limitations to an approach that determines the signification of animals based solely upon a study of their names as part of a semiological system. The names themselves are determined by a combination of material, symbolic, and functional aspects of

the animal's relation to humans. It should be added that function, conformation, and color of horses are not merely metaphorical extensions of
differences in occupation, morphology, and color of people. There is also a
metonymical identification between the temperament, origins, and functions of particular horses and the corresponding would-be or aspired-to
characteristics of social groups. This kind of identification has only been
suggested in this essay, and deserves further study.

11. Gorman (1958:313) elaborates the levels of categorization used
in speaking about individuals who are partially or fully part of a specific
breed. A purebred "is a horse whose ancestors have been recognized as a
breed for several generations. They are generally registered in a breed
association." "A registered horse is one that has been recorded in a registration association by name and number." "A crossbred is a horse whose
sire and dam are of different purebred breeds." A *grade* usually means a
horse that had one purebred parent and one of unknown or mixed breeding. A more basic distinction is often made between hot-blood and cold-
blood, which roughly corresponds to the light-horse/draft-horse division.
Haynes describes a hot-blood morphologically, as having "smooth body lines,
trim legs and feet, quick movement, maneuverable speed" (1976:62).

12. For a perspective on the extensiveness of an inspection program,
note the following two years of statistics for the Quarter Horse (Sikes
1958:12):

YEAR	MILES DRIVEN BY INSPECTORS	HORSES ASSIGNED FOR INSPECTION	PERCENTAGE ACCEPTED	PERCENTAGE REJECTED
1956	199,011	5,888	68	32
1957	264,890	9,007	70	30

13. Although the pattern to be sketched is generally true for the
Continent as a whole, I am limiting the discussion to Germany and France.
Germany is today the recognized exemplary center of international horse
competition, of dressage in particular, and a center of breeding for this
purpose. Yet, it is in seventeenth- and eighteenth-century France that
light-horse riding as we know it today became codified, and for this reason,
the development of French breeding and showing served as an exemplary
center for the rest of the Continent.

14. In an article on sport and social class, Bourdieu makes several
related observations about the French case. He maintains that the "extension of the public beyond the circle of amateurs helps to reinforce the reign

of the pure professions," and he attributes "decisive political effects" to "the division it makes between professionals, the virtuosi of an esoteric technique, and laymen, reduced to the role of mere consumers" (1978:829, 830). While democratization and popularization of certain sports (that is, the extension of participation from royalty in elite schools to military to mass sporting associations) in Europe may have led to the solidification of status differences, the process in America is different. This is because, first, many sports in America were not initially confined to an elite or to a group of amateur connoiseurs (for example, racing, Western riding); rather they were initially quite democratic. Second, the movement has been toward a proliferation of breeds, sports organizations, and shows, all roughly hierarchically ranked and indexically related to the creation of class and status distinctions in the general population. The consequence has been an appropriation of particular breeds by particular social classes.

15. The account here of this history follows the similar, although more detailed, accounts in the following texts: Seunig 1956; Wynmalen 1966; Kellock 1975; Skelton 1978; Goodall 1982.

16. Xenophon's texts appear enlightened and contemporary when compared to documents published in the Middle Ages. Laurentius Rusius, in *Hippiatrica sive marescalia,* printed in Paris in 1533, notes: "The nappy horse should be kept locked in a stable for forty days, thereupon to be mounted wearing large spurs and a strong whip; or else the rider will carry an iron bar, three or four feet long and ending in three well sharpened hooks, and if the horse refuses to go forward he will dig one of these hooks into the horse's quarters and draw him forward; alternatively an assistant may apply a heated iron bar under the horse's tail, whilst the rider drives the spurs in with all available strength" (quoted in Wynmalen 1966:27).

17. For detailed and theoretical treatment of the history of manners in France and Germany, see Nobert Elias (1978, 1982). Elias emphasizes both the internalization of norms and the external, policing efforts toward making particular cultural standards uniform. Although, for reasons of length, I am not dealing with the social conditions that made possible the reception and adoption of a national standard, imposed from without, the social levelling processes that preceded and subsequently accelerated after the French Revolution are acknowledged as important in the creation of French nationalism.

18. Arguments concerning the effects of French political centralization on cultural development are put forth by Pierre Bourdieu and Jean-Claude Passeron (1977) on national education, and by Eugen Weber (1976)

on the creation of national identity among French peasants. Pierre Birnbaum makes the strongest theoretical statement, claiming that the French state is an independent variable, setting the limits for cultural and social processes (1980; Badie and Birnbaum 1983).

19. Max Weber, commenting on the importance of bureaucratization in the development of Germany, notes that the lack of powerful status groups of notables in Germany was in part responsible for the absence of political centralization (1978:976–977). In an extended treatment of the Prussian experience, Hans Rosenberg maintains that during the *ancien régime* the bureaucracy "ceased to be responsible to dynastic interest" and "recast the system of government in its own image" (1966:vii). By 1815, the "political hegemony of the bureaucracy . . . was firmly established" (1966:227). By 1871, German political unification was complete. The interesting aspect of German breeding is that even without political centralization, each German breeding program (*Landgestüt*) bureaucratized and rationalized separately. The history of German breeding is too lengthy to deal with here; however, I might note that the Teutonic Order of Knights already owned sixty-one stallions in 1400. In 1732, Frederick William I started the Trakehner Royal stud which was later taken over by the Prussian state upon the death of his son, Frederick the Great. Yet during the nineteenth century eighty percent of breeding still lay in the hands of small breeders, and the Trakehner horses were not branded until 1888. The Oldenburg breed was constituted in the seventeenth century by Count Gunther, but not subject to licensing of stallions and breeding control until 1819. This can be compared with the early date, 1621, of the Swedish Royal Stud (Goodall 1973, 1982; Skelton 1978).

20. The infantry, not the cavalry, was the backbone of the Prussian army. Yet the Prussian cavalry enjoyed royal patronage and "in the eyes of Europe (since Frederick the Great) was the most famous branch of the Prussian armed forces" (Shanahan 1945:17, 19). Perhaps because of the lack of political integration there existed great regional autonomy in breeding and training until the time of Bismarck.

21. Birnbaum maintains that "the German state was unable to differentiate itself from the aristocracy" (1980:675), whereas in France "the institutionalization of the state was accompanied by marked differentiation from the dominant class" (1980:676). This may explain in part some of the differences between German and French horse breeding that run contrary to what one might on the surface predict. The German standard is more uniform than the French, deriving from the close links among the German aristocracy, the military, and the bureaucracy. Yet the French, who have more centralized political administration than the Germans,

88

also have more marked differentiation among the aristocracy, the military, and the state. Thus, the French exhibit somewhat more regional diversity in horse breeding and usage than do the Germans.

22. See Benedict Anderson's *Imagined Communities* for an extended argument on the conditions under which imagined national communities have arisen.

REFERENCES

ASHA
>
> 1982–83. *Rule Book, The American Horse Shows Association, Inc.* New York: American Horse Shows Association, Inc.

Altschuler, Glenn C.
>
> 1982. *Race, Ethnicity and Class in American Social Thought, 1865–1919*. Arlington Heights, Ill.: Harlan Davidson, Inc.

Anderson, Benedict
>
> 1985. *Imagined Communities: Reflections on the Origin and Spread of Nationalism*. London: Verso

Badie, Bertrand, and Pierre Birnbaum
>
> 1983. *The Sociology of the State*. Chicago: University of Chicago Press.

Barthes, Roland
>
> 1983. Myth Today, *Mythologies*. In *A Barthes Reader.* Susan Sontag, ed. New York: Hill and Wang.

Birnbaum, Pierre
>
> 1980. "States, Ideologies and Collective Action in Western Europe." *International Social Science Journal* 4:687–716

Bourdieu, Pierre
>
> 1978. "Sport and Social Class." *Social Science Information* 17 (6):819–840.
>
> 1984. *Distinction: A Social Critique of the Judgement of Taste*. Richard Nice, trans. Cambridge: Harvard University Press

Bourdieu, Pierre, and Jean-Claude Passeron
>
> 1977. *Reproduction in Education, Society, and Culture*. Beverly Hills: Sage

Copeland, L.
>
> 1959. The Negro as a Contrast Conception. In *Race Relations and the Race Problem*. E. Thompson, ed. Durham: Duke University Press

Craig, Gordon
> 1978. *Germany,* 1866–1945. New York: Oxford University Press

Davis, Deering
> 1962. *The American Cow Pony.* Princeton: D. Van Nostrand Company, Inc.

Denhardt, Robert
> 1967. *Quarter Horses: A History of Two Centuries.* Norman: University of Oklahoma Press

Dinsmore, Wayne
> 1978. *The Horses of the Americas.* Norman: University of Oklahoma

Doyle, Bertram Wilbur
> 1937. *The Etiquette of Race Relations in the South.* Chicago: University of Chicago Press

Elias, Norbert
> 1978. *The Civilizing Process,* Vol. 1. New York: Pantheon Books
> 1982. *The Civilizing Process,* Vol. 2. New York: Pantheon Books

Evans, J. Warren
> 1977. *Horses.* San Francisco: W. H. Freeman and Company

Foucault, Michel
> 1973. *The Order of Things: An Archaeology of the Human Sciences.* New York: Vintage/Random House

Glazer, Nathan, and Daniel P. Moynihan
> 1975. *Beyond the Melting Pot.* Chicago: University of Chicago Press

Goodall, Daphne Machin
> 1973. *The Flight of the East Prussian Horses.* New York: Arco Publishing Co., Inc.
> 1982. Breeds of Horses. *Encyclopedia Americana.* Connecticut: Grolier, Inc.

Gorman, John A.
> 1958. *The Western Horse.* Danville, Ill: The Interstate

Gossett, Thomas
> 1963. *Race: The History of an Idea in America.* Austin: University of Texas Press

Gumperz, John
> 1982a. *Discourse Strategies.* New York: Cambridge University Press
> 1982b. Introduction: Language and the Communication of Social Identity. In *Language and Social Identity.* J. Gumperz, ed. New York: Cambridge University Press.

Haddle, Jan
> 1975. *The Complete Book of the Appaloosa.* New York: A. S. Barnes and Company

Harrington, Michael
> 1980. *Decade of Decision: The Crisis of the American System.* New York: Simon and Schuster
> 1984. *The New American Poverty.* New York: Holt, Rinehart and Winston

Hartz, Louis
> 1955. *Liberal Tradition in America: An Interpretation of American Political Thought since the Revolution.* New York: Harcourt Brace

Haynes, Glynn
> 1976. *The American Paint Horse.* Norman: University of Oklahoma Press

Hechter, Michael
> 1978. Considerations on Western European Ethnoregionalism. Paper presented at conference on Ethnicity and Economic Development, University of Michigan, Ann Arbor, October 1978

Higham, John
> 1967. *Stangers in the Land: Patterns of American Nativism 1860–1925.* New York: Antheneum

Hintze, Otto
> 1973. The State in Historical Perspective. In *State and Society.* Reinhard Bendix, ed. Berkeley: University of California Press

Horse Identifier
> 1980. New York: Sterling Publishing Company

Huntington, Samuel P.
> 1973. Political Modernization: America vs. Europe. In *State and Society.* Reinhard Bendix, ed. Berkeley: University of California Press

Kays, John
> 1982. *The Horse.* New York: Arco Publishing, Inc.

Kellock, E. M.
> 1975. *The Story of Riding.* New York: St. Martin's Press, Inc.

Leach, Edmund
> 1976. *Claude Lévi-Strauss.* New York: Penguin Books

Le Roy Ladurie, Emmanuel
> 1979. *The Territory of the Historian.* Chicago: University of Chicago Press

91

Lévi-Strauss, Claude
    1963. *Totemism.* Boston: Beacon Press
    1966. *The Savage Mind.* Rodney Needham, trans. Chicago: University of Chicago Press
    1975. *The Raw and the Cooked.* New York: Harper & Row
Manual of Horsemanship
    1972. Kenilworth, England: The British Horse Society
Mellin, Jeanne
    1973. *The Morgan Horse.* Battleboro, Vermont: Stephen Greene Press
Radcliffe-Brown, A. R.
    1952 [1929]. The Sociological Theory of Totemism. In *Structure and Function in Primitive Society.* New York: The Free Press
Rosenberg, Hans
    1966. *Bureaucracy, Aristocracy, and Autocracy: The Prussian Experience 1660–1815.* Boston: Beacon Press
Sahlins, Marshall
    1976. *The Use and Abuse of Biology.* Ann Arbor: University of Michigan Press
    1977. Colors and Cultures. In *Symbolic Anthropology.* Janet Dolgin, David Kemnitzer, and David Schneider, eds. New York: Columbia University Press
    1981. *Historical Metaphors and Mythical Realities: Structure in the Early History of the Sandwich Islands Kingdom.* Ann Arbor: University of Michigan Press
Seunig, Waldemar
    1956. *Horsemanship.* New York: Doubleday & Company
Shanahan, William O.
    1945. *Prussian Military Reforms, 1786–1813.* New York: Columbia University Press
Sikes, L. N.
    1958. *Using the American Quarter Horse.* Dayton, Texas: Saddlerock Corporation
Skelton, Betty
    1978. *Pictorial Encyclopedia of Horses & Riding.* Chicago: Rand McNally & Co.
Thurow, Lester
    1975. *Generating Inequality: Mechanisms for Distribution in the U.S. Economy.* New York: Basic Books
    1980. *The Zero-Sum Society: Distribution and the Possibilities for Economic Change.* New York: Basic Books

Tocqueville, Alexis de
  1955. *The Old Regime and the French Revolution.* New York: Doubleday & Company
Todorov, Tzvetan
  1984 [1982]. *The Conquest of America.* New York: Harper & Row
Trench, Charles *et al.*
  1972. *The Treasury of Horses.* London: Octopus Books
Warwick, Everett J., and James E. Legates
  1979. *Breeding and the Improvement of Farm Animals.* New York: McGraw-Hill Book Co.
Weber, Eugen
  1976. *Peasants into Frenchmen: The Modernization of Rural France 1870–1914.* London: Chatto & Windus.
Weber, Max
  1978. *Economy & Society: An Outline of Interpretive Sociology.* Guenther Roth and Claus Wittich, eds. Berkeley: University of California Press
Wehler, H.-U.
  1973. *Das deutsche Kaiserreich 1871–1918.* Göttingen: Vandenhoech u. Ruprecht
Wynmalen, Henry
  1966. *Equitation.* London: Country Life Limited

PART II

National Identities in a Disintegrating Political Order

4

Time-Space Compression and the Continental Divide in German Subjectivity

Opened Wall, Quickened Time, Collapsed Space

Concepts of time and space orient the way we perceive and understand the world around us and are fundamental to a sense of self. They also differ across cultures and over time. Thus, a shift in either category is always experienced as alternately challenging and unnerving, exhilarating and stressful, disorienting and reorienting, in any case, as deeply troubling. The opening of the Wall in November 1989 precipitated a fundamental shift in the categories of time and space, for Berliners specifically, for Germans more generally, and even, one might say, for the world. What follows is an analysis of the way in which the occasion of the opening as well as events in the year following it—primarily the currency reform and elections—affected a reordering of temporal and spatial categories in both East and West Berlin.

Life in Berlin since November 1989 has been characterized by what Oxford geographer David Harvey calls "time-space compression." By this he means processes—revolutions are perhaps the paradigmatic example—that simultaneously quicken time and collapse spatial distinctions. "Space," he writes, "appears to shrink to

97

a global village of telecommunications and a 'spaceship earth' of economic and ecological interdependencies. ... Time horizons shorten to the point where the present is all there is." Harvey argues that time-space compression is peculiar to capitalism, in that both everyday tempo is speeded up and spatial barriers are overcome so that "the world sometimes seems to collapse inward upon us." He dates this phenomenon back to the Renaissance, identifying it with the historical transformations accompanying Modernity. But, more generally, "compression" is a process that can occur at any historical moment or in any place. It should not be conceptualized in an evolutionary sense but merely in terms "relative to any preceding state of affairs"(Harvey 1989: 240).[1] The most immediate consequence of the opening of the Berlin Wall, and of the economic and political events staged to unite the two German states, was a time-space compression involving a basic disorienting and reordering of the spatial and temporal universe. This compression, I will argue, was experienced quite differently by East and West Berliners, Ossis and Wessis, and has been fundamental up to the present in accentuating the already existing asymmetry between East and West. The expression, repeated especially by East Berliners in 1990 and 1991, that best captures this experience is "Alles auf einmal" (everything at once).

Cold War Categories of Time and Space in Berlin

Prior to November 1989, East and West Berliners had come to experience time and space through cognitive categories framed by, if not often directly derived from, Cold War order. These categories were constructed from 1945 to 1989 in an intense process of mirror-imaging and misrecognition whereby East and West Berliners were thought of, and often thought of themselves, as prototypes of specific East and West German, if not more generalized East and West, patterns.[2] However, East and West states and societies were never as autonomous as they often represented themselves to be, but rather symbiotic constructs, perhaps best expressed by the adage: when one side sneezed, the other caught a cold—while denying both the cold and its relation to the sneeze on the other side.

98

Although characterized by mutual interdependencies and antagonisms predicated on an assumption of formal equality, East and West Germans were in an unequal relationship that increased in asymmetry over time. The grotesque examples of this asymmetry include exchange of (East) people for (West) money, private gift-giving from West to East, sale of (West) garbage to (East) dumps, West state loans to maintain political and economic stability in the East. In short, the self-conceptions of the two states and their citizens corresponded to the Hegelian dialectic of one-sided recognition: to be recognized without in turn having to recognize the other. Yet I will be arguing that while the West and East created the effect of being outside and external to each other, they were in fact inside and internal: the other was always already there. Schematically, then, what were the differences in the fundamental orienting categories or ways of knowing in East and West that enabled the two sides to misrecognize each other?

In the East, after the end of the *Aufbau,* the early stage of (re)construction of the economy lasting to approximately the mid-1960s, time was experienced as petrified or artificially slowed down. Both the state and the citizen had good reason to reject the modernist vision of industrial time, the vision that presupposed an unstoppable race toward a progressive future. On the one hand, the regime had exhausted its economic base in a policy that favored the building of heavy industry over investment in domestic infrastructure or consumption. No longer able to maintain the ideological mirage that it could compete economically with the West, it increasingly sacrificed "production" goals in order to slow down time so that it could record and monitor people's behaviors, tastes, and appetites. It feared the overstimulation of its citizens, the appearance of desires or wishes that it had not already anticipated and thus potentially would be outside its control. Two examples may suffice. The *Stasi* (state security) continually expanded its reach during the seventies, eventually accumulating reports on one-third of all citizens. We now know that most of these reports concerned mundane activities that were thought to index potential critical thought or political dissatisfaction: stray comments at a meeting in a youth club, passing remarks made on the telephone, the kinds and numbers of friends one kept, or even daily rhythms such as the time it took one to empty one's garbage in the dump. A second means by which the state monitored citizen desire was the *Eingabe*, a legally sanctioned petition to a person with authority over the request. These petitions expressed directly the perceived needs and wishes of the citizen, ranging from complaints about service in a restaurant to requests for a pair of ski pants or an apartment, or to travel to the West. The regime read these wishes with great interest, sometimes responding like a Santa Claus, sometimes responding by referring the person to the state security for further, more intimate monitoring. Both of these examples indicate the state's enthusiasm for Lenin's oft-repeated maxim: Trust is good, but control is better.

On the other hand, citizens in the German Democratic Republic (GDR) also wanted to slow down time, partly because they had no incentive to speed it up. Accelerated productivity on the job, and thus faster work, was not the principle by which people were rewarded in everyday life in the East. Instead loyalty, stability, political acquiescence, and teamwork formed the bases for rewards on the job, to the extent there were any. Punitive sanctions for slowing down time were nearly nonexistent, since people were rarely fired. Nor were citizens part of an orthodox class system, of the sort Pierre Bourdieu has outlined for France, where constant distinction making is the principle that generates and reproduces the system of class hierarchy (Bourdieu 1984). Hierarchies in the GDR were based on principles other than social climbing and productivity. Opportunities for status through conspicuous consumption were simply not readily available, much less pandered to and advertised as in the West. Commodities were in one way or another either available without much ado, or unavailable even with concentrated effort. As János Kornai has argued, Eastern European socialist economies distinguished themselves from capitalist ones in that they were supply-constrained (seeking to control the allocation of goods), whereas capitalist economies are demand-constrained (based on control of resources and manipulation of demand) (Kornai 1980; Verdery 1991: 74–83). A demand-constrained economy depends on a constant displacement of consumer desire and thus tends to accelerate the activity of exchange. A supply-constrained economy could best achieve its goal, distribution control, by retarding the pace of exchange. Thus, since the mid-1960s, time in the GDR was experienced as petrified.

With the building of the Wall in August 1961, space in the East was shaped by a sense of confinement and closure. The East German state then developed into the paradigmatic example, the mirror-image, of the American policy called "containment of Communism." It encircled West Berliners with the Wall and contained most of its people in its own unambiguous and heavily guarded borders. Additionally, the GDR gradually increased the size of its state security to watch over citizens within those borders. When wanting to go abroad, most East Germans could travel only within socialist bloc countries. Unrestricted travel was possible only in Czechoslovakia, Hungary, and Romania. One could travel to the other socialist countries only with official permission, most often within a group. Much of the Soviet Union was always off-limits; and with the rise of Solidarity in Poland, travel there was also severely curtailed. Cuba was open, but quite expensive. Although the regime modified this pattern of containment in 1987 and 1988, allowing more than a million visits of its citizens to West Berlin and the FRG, it still denied this right to the majority. Of those granted the privilege of travel to the West, the majority were pensioners, and, when those of working age were allowed to travel, they rarely could take with them a spouse, relative, or friend.

Furthermore, the GDR adhered to the socialist principles regarding property: one could possess (besitzen) buildings but not land. The ability to occupy space (besetzen) was extremely restricted. This limitation in the possibilities for private valuation, through occupying, owning, or making public one's own space in the GDR, created a peculiar relationship to what Freud called Besetzung and in English is translated as "cathexis." The libidinal attachment and investment in an object, specifically property, was truncated. This truncated "cathexis," in comparison to the West, resulted in a projection of "real" value onto two other spaces: valuable space was either totally private (a Western automobile or a country house, for example), or it existed outside the confines of the GDR, such as (and especially) in West Germany.

In the West, time was not experienced as petrified but as quickened. Capitalism as a process accelerates the pace of life, with all

101

things and spaces being continually re-commodified, made different from and exchangeable with one another on an impersonal, abstract market. Driven relentlessly to desire and occupy, or cathect with, new objects for personal consumption, to shift and replace old desires with new ones based on market principles of replaceability and endless supply, West Germans had, during the Cold War, been integrated into a hierarchical class society with a very large and affluent middle class. Rather than being confined and slowed down, they were encouraged to open up and speed up. Two of the most distinctive postwar symbols of this were the preferred vacations abroad (as the opening-up to the outside) and freeways without speed limits (Borneman 1992a: 231–235; Borneman 1992b: 44–61).

Moreover, space for the *Bundesbürger* was not closed inside fixed boundaries as in the GDR, but open, ambiguous, and imperial. The Federal Republic (FRG), along with some of its citizens acting as members of refugee organizations, contested the land in Poland and Czechoslovakia lost in World War II when Germans in these *Ostgebiete* were driven from their homes. (The fact that some of this land had been initially gained by driving Poles and Czechs from their homes was rarely mentioned.) Contested space was the basic issue in the West German refusal to sign a peace treaty with Poland up until 1990. In fact, the Federal Republic went so far as to claim the entire territory of the GDR along with its people as a rightful part of itself. Hence, during the Cold War neither the FRG nor its citizens made open reference to fixed boundaries, for this territorial ambiguity was a source of potential power for the state, especially in its relations with Poland and Czechoslovakia. (For example, no reparations had to be paid to the nearly one million Poles for their forced labor or for war damages. By disputing the postwar land settlements agreed upon by the Allies at Yalta, many West Germans could claim that they, like the Poles, had been victimized by the war.) In conceptualizing space, West German citizens oscillated between two extremes, those of the cosmopolitan and the provincial. Those who identified as cosmopolitan denied the necessity of place, desiring instead to transcend space altogether, to feel at home either nowhere or everywhere. Those who identified as provincials remained loyal to the local place of either birth or residence, meaning that up to one-fourth of all West German citizens had a right to some type of future settlement over disputed space that lay outside the territorial boundaries of their state. Uniting the cosmopolitan and the provincial was an imperial attitude toward space: West Germans were not to be confined within the borders of the Federal Republic. They were also united to a large extent in pushing strenuously for European unification, even on the issue of refugee policy. This attitude, in turn, demarcated them from the East Germans, for whom space was closed and confining.

The Close-up of the Wall, Shortened Time Horizons, and the Imaginary

With these category differences in mind, let us go back to the sequence of events on the evening of November 9, 1989. Already since August 1989, the time horizon between initiatives of the East German Politburo and citizen response had been shortening, so that who was initiating and who responding became irrelevant. In fact, both citizen and state were responding to the close-ups on TV: from August to September to the unmanageable and, for many, embarrassing flight of young citizens into the East European embassies, and again on November 9th, to the chaos at the Berlin border crossings. The opening itself was an accident—a misunderstood response by reporters in the evening news to a poorly formulated Politburo ordinance concerning changed visa regulations (Borneman 1991: 1–4, 20–37).

In this respect, the opening of the Wall was similar to opening events culminating in the other "revolutions" of 1989 (which, we might note, began with the Philippine ouster of Ferdinand Marcos in 1988): it was mediated by television, by the cinematic form possible with filmed images. Stationing itself on the border-crossing Bornholmer Straße, West German television enlarged and magnified through close-ups every move on the other side. These filmed revelations initiated a process of re-imaging the Wall and the perceptions of those on the other side. For most East Germans, who had foregrounded an image of the West as other to whom you do not have access but who has access to you, this event radically questioned their subjectivity as mirror-image of the West. The opening disrupted the stable binary of the Cold War, the fantasies of protagonists and antagonists in complementary opposition. East and West were suddenly brought into a new relation with one another, or, in Lacanian terms, the Imaginary was destabilized by confrontation with a self other than that which had been imaged.

In its twenty-seven years of history before the TV portrayal on that evening, the Wall was imagined in terms of its stolidity and concreteness, its impenetrability, its clean and scrubbed whiteness on the East side—with an opposite set of associations on the West side: of a penetrable, graffiti-covered illegality. In other words, the Wall was part of the Imaginary register, a perfect authoritative closure, secure, contained, orderly, stable. This register of images, both conscious and unconscious, had been reinforced in actual experiences with the Wall, for very few East Germans had been allowed to pass to its other side (though people from the Western side would suddenly appear out of a chaotic Nowhere, and within a day, disappear behind the Wall again). Hundreds of East Germans died, and hundreds more were imprisoned, in escape attempts while challenging this image of the wall. On November 9, television cameras confronted this Wall in the Imaginary with a cinematic portrayal that revealed its fragility and human scale through repeated showing of movements, previously hidden, of guards and people at the border. People's own signifiers and linguistic conventions, their perceptions of this Wall and the Cold War and themselves in a divided Germany, in short, their entire Imaginary, proved inadequate to comprehend this new event, this sudden chaos at the very site of Order itself.

East and West Berliners, specifically, most clearly expressed this confusion by claiming that with the opening they were *sprachlos*, speechless, and that this was an experience of *Wahnsinn*, madness, or literally, delusional sense. The images projected on the TV screen initially functioned as a "third" dimension, interrupting the stability of the mirror-imaging process; they became the standard of reality for citizens and leaders alike. Thus, the citizens, thrown out of the closed and complementary order of the Cold War, had to find a language and reformulate their relation to "knowledge" of the world and of their selves.

Within days of the opening, the joke I heard was that foreign policy was being made not by the Politburo at the center of power but by the border guards on the periphery. Although it seemed as if periphery had replaced center as the seat of power, this was not in fact the case. The guards had initiated nothing: they merely responded to the people who were responding to their own images on television. Indeed, as the time horizon between initiative and response shortened, East German leaders were required to react more quickly; they acted in a new tempo in which they were constantly forced to acknowledge events already displayed on the screen. In an age of mechanical and electronic reproduction, the question of the *origin* of the image becomes secondary, if not irrelevant, to the issue of the image as simulacrum, to the image's *reproducibility* and *audience*.

The TV close-ups did not simply render more precise a reality that people could see by going to the Wall and viewing it for themselves. That they had done many times before. Rather, the close-ups revealed possibilities for, to cite Walter Benjamin, "entirely new structural formations of the subject"(Benjamin 1978:237). That subject, the East German, was a person in time and space who prior to these events could cross that border, if at all, only with a visa, for which one had to apply months, even years ahead. Now one could cross that border without preparation twice, or three, or four times within a single day. The East German became a new subject with a changed relationship to time, to space, and to power. Instead of being overwhelmed by the Wall with its Cold War aura of cleanliness, fixity, and closure, the masses penetrated the Wall, climbed on it, chopped at it, poured champagne on it. They opened it up, moving it from the Imaginary to the Symbolic order, revealing the East-West binary to be unstable and asymmetrical.

For West Berliners, as I have argued above, openness and ambiguity were already shared spatial categories, as was quickened time. They experienced this moment of time-space compression as reaffirmation of what they already were. The opening of the Wall may have involved some disorientation for them, but it provoked no fundamental reordering, at least not initially. Rather, they soon acted on the third spatial category held in common, that of imperial space. The FRG had consistently maintained that it was the only legitimate Germany, thus whole and complete in itself, but also that the GDR had always belonged to it, thus a necessary addition in order to complete itself. Hence West Germans did not initially get very excited about unity with their supplement. The Federal Republic was just enlarging, completing itself, and Chancellor of Unity Helmut Kohl had promised them that unity would be costless.

Creating National Space through Economic and Political Union

Two subsequent events have been integral to the restructuring of temporal and spatial categories since the opening: the unification of the economies and the governments—perhaps the only two domains where East and West Germans are unified. On July 1, 1990, eight months after the opening, a currency union took place. Three months later, on October 3, 1990, political union was completed. During these initial eight months, anyone living in or travelling through the East could use both currencies. This "territorial unity" at the monetary level severely weakened the already inferior East German currency, as it eliminated the state's ability to control its value on its internal markets. This happened through a compression of space. Three examples may be cited: the incorporation of East German people and things into West German markets; the (ongoing) breakdown and pulverization of coherent space within the GDR by privatizing former East German holdings (after October 1990, through the actions of the Treuhandanstalt, a para-public trustee); and the huge population transfer of skilled labor from East to West.

The creation of a single market and single national space enabled many West Germans to exploit their superior position by buying labor, real estate, and other East German goods in the increasingly fragmented and unprotected spaces of the GDR. But, significantly, East Germans could not do the same in West Germany. They were still paid in East German Marks. At most they could flee to West Germany to secure a D-Mark return for their increasingly devalued labor. The result of economic unity was not an "imagined community" in the sense explicated by Benedict

106

Anderson, but a territorial and fiscal community in a homogeneous space with quickened time (Anderson 1983). No matter how much people imagined and experienced a national unity by reading a tabloid *Bild Zeitung* together in the morning, they were divided by their differential orientation and access to the new temporal and spatial world in the afternoon. Moreover, though Anderson may be right that print capitalism made people into nationals in the eighteenth century, its function in the late twentieth century German unification process was to exploit, not to overcome, a set of preexisting distinctions for the purposes of expanding market shares. Creating the united nation—or at least its image—was a task more suited to those in control of visual technologies, a union of media consultants and politicians.

Nonetheless, East Germans initially seemed pleased that they could finally buy goods in the West, outside of the state-controlled Intershops. Paradoxically, though, East Germans actually weakened their own positions within Germany by eliminating the need for their own labor, for purchases in the West reduced demand for the goods that they themselves were producing. The introduction of a single currency in July 1990 inflated the price of East German goods for the East Germans, but made these same goods cheaper for the West Germans. As the goods they produced lost their value, East German labor was also further devalued, which promoted a further flight of young skilled labor to the West. This entire process both quickened the collapse of what was spatially the East and enlarged the space in which West Germans could maneuver.

While the territory of the Federal Republic actually enlarged with unity, the sense of space paradoxically contracted and time horizons shortened. With the opening of the Wall, people could suddenly move back and forth without long waits before state authorities. This ease of movement effaced the distances between West and East, prompting immediate demands for improvements in telecommunications. It also facilitated the creation of a single labor market that increased labor mobility in both directions. A trip from East to West or vice versa that had previously taken six months or even several years to plan (and without guaranteed success) was suddenly possible overnight. Whereas the initial experience of most West Germans in the East was of an imperial space,

formerly withheld from them but now open for use and development, the initial experience of East Germans in the West was colored by *Begrüßungsgeld*,—the 100 D-Mark of "greeting money" (more
for families) each East German was to receive yearly from the FRG
to help finance travel in the West. This fund had been created
when less than one percent of all East Germans could travel in the
West. Suddenly all seventeen million East Germans were free to
travel. The gift had lost its purpose. Yet West German politicians
and bureaucrats, who were not prepared for the opening, did not
immediately rescind the law. This "greeting money" set the tone for
future relations between East and West: the West German government giving money, East German citizens receiving.

The other major event leading to unity was the election of March
18, 1990, when the majority of East Germans voted to eliminate
the GDR and swiftly become part of the Federal Republic. In the
previous five months, the authoritarian political structures had
been crumbling. East Germans responded with a groundswell of
democratic will-formation, expressed, for example, in the creation
of the interim roundtable, the registration of 800 "civic" organizations, the development of a critical and diverse press and electronic
media, and the formation of twenty-four political parties. Beyond
the winners and losers of this March election, it was decisive in
replacing two semi-sovereign spaces with a single national space.
Unification was thereafter understood no longer as a question about
ends or goals, but as one about means and procedures toward the
unquestioned goal of national unity. Moreover, these procedures
could be handled as administrative problems to be solved by German bureaucrats and politicians. By the third and final election of
1990, a pan-German election on December 2, the twenty-four East
German parties that competed in the first bout were reduced to
five. The media reporting on these elections also assumed more
uniformity in the East: one of the two television stations was closed,
the sole film conglomerate was put up for sale, and nearly all of the
major newspapers, journals, and presses were either bought up by
West German (and British) concerns or simply closed. Primarily
responsible for shrinking this spectrum of representable interest
and molding political will into West German form were West German political professionals and an intellectual elite. At stake in the

108

election rituals was legitimation for the political and economic steps—primarily with respect to shifting ownership and regulatory authority—already being taken to dissolve the GDR. The process of assessing value, restructuring, selling, and closing corporations, factories, academies, day care centers, and the like came to be known as *die Abwicklung* (a carrying to completion or unwinding—both temporal metaphors) (on *die Abwicklung*, see Arnold and Meyer-Gosau, eds. 1992; on the Treuhand, see Christ and Neubauer 1991; Luft 1992).

Unity Imagined

If observed abstractly or "objectively"—in other words, from the perspective of no one in particular—the creation of a single national space and economic market opened up many new opportunities for "Germany." Some Germans in the new "Germany" have undoubtedly capitalized on these opportunities, as have some non-Germans. Nonetheless, I would argue that for most East and West Germans, unity has been experienced as a loss—though for different reasons by those on each side of the Wall. One of the major losses for West Germans has been that of their East German Other, which has now reconstituted itself in altered form with respect to the West. If West Germans during the Cold War had always thought of themselves as central, they were only so with respect to their inferior, supplementary mirror-image in the East. And although this East had its own state and form of social organization, constituted as the antithesis of the state and society in the West, the Federal Republic insisted that it was itself the only territorial state that represented German nationals. Thus, the West in the Cold War maintained a double fiction: of the East as a spatially distinct and antithetical Other outside of the territorial West, and of the East as a lost part of the West, rightfully belonging inside the West and needed for completion of self. Unity has meant that the East—land, people, machinery, debt—has been fully absorbed inside the Federal body. East Germans may have initially felt that they were coming in from the cold, but West Germans are being asked, or forced, to provide the heat. The insider joke repeated by both sides goes: An East German says to a West German, "Wir sind ein Volk" (We are a/ one people), and the West German replies, "We are too!"

With respect to time, the accelerated tempo of unity with the East was soon paralleled by a slowing down of the pace of unification within Western Europe. Furthermore, the impatience and *rush* to unity with both East Germany and the other European Community countries was due less to popular pressure than to strategic manipulation of both national feeling and superior economic and cultural capital by West German elites (Offe 1990: 42). As a result, this unity was realized only with respect to East Germany, whose citizens, unlike the Danes, for example, were not only disoriented but divided among themselves and thus incapable of articulating a credible opposition. Moreover, West Germans were immediately confronted with real costs in their unity with the East: The FRG was forced finally to cede the territory it had lost during and after World War II, pay money to Poland and the former USSR, and thus acknowledge fixed boundaries. Hence, for West Germans, although their state had gained territory and enlarged in size, space was no longer open and ambiguous. They, of course, experienced this territorial circumscription as a loss. Slowly this loss was compounded for many by an anticipated decline in the standard of living or threat to prosperity. West German postwar identity, which had been based in part on the ability of the political system to deliver economic goods, to protect Germans as consumers, and to integrate them into the West, has now been threatened. Furthermore, incorporation of part of the East into the old Federal Republic has meant a territorial movement East instead of West, thus reluctantly reorienting the attention of the affluent and complacent West Germans from Western Europe to the East. In short, while formal unity with the East (Germans) has gone ahead, formal unity with the West (Europeans), as prescribed by the Maastricht Accords, has stalled.

West Germans to some degree have been compensated for their ego anxiety, for the loss of coherence and direction, by a successful projection of the East Germans as *inferior* in space and *behind* in time.[3] Most East Germans have remained speechless and have largely internalized these projections.[4] Having already signalled a desire for and a prioritizing of the material wealth enjoyed in the West, most East Germans are hardly positioned to engage in a critique of Western consumer culture. With West Germany now the desired End, East Germans are conceptualized and have conceptualized themselves as merely needing to recapitulate steps already taken since the fifties in the FRG. Critical to this positioning of the East Germans as inferior and behind has been the notion, also applied to the other (former) East Europeans and Soviets, that their revolutions were *nachholende* or catching-up revolutions, aimed at recovering freedoms enjoyed by Western Europeans since 1945. An article by Jürgen Habermas published shortly after the events in the fall of '89 seemed to capture this new positioning of peoples. These revolutions, he claimed, were driven by a desire to make up for lost time. Of primary importance in this recovery, he wrote, are the political and economic freedoms guaranteed in civil society by Western capitalist, liberal democracies (Habermas 1990: 3–23). Whether this was the initial motivation behind the revolutions is debatable, but I do agree that within months after the overthrow of the regimes, most East Europeans began expressing their motivation in these terms. They sought to recover lost time and regain what was denied to them by the Russian occupation and the pseudo-socialist systems they had lived under.

This placement of the recovering East versus the advanced West, employed in all domains, is reminiscent of the structure Norbert Elias (1978) posits for the development of the Western world in *The Civilizing Process*. All of the former socialist states and their citizens, including the East Germans, are now expected to undergo a similar process of changing etiquette, work habits, and individual psychology, marked above all by an internalization of forms of authority that previously had been exercised by coercive means from an external source. Much like Elias's presumptions about civilizing the West, however, assumptions about the new civilizing process with regard to the former socialist societies involve a fundamental misunderstanding of the direction of psychological change. Elias assumes that, with civilization, tighter controls over affect are accompanied by an increase in shame and a postponement of gratification, and that this results in a processual strengthening of the superego. In fact it is not superego but ego controls that are strengthened under capitalism and the civilizing processes that accompanies it. To the extent that the East Germans are being "civilized," they are encouraged to drop any inhibitions or ties to tradition they already have, and instead to abandon themselves to

111

an external authority (capitalist managers, political and educational policy experts, primarily from the West) and submit their egos to a general reformation. Indeed, East Berlin is witnessing a wave of newly opened beauty parlors, aerobic and nautilus centers, and "finishing schools" for adults to aid in this process.

As Michael Weck has shown in a recent illuminating analysis, this reformation entails an "orientalizing" of the East Germans (Weck 1992: 76–89). They are constructed as the *"wild"* and *"ungezähmt"* (wild and undomesticated), in contrast to the model civil society of West Germany. East "authoritarian" or "autocratic" (more Prussian and more *Urdeutsch* [primordially German]) habits are to be eliminated and replaced by the democratic principles of enlightened and tolerant citizens and by the "free market" that characterize the Federal Republic. Politically, East Germans are assumed to be unable to speak for or represent themselves. Since formal political unification in October 1990, four of the five elected Minister-Presidents from the East have been replaced by West German cronies. And legally, the *Unrechtsstaat* (illegal state) of the Nazi period is constantly equated with the *Unrechtsstaat* called the GDR, both of which are then compared to the *Rechtsstaat* (legal state) called the Federal Republic (Borneman 1993: 1–24).[5]

From an economic perspective, the Deutsche Bank has conceptualized the former East Germany as undergoing "a time of transition and stabilization . . . before the onset of a growth phase" (Deutsche Bank 1991). Immediately after the opening, East Germany was envisioned as an arena for new markets for West German goods, a land of virgin consumers eager to buy from the West. With "open markets" and West German leadership, it was generally assumed that the "five new states," as they are called, would undergo an economic miracle much like the West did in the 1950s. Although we might think of the chaos, imbalances, and "considerable risks" in this transition as lurking tragedies, where the protagonist is engaged in a morally significant struggle that might end in ruin and personal disaster, liberal economics is at base not a tragedy but a comedy. The plot always leads through the "time of transition" to a positive "growth phase." Such obstacles as declining GNP, growing unemployment, environmental pollution, and cultural displacement are unintended costs attributable to past (ergo Communist) inefficiency. They can and will be overcome, however, as economic laws—the scientific "laws" of the market or, alternately, the "laws" of prosperity theology—predict a reassertion of liberal order. East Germans are, on the one hand, expected to initiate personal changes like characters in a *Bildungsroman*, but on the other hand, the specific rites of passage are elements of enlightened stages of development already predetermined by economic laws. The logic of its plot is engaged in a double paradox, for, to paraphrase Jonathan Culler, the story's ending, or the result of the "free market," is both the effect and the justification of the plot (Culler 1981).[6] In other words, the ending (freedom of choice and national economic wealth) is supposed to be the result of the workings of a "free market," but the free market is also supposed to be the cumulative result of free choices. Thus, cause and effect are obscured—both presuppose one another; this circularity makes it impossible to ascertain the relative efficacy of economic policy during "the transition."

Finally, this process of unity, wherein the East is positioned as spatially inferior to and temporally behind the West, has another level, a psychoanalytic one. This psychoanalytic level has nothing to do with the essentialist pathologies posited for East and West by Hans-Joachim Maaz, an East German psychologist who became a pan-German media darling after the opening. Appearing endlessly on TV talk shows, Maaz has repeated the conclusions he drew in his books: East Germans are "psychologically defective," infected by a "'virus' of a pathological social deformation." West Germans, he claims, are engaged in a merciless striving for domination. The revolution itself he characterizes as an "uprising in neurosis" (Maaz 1990: 104, 137–169; Maaz and Moeller 1992).[7]

Where Maaz finds the most public resonance, I suspect, is in his use of familiar cliches and kinship metaphors to describe the process of unification. He assumes, as do a majority of German pundits across the political spectrum, that East and West are like siblings separated or a divorced couple, in any case male and female, preparing to reunite. The new union involves bringing together or founding a family, half of whose members have been deformed, argues Maaz, by premature separation of the child from the mother and by authoritarian education. A West German Social

113

Democratic Party politician recently put it this way: "We Germans from the East and from the West have contracted a marriage—and not without a certain liking for each other—which is indissoluble. Even genuine love, at some later point, can't be ruled out altogether. It was a nice wedding, really, but now we have to get to know each other" (Die Zeit 1990: 5).[8] Nothing could be more misleading than uncritically replicating this cultural metaphor at the analytical level. East and West Germans are not kin reuniting, but two separate peoples, each with its own set of dispositions, who are suddenly, in one of those accidental moments in history, thrown together in a national whole.

Eroticization, Striptease, Death/Burial

The cultural encounter between East and West Germans made possible by the opening of the Wall has followed a sequence that in many ways is reminiscent of other first contacts between two differently imagined communities. Before unity, East and West were partly hidden from each other, full of private secrets, each part hiding behind the Wall. Secrecy and hiding, partial covering, as we well know, infuses an object with desire, makes it more desirable than it would have been had it been uncovered and revealed. Thus, during the Cold War, East and West always exhibited some curiosity for and erotic interest in each other. Moreover, with the massive migration of people from East to West throughout the Cold War, many kin who were initially separated by the Iron Curtain would reunite in West Berlin or the Federal Republic. Among the West Berliners I met during fieldwork from 1986 to 1989, it is my impression that approximately two-thirds had relatives in the East in the 1950s, but this dropped to less than one-third by the time of my research. Thus, the simultaneous excitement and repugnance of incest became less of a factor over time in the eroticization of the other. For several weeks— even months for some—after the opening, the erotic differences were explored in a series of both spontaneous and organized private encounters, parties, and ceremonial gatherings. Within six months, however, the two sides stood naked before a disassembled border, and with this uncovering, the erotic investment in the other was gone.

Pre-contact erotics were quickly replaced by a process that might be likened to an East German striptease—again, with each side perceiving the event differently. Ossis see their strip as a narrative process, much as Roland Barthes described narrative as striptease (Barthes 1972: 84–87). They are not really interested in the end but in all the moves along the way, in the shedding of props acquired since the end of World War II. Obsession with their own history, constant exposés about the Stasi, rehabilitation commissions, and reexamination of individual relations are not seen as end products but as a process of reflection whereby they discover their own significations. It is a coming-to-consciousness of the semiotic properties of the body, a body inscribed over forty-five years by Russian occupation and the GDR. Time is a crucial medium of desire in this strip, for without time there is no eroticization; the performance will be flat and meaningless. For Wessis, however, the East must engage in a quick ritual shedding of its props: law, politicians, industries, research institutes, daycare centers—all must go. Thereafter East Germany can be envisioned as a newly discovered pristine body, an unmapped and chaste body, a blank space waiting to be signified, ready to be remade by them. "Privatization," primarily by the Treuhand, is the process they have initiated to disassemble this body, to remove the "deformed culture" and reduce the body to a state of raw materials. West Germans, moreover, tend to view the repeated East German exposés along the way, all the Stasi stories and whining about injustice suffered in the GDR, as deflections from the course of history. They are not interested in the strip as a narrative that unfolds. The whole thing should be sped up so the show can go on. They are interested only in the end result, the goal of producing a replica of the body and ego in the West.

Yet, it is "only the *time taken* in shedding clothes," as Barthes notes, that "makes voyeurs of the public." Nearly everyone agrees that the striptease will soon end, and East Germany will stand unveiled before Western eyes—to cite Barthes again,"desexualized at the very moment when [s/he] is stripped naked." Part of this disassembling has included, for example, making East German markets some of the most open and unprotected in the world, eliminating twenty percent

115

of all jobs in the service and public sectors, fifty percent in state-owned industrial enterprises, seventy percent in agriculture (GIC 1992: 4). Its automobile industry is dead, and its shipbuilding industry has been destroyed—justified largely in terms of eliminating subsidies for inefficient businesses. This baring and "bringing to completion" is accompanied by a metaphorical shift in representation. Three years after the opening, East Germany has ceased to be a wild or virgin territory waiting for development. Unification increasingly resembles more a funeral than a striptease, and this funeral metaphor, always latent in representations of the East, has come into common usage. In fact, recently East German author Werner Heiduczek offered the following picture: The East is a corpse that the West expected to bury. Instead, the West is not only carrying that cadaver on its back, but the corpse keeps showing signs of life (Heiduczek 1992).

Anthropologists have often stressed that when "death and rebirth" become dominant tropes—in this case, replacing "development and growth" as metaphors for "the transition"—then women and gender symbolism tend to be pronounced. In many different cultures, the putrescence of the dead body is associated with women, who in funerary rites must literally carry the corpse in order to transform the death into life (Bloch and Perry 1982). This holds true across a wide geographic range of cultures, among others, the Merina and Bara in Madagascar (Bloch 1982: 211–231; Huntington and Metcalf 1979: 93–119), the Zulu in South Africa (Ngubane 1976: 274–283), the Gimi and Melpa in New Guinea (Strathern 1982: 111–133), Greeks and Andalusians in Western Europe (Seremetakis 1991: 99–125; Pitt-Rivers 1977: 43–47). In many of the ex-"actually existing" East European socialist countries, including Hungary, Poland, Bulgaria, and Romania, a similar association is often made of women with Communism and its legacy (Creed 1991; Gal 1991; Hauser 1991; Kligman 1991; Rosenberg 1991; Verdery 1996). In contemporary Germany, however, the deficits of communism in the ex-GDR are not linked specifically with women, but with a generic, geopolitically placed person, the Ossi. Another frequent cross-cultural distinction, noted by Maurice Bloch and Jonathan Parry in their seminal essay on death symbolism, is that between "bad death" and "good death" (Bloch and Perry 1982). A bad death tends to occur when a

116

social death precedes its physical or biological counterpart. Likewise, the GDR is a "bad death" in that its death sentence at the social and rhetorical level has not completely killed it, as mentioned above, but instead seems to have transformed it into a Schwarzenegger-Terminator figure that keeps resurrecting itself.

In most of the cultures mentioned above, after women take on and embody the death symbolism, the funeral comes to a completion with the transformation of the death into a life-giving process. In these cultures, women's reproductive abilities are so central to the reproduction of the society that in the process of transforming the death into life, women are also "reclaimed" for the social. In Germany, however, most East Germans—both men and women— carry the stigma of being the agents and the dross of a failed system. They are considered not only prior and behind, but also untrainable and costly. It is not their reintegration that is imagined after the not-yet-completed burial of the GDR, but their expulsion. Indeed, more Ossi labor is not needed in the new Germany, and Ossis-as-workers, who since the opening have continued to migrate West at the rate of approximately 2,000 a week, threaten to crowd an already tight labor market in the West, thus undermining the postwar corporatist agreement reached between West German labor and management.

This crisis in representing and integrating the East has even wider implications, however, for the East is no longer conceived as outside of and supplementary to the Federal Republic, but as on top of or inside the formerly healthy (West) German body. Thus, we might understand the necessity of the "death of the GDR" and its burial to West Germans, for how else will unification with the East be transformed into a more general life-giving process? This particular vision reinforces the salience of economistic metaphors, like those of Dr. Hans Tietmeyer, head of the Deutsche Bank, and other mainstream economists, who insist that only after the destruction and death of the old GDR, seen as an undifferentiated whole, will rebirth and growth be possible (Tietmeyer 1991). The flaw in this picture, as Heiduczek notes, is that Ossis are not properly dead; they are still kicking. If we take the metaphors of the psychologist Maaz and the banker Tietmeyer and other public figures at their face value, then West Germany is the male life-giver and East

117

Germany a female body that refuses to submit to death and burial. By refusing to accept its role in this process, East Germany becomes a hermaphroditic parasite, a part male–part female, part dead–part alive thing—a species in-between that feeds on the living. Such ambiguous creatures, like amphibians, are neither fit for eating nor good as domestic pets. Rather, they are zombies who signal danger and elicit fear.

A Civil Transition to Unity

I have merely taken us through the effects of time-space compression and the sequence of events during the first several years of the so-called transition. Other processes having to do with property disputes and status reallocations are not placed in the center of this analysis, though they are equally significant in their long-term effects on the restructuring of everyday life in Berlin and in Germany at large. I hope to have shown that East and West Germans have moved into unity with very different categories of time and space. And although these old categories have indeed been transformed since November 1989, they still do not comprise a consensual set of classificatory devices by which Ossis and Wessis perceive the same reality. Rather, new differences have replaced the old ones.

For Wessis, space is no longer open and ambiguous, though still imperial. Furthermore, they fear that their material progress is being endangered by the integration into the FRG of the Ossis, whose petrified time is likely to bring growth to a halt. For Ossis, space is no longer confined, and valuable space is no longer projected onto the West or maintained in their own private spheres. Rather, their own spaces, including private ones, have been penetrated and pulverized, bought up, reclaimed, resignified, and reterritorialized, quite often by Wessis who were better situated to take advantage of the quickened tempo and rapidly changing conditions produced under time-space compression.

I am tempted to go further and argue that East German assimilation into the West German state, its entrance into the world of late capitalist liberal democracies, is an extreme case of the "civil transition" being made to some extent in all the formerly socialist countries. Whether the specific features and effects of time-space compression outlined here are generally true of other "first-contact" situations, or of other contexts analogous to a colonial situation where a smaller social Other is absorbed by a more powerful social unit, is, however, a matter for further research. Likewise, the particular plot sequence in this encounter—"pre-contact" eroticization, striptease, funeral/burial—may well hold true for similar encounters of this type. In any case, the East German transition is less accurately characterized as a movement from an undeveloped stage to a civilized one than a union of unequals in a Dadaesque pastiche, assembling different elements of the past in a present collage that produces entirely new subjects. This new German subject is still a plural one, as it was in the Cold War, with East and West counterparts. Though Germans are formally united, they are far from being unified.

Perhaps the major obstacle to unification lies in the refusal in both East and West to recognize how the Hegelian dialectic of lordship and bondage continues to construct interactions. East and West Germans had no independent consciousness during the Cold War, but in fact constituted themselves as self and other in a relationship marked by domination. The dissolution of the East has done two things: first, it has denied the West an object capable of reflecting back its conception of itself as a free self, and second, it has strengthened the dependence of the East on the West by undermining the East's sense of self-worth. If, as Hegel argues, selfhood or self-worth involves the desire for self-certainty, and if this self-certainty requires recognition by the other, then the one-sided recognition that characterized the Cold War and that now characterizes actions of the dominant West cannot succeed (Hegel 1977). The West can maintain its self-certainty only at the cost of the self-certainty of the East, in other words, through domination. Furthermore, West Germans conceal from themselves their dominion over the East by representing the Ossis as formally free and equal to Wessis when this pretense does not in fact structure the relation of the two parts to each other. Indeed, a "more perfect union" will be possible only when the diverse histories and orientations of East and West as manifested in the present, the continental divide in their subjectivities, are fully acknowledged and respected, with an orientation to understanding the nature of these differences and the conditions of their production rather than clinging to the illusion of national unification.

NOTES

1. Harvey tends to reduce conditions like "time-space compression" to a function of political-economic factors, specifically, to phases of capitalism. I am trying to account for the differential "experiencing" of time-space compression and its consequences. These experiences cannot be accounted for solely, or even primarily, in terms of the dynamics of political economy or capitalist process.

2. I examine the development of mirror-imaging processes in Borneman 1992. See the superbly concise essays in the catalogue accompanying the 1992 museum exhibit of German ideology during the Cold War, edited by the Deutsches Historisches Museum 1992.

3. For a critique of this form of temporalizing the other, see Fabian 1983.

4. Hans-Michael Diestel, former Christian Democratic Minister of the Interior under the de Maiziére regime, referred in public to himself and his compatriots as "aus den Früheren," (out of the former/earlier). Perhaps the most widely read published works that portray an internalization of these representations are those by Hans Joachim Maaz, dealt with later in this essay.

5. Political unity was expedited by using Article 23 of the Basic Law instead of Article 146, for Article 23 enabled an immediate transplantation of (superior) West Germans structures onto the (inferior) East and avoided any extended negotiation of the terms of unity.

6. I owe this suggestion to Irmela Krüger-Fürhoff.

7. Maaz and Moeller, in their most recent book, take an explicit family therapy model and project it onto East and West relations. They argue that Ossis play the traditional role of the woman (depressive, hesitant, and dependent) while the Wessis play the role of the dynamic, dominant, and aggressive male.

8. When unity is thought of as a wedding, the bride always becomes the GDR. In this vein, the Frankfurt sociologist Karl Otto

120

Hondrich (1993: 29–30) recently wrote that the GDR's *Mitgift* (dowry), which it has brought into the unification process, was a revival of the identification of Germans as one *Volk*. The German word *Gift* means both poison and gift.

REFERENCES

Anderson, Benedict
> 1983. *Imagined Communities: Reflections on the Origin and Spread of Nationalism.* London: Verso

Arnold, Heinz Ludwig, and Frauke Meyer-Gosau, eds.
> 1992. *Die Abwicklung der DDR.* Göttingen: Göttinger Sudelblätter

Benjamin, Walter
> 1978. *Reflections.* Peter Demetz, ed. New York: Harcourt, Brace, Jovanovich

Bloch, Maurice
> 1982. Death, Women, and Power. In *Death and the Regeneration of Life.* Maurice Bloch and Jonathan Parry, eds. Pp. 211–231. Cambridge: Cambridge University Press.

Bloch, Maurice, and Jonathan Perry, eds.
> 1982. Introduction: death and the regeneration of life. In *Death and the Regeneration of Life.* Maurice Bloch and Jonathan Parry, eds. Pp. 1–45. Cambridge: Cambridge University Press

Borneman, John
> 1991. *After the Wall: East Meets West in the New Berlin.* New York: Basic Books
>
> 1992a. *Belonging in the Two Berlins: Kin, State, Nation.* Cambridge, Mass.: Cambridge University Press
>
> 1992b. "State, Territory, and Identity Formation in the Postwar Berlins, 1945–1989." *Cultural Anthropology* 7:44–61
>
> 1993. "Uniting the German Nation: Law, Narrative, and Historicity." *American Ethnologist* 20(2):218–311

Bourdieu, Pierre
> 1984. *Distinction.* Cambridge, Mass.: Harvard University Press

Christ, Peter, and Ralf Neubauer
> 1991. *Kolonie im eigenem Land.* Berlin: Rowohlt

Christa, Luft
> 1992. *Treuhandreportt.* Berlin: Aufbau

121

Creed, Gerald
    1991. Civil Society and the Spirit of Capitalism. "Civilizing
    Eastern Europe," a panel chaired by Gail Kligman. 1991 An-
    nual Meeting of the American Anthropological Association,
    Chicago
Culler, Jonathan
    1981. *The Pursuit of Signs*. London: Routledge and Kegal Paul
Deutsche Bank
    1991. *Unification Issue No. 51*. Frankfurt am Main: Deutsche
    Bank
Deutsches Historisches Museum, eds.
    1992. *Deutschland im Kalten Krieg, 1945 bis 1963*. Berlin: Argon
    Verlag
Elias, Norbert
    1978. *The Civilizing Process: The History of Manners*. New York:
    Urizen Books
Fabian, Johannes
    1983. *Time and the Other: How Anthropology Makes its Object*.
    New York: Columbia University Press
Gal, Susan
    1991. Questions about women and gender after socialism: the
    abortion debate in Hungary. "Civilizing Eastern Europe," a panel
    chaired by Gail Kligman. 1991 Annual Meeting of the Ameri-
    can Anthropological Association, Chicago
GIC (German Information Center)
    1992. *This Week in Germany, October 16*. New York: German
    Information Center
Habermas, Jürgen
    1990. "What Does Socialism Mean Today? The Rectifying Revo-
    lution and the Need for New Thinking on the Left." *New Left
    Review* 183: 3–23
Harvey, David
    1989. *The Condition of Postmodernity*. Oxford: Oxford Univer-
    sity Press
Hauser, Eva
    1991. Politics of feminism in Poland. "Civilizing Eastern Eu-
    rope," a panel chaired by Gail Kligman. 1991 Annual Meeting
    of the American Anthropological Association, Chicago
Hegel, G.W.F.
    1977. *Phenomenology of Spirit*. A.V. Miller, trans. Oxford: Ox-
    ford University Press

122

Heiduczek, Werner
    1992. Germany: NOT a "Winter's Tale," Rather the "Outsider." Symposium on "Restructuring our Lives," organized by Robin Ostow, sponsored by the Goethe Institute- Toronto, Canada, September 26–27

Hondrich, Karl Otto
    1993. "Das Volk, die Wirt, die Gewalt." *Der Spiegel* 1/47: 29–30.

Huntington, Richard, and Peter Metcalf
    1979. *Celebrations of Death*. Cambridge: Cambridge University Press

Kligman, Gail
    1992. When abortion is banned: the politics of reproduction in Ceausescu's Romania. Report prepared for the National Council for Soviet and East European Research

Kornai, János
    1980. *Economics of Shortage*. Amsterdam: North-Holland Publishing Company

Maaz, Hans Joachim
    1990. *Der Gefühlsstau. Ein Psychogramm der DDR*. Berlin: Rowohlt
    1991. *Das gestürzte Volk*. Berlin: Rowohlt

Maaz, Hans Joachim, and Michael Moeller
    1992. *Die Einheit beginnt zu zweit*. Berlin: Rowohlt

Offe, Claus
    1990. "Vom taktischen Gebrauchswert nationaler Gefühle." *Die Zeit* 51/14:42

Ngubane, H
    1976. "Some notions of 'purity' and 'impurity' among the Zulu." *Africa* 46:274–283

Pitt-Rivers, Julian
    1977. *The Fate of Shechem or the Politics of Sex: Essays in the Anthropology of the Mediterranean*. Cambridge: Cambridge University Press

Rosenberg, Dorothy
    1991. "Shock therapy: GDR women in transition from a socialist welfare state to a social market economy." *Signs* 17:129–151

Seremetakis, Nadia C.
    1991. *The Last Word: Women, Death, and Divination in Inner Mani*. Chicago: University of Chicago Press

123

Strathern, Andrew
>1982. Witchcraft, greed, cannibalism and death: some related themes from the New Guinea Highlands. In *Death and the Regeneration of Life*. Maurice Bloch and Jonathan Parry, eds. Pp. 111–133. Cambridge: Cambridge University Press

Tietmeyer, Hans
>1991. The Economic Unity of Germany: An Assessment one year after the monetary union. Paper delivered at, and published in, the First Stanford Berlin Symposium on Transitions in Europe: Economic Transformation in Germany—Social, Political, and Psychological Dimensions, Berlin, July 4–6, pp. 16–22

Verdery, Katherine
>1991. *National Ideology under Socialism: Identity and Cultural Politics in Ceausescu's Romania*. Berkeley: University of California Press
>1996. *From Parent State to Family Patriarchs: Gender and Nation in Contemporary Eastern Europe*, pp. 61–82
>*What Was Socialism, and What Comes Next?* Princeton: Princeton University Press

Weck, Michael
>1992. "Der ironische Westen und der tragische Osten." *Kursbuch* 190: 76–89

Die Zeit
>1990. "Spätere Liebe nicht ausgeschlossen: Die Deutschen in Ost und West müssen einander erst kennenlernen." *Die Zeit* 51 (December 21, 1990): 5

5

Narrative, Genealogy, and Historical Consciousness: Selfhood in a Disintegrating State

In response to the general loss of confidence in the truth-value of representations by social scientists, anthropologists have increasingly turned to narrative analysis, a subfield of literary studies long involved in understanding textual representations and the concomitant processes of authorship, writing, and reading. At this time of increased doubt and reflexivity, judicious borrowings from literary theory are now, more than ever before, attractive to anthropologists (e.g., Clifford 1988; Marcus and Fischer 1986; Clifford and Marcus 1986; Herzfeld 1985).[1] While literary critics offer anthropologists no dominant paradigms by which to decide exactly what to study in the field, nor new techniques that might improve the ways to go about such work, they have developed a rather sophisticated understanding of how data—utterances, actions, events, and happenings—are made assimilable to structures of meaning by assuming narrative form (see the essays in Mitchell 1981). The key to representational form, we are told, is never merely a neutral evaluation and recitation of facts, but also a narrativization of them (Mink 1978: 129–149; White 1978, 1973). By making stories out of fieldwork data, we are, then, not involved in deception or distortion, but availing ourselves of the only means we have of making the facts comprehensible (Borneman 1993: 218–311; Bruner 1986: 139–158; Ricoeur 1984).

In this essay, I wish to focus not so much on the ethnographer[2] and text as on the processes of narrativization during the telling, that is, the act of authorship or inscription.[3] I hope to show that the relationship between anthropology and literary studies is not merely one of convenience, but necessary and indispensable. In fact, the two disciplines, interrelated through the process of narrativity, the method of genealogy, and the condition of historical consciousness, presuppose one another in a mutual practice centered around the production and interpretation of narrative texts.[4] I shall demonstrate this by investigating how narrative form is put to work and made to act during narration. How, in other words, is form (per)formed?

First, we will examine the autobiography of East Berliner Susan R., an ethnographic text about the struggle for self-articulation and definition told at a moment in time when Susan's self and the world around her—in particular, her citizenship and nationality—are rapidly losing coherence.[5] Her autobiographical life history typifies many of the properties of narrative—a reconstruction where the end writes the beginning and shapes the middle, told in temporally sequenced clauses, always anticipating her own retrospection—and of genealogy—an account related from present to past as a series of disjunctive and accidental events, with no universal History in mind, selectively fashioned into a relative coherence concerned more with descent (*Herkunft*) than origin (*Ursprung*).[6] Second, we will be situating this story in the fieldwork context of its narration. I do not separate Susan's story from my own analysis, but rather bring both the fieldwork context and my analytic voice to bear on her text when it illuminates the relationship of genealogy to narrativity. Thereby I hope to address a theoretical issue central to the social sciences and humanities: how to reconcile Hans-Georg Gadamer's understanding of *historical consciousness* (taking into account the presentness of historical reconstruction) with Michel Foucault's notion of history as *genealogy* (a history of the present), which I take to be different but essentially complementary aspects of any project in the human sciences.

126

Before presenting Susan's narrative, let me define more precisely the analytical terms I will be employing. A genealogical approach is fundamental not only to ethnology but also to self-understanding. All memory, in fact, proceeds via genealogy, even though the result of memories, their final representations, may be made to appear like constructions of an original movement from past to present rather than reconstructions done in reverse. Ethnographers have long derived their authority from fieldwork situations where they assemble knowledge genealogically told or performed. Even observed live performances, before they can take textual form, must be reconstructed at a point in time after the event. The particular genealogies for which the discipline of anthropology has become renowned have been accounts of kinship, often represented as affines and consanguines fanning out in ordered rows beneath an "ego." Kinship genealogies resemble all other reconstructions (e.g., of objects, life stages, group memberships) in that their historical nature "does not consist in the restoration of the past, but in thoughtful mediation with contemporary life" (Gadamer 1979: 150). In other words, all genealogies share the fact that, from a position in the present, someone imaginatively reconstructs the forms that preceded the current one.

What links the genealogical method to narrativity is that the ethnographer's method produces texts, some of which will invariably take narrative form, that is, sequentially ordered with a beginning, middle, and end. In short, narrative and genealogy, much like literature and anthropology, predicate each other: narration always proceeds via a genealogical ordering, but a genealogical mode of inquiry requires narrative for its representation. The study of this form of representation, and the process whereby it translates something told into something known, is precisely the shared object of literature and anthropology.

Finally, historical consciousness, which I take to be a condition to which one strives and not a state of being, involves the recognition and knowledge of one's own historicity. Following Gadamer, we are unable to confront the Other except through our own cultural prejudices. This of course implicates the present in any narration, or understanding, of the past. When anthropologists do fieldwork, they are doing precisely such histories of the present. They are

127

engaged in a genealogy of forms that assumes no necessary movement from the past to the present, but instead concedes that the
present is an arbitrary result of past forms arrived at often willy-
nilly and often through unintended consequences of past actions
having little to do with the motivations at the original time of
action. Although anthropologists always invert the usual historical
method and proceed from the present to the past, they usually
understand this inversion as a constraint, and rarely see it as
productive of a particular form of knowledge. Indeed, if we become
conscious of what follows from our method, might we not better
understand our own historicity and integrate that into the questions we ask? Might this consciousness make us less liable to read
the past as teleologically unfolding according to some prior plan?
Might we not gain from a recognition that, in the words of Edward
Said, we are not "commanded by [some silent past] to speak in the
present," but rather describe the present "in the course of its articulation, [in] its struggles for definition" (1983: 51)? What, then,
can we learn about narrative, genealogy, and historical consciousness by concentrating on the act of inscription itself—on Susan R.'s
genealogical narrative at the moment of telling?

Susan R. told her life story to me and Jeffrey Peck on September
10, 1989, exactly two months before the opening of the Berlin Wall.
Like many anthropological documents, hers is a narrative primarily about kinship construction, genealogically told. Yet while she
was telling us the details of personal history, other events forced an
awareness of the present moment and thus knowledge of historicity, which then threatened to undermine her narrative voice and
change her story. During the late summer of 1989, other East
Germans vacationing in Prague and Budapest had begun taking
refuge in West German embassies in those cities, choosing to exit
their own society and state. Just one month after we met with
Susan, on October 8, 1989, about 500 East German citizens took
advantage of a local fair where Hungarians and Austrians were
celebrating the dismantling of their border, to flee to Austria. The
trickle turned into a flood; thousands poured over daily; the Austrian government then sent them on by bus to automatic citizenship and social welfare payments in West Germany (see Borneman
1991). This flight destabilized the political and domestic situation

in which Susan lived; her world was being transformed with neither her approval, resistance, or complicity. At the very moment when Susan was being asked to construct a coherent narrative about her identity, her social context—the state and forms of belonging in which she lived—was disintegrating.

Paradoxically, what most intruded and disturbed her account was the loss of a form of membership that she had never shared. She had never taken on citizenship of the German Democratic Republic (GDR), but merely maintained residence within its protective and confining borders. Yet she was embedded in a kinship network that included members of that state—parents, siblings, husband, children; it ultimately also contained her through her own lived experience. Despite being formally an outsider in the GDR, she could not escape a confrontation with its position in the inter-national order of things. Both the construction and the disintegration of the East German state, along with its system of memberships, affected her equally. Hence, kinship and the state provide the central tropes for her story.

We might begin with a formal representation of her late summer 1989 genealogy of kin and state membership, what I call, to borrow a term from Nietzsche, "effective historical" kin (figure 5.1).

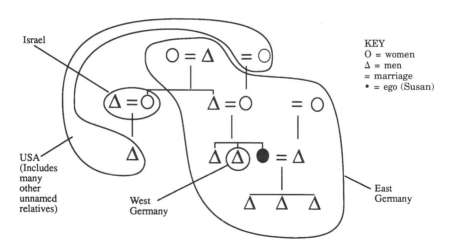

Figure 5.1. Susan R.'s "effective historical kin," late summer 1989.

I have included only those kin specifically mentioned by Susan. Her omissions were not due to a bout of "genealogical amnesia," nor is her failure to distinguish between "fictive" and "real" kin— which anthropological accounts have been prone to do—a result of category error. Rather, she began by focusing on what was near to her, meaning significant for or memorable to her. At another point in time, she might have even narrated a different genealogy. An abstract lineage model, which, had I insisted, she certainly could have constructed, would have had little relation to the structures of her history. Illumination of these structures, represented by her "effective historical kin," was, after all, the point of her narrative. Note that of the four states in which her kin resided at the time of the interview, only three exist as of this writing (East and West Germany have since been reunited).

Susan R.'s Genealogy of Kin and State Membership

Susan was born in 1949 in the United States, but fled with her parents to Austria in 1950, to the GDR the following year. "They had to leave," says Susan, "My father was very active politically, a member of the American Communist Party, and because my mother was with him, and then also had become a member of the Communist Party, she too had problems because of this at that time." While attending an international medical conference in Switzerland, her father suspected a return to the United States would result in his arrest. He allowed the party to decide for him whether to return; they told him to stay in Europe. "Therefore my mother had to arrange everything, which wasn't so easy, ... because getting passports"—Susan introduces the word that tropes so much of her experience: "pass-ports," implying state borders, citizenship, freedom of movement—"for the children was problematical." In particular, she explains, it was a problem for her second oldest brother, who was three years old at the time. He never was told that he had an American passport, "but he found out about it later. [While in the GDR] he had been forced to swear that he never did have a passport and never was an American." But on his last visit to the United States, the computers found him registered as a citizen, much to his surprise! After his return to the GDR, his no-longer-secret membership was a source of considerable tension between him and his parents.

Nearly half of Susan's two-hour-long narrative is about resisting and resigning oneself to the boundaries imposed by states. She tells this plot genealogically, in the sense both of a history of familial descent and of an archeology of past events that anticipate her present. Reconstructing the history of interactions between legally inscribed memberships and the movements and motivations of her kin, she "effectuates a mediation between the once and the now" by describing, as Gadamer writes of historical consciousness, "a continual series of perspectives through which the past presents and addresses itself to [her]" (Gadamer 1979: 159).

"My father was born in 1912 in the Soviet Union," she began, immediately adding, "in the territory of Ukraine." Since then, of course, Ukraine was absorbed into the Soviet Union; in 1912, it was a sovereign territory. And two years after this interview, Ukraine again became a sovereign state. His personal diaspora began in 1920, when a pogrom directed against the Jews drove his parents—who, like his other relatives, were primarily Jews—to Austria. The rest of the kin group resettled in the United States. Although subject to antisemitism in Austria, Susan's father nonetheless succeeded in going to a private school, and later the university, studying medicine and chemistry. Meanwhile, he joined the Communist party in 1930, at the age of eighteen, something about which "he doesn't speak too much," and "insofar as [she] knows, also was imprisoned [for his activities] twice." He lived in Austria until 1937, when he left to accept an offer to study and research in the United States. To Susan, and, I suspect, to her father, it is unclear whether he had to leave Germany because of his communist activities or because he was a Jew—the two identities being entwined. He was identified by the authorities as an enemy of the state not on racial grounds but because of his political activities. It is clear, however, that his Jewish background would have eventually also placed him in danger and forced him to leave.

Susan's mother, born in 1912 to a German father and Jewish mother who converted to Christianity, traces her natal home to Africa, where her maternal grandfather did business. This African part of the Jewish family's participation in German colonial history is left unelaborated. Her parents divorced, "not because of the Jewish thing, although it was 1934, but because of another woman who my grandfather wanted to marry—who then also left him sitting alone."

"My grandmother," Susan explains, "had to earn money herself then, in 1934, [even though] she came from a wealthy family. My grandfather controlled her money and squandered her entire inheritance." Susan lowered her voice and said softly, "She didn't speak too well of him."

Susan's mother grew up in Hamburg, Germany, also studied medicine there, and "first through the National Socialists became interested in Jewishness. She definitely knew nothing about it before." German Jews were perhaps the most "assimilated" of the European Jewry around the turn of the century. Hitler's racial programs forced many fully assimilated Jews to reconstruct an identificaton that had been partly or wholly superseded by others. Susan is careful not to impute an identity to her mother that wasn't part of her mother's own identifications. In the period before the Nazis came to power, Jewishness, for her mother as well as for many German Jews, was not part of a universal History to be recovered, but rather one identification, among others, to be *selected* and reconstructed. After 1934, however, German Jews had little or no "choice" about determining their own selfhood—their Germanness was denied to them; their Jewishness was elevated to a primordial category of being.

"[Sometime later]," she continues, "[my mother's] belief in God was broken and since then she's been atheist." Though her mother had not been politically or religiously active, living with a Jewish mother classified her as "full Jew." On this basis, she was denied her doctorate in medicine. In 1938, she emigrated to the United States, with her mother following shortly after. Susan's uncle from this side of the family managed to survive the Nazi period living in Germany and emigrated to the United States in 1950. "Since my parents had already returned [to Germany]," adds Susan, "they never even met [each other] here." Like ships without a compass crossing in the night, Susan's kin in this century were in constant motion but never sure about direction, fleeing from and escaping to

132

territorial units which themselves had shifting residents and boundaries, recovering old identities and shedding new ones, often with no plan or design for life other than survival.

According to Susan, her parents remember the period of twelve years in the United States as "the happiest years of [their] lives. But why they were so happy is because they met there and it was the first love [for them]; my father had his work. And the people there, they had their most friends, either old comrades [from the Party], or friends from youth who either live in the GDR or Austria now." The great master narratives of the American experience—freedom, liberty, wealth—were not central to her parent's experience. It was something more parochial and concrete—love and friendship—that imprinted itself as America on the memory of her parents.

In this act of recalling the remembrance of her parents, Susan is in effect doing a Nietzschean or Foucaultian genealogy, and she is reaching for a mode of historical understanding of the sort explicated by Gadamer. She seeks out "the singularity of events outside of any monotonous finality," and finds them "in the most unpromising places, in what we tend to feel is without history—in sentiments, love, conscience . . ." (Foucault: 1977: 139). Her story is not the progressive realization of an ideal, such as choice or freedom. Genealogical analysis, argued Nietzsche (1964: 9), shows that the concept of liberty is an "invention of the ruling classes," neither fundamental to nature nor connected to being and truth. Susan cannot reconstruct her life with reference to a tale about freedom being realized. Rather, as she descends into the past, she talks of disrupture, dispersion, discontinuity. Yet for Susan this historical knowledge is not part of a nihilistic project, as is often claimed to be the tendency when employing the genealogical approach of Nietzsche or Foucault. For her, it "does not necessarily lead to the dissolution of the tradition in which [she] live[s]," but, as Gadamer (1979: 107) has maintained, enables her to discover alternative possibilities of identification by enriching this tradition, either by "confirm[ing] or alter[ing] it."[7]

Exactly why her father had to leave the United States remains unclear. He was sent to Japan by the American government for six months in 1947 to deal with the outbreak of an epidemic. While there, the army discovered that he was a member of the Communist Party, and called him back. Meanwhile, in America her mother "distributed leaflets in some apartment area, arguing that blacks should be able to live there. She had her children [especially the oldest son] help her. People shot at her with rifles to terrify her into giving up." This story trails off into micro-events, episodes of what, in retrospect, seem minor political fights, but which undoubtedly formed the basis for, as Susan argues, "getting the entire family put on the Black List." Susan's dispersed narrative parallels the uncertainty at the moment of her telling. The trope of disintegration figures both her text and context. Her search through descent in time for the beginning of her family's persecution in America does not settle and provide solace, but rather "disturbs what was previously considered immobile," as Foucault characterizes genealogy more generally. "[I]t fragments what was thought unified; it shows the heterogeneity of what was imagined consistent with itself" (1977: 147). Accompanying her recognition of the fragmentation around her, Susan is confirmed in her sense of self as relative and incomplete. By not forcing events into a coherent plot that would allow a single interpretation—which, in any case, appears unavailable to her—Susan finds herself able to narrativize her past. She concludes simply that something happened making her parents enemies of the United States. They left America before she had reached her first year; they ended up in East Germany.

From the United States, the family first fled to Austria. Her father then applied for work: in Austria, France, Israel, and the Soviet Union. Despite his international preeminence in the field of medicine, he found no takers. After nearly a year, he received and accepted an offer from the GDR to found a research institute. Since her parents took the pursuit of science to be central to their identities, their work made them integral to East Germany. And they integrated rather quickly—but they did not assimilate. Even during the height of division in the Cold War, they enjoyed a cosmopolitan identity, moving freely from East to West and West to East. In the early 1970s, her father was invited back to the United States to receive an award from the U.S. Army for an invention still in use that improves blood conservation. Not until 1978 did they take on GDR citizenship—for what reasons Susan is still unsure. During family dinners possibilities to go elsewhere were discussed constantly. "My mother raised us as if this was a waystation," exclaims Susan, "that we'd eventually leave, that we weren't German."

Her mother, also a medical doctor, found the adjustment to life in Germany more difficult than did her father, precisely because she had once felt fully assimilated, and then was branded as a foreigner during the Third Reich. "My mother hated the Germans; my father was actually not so nationalistic as my mother. He hadn't actually lived here. He had other things for which he fought, which he had already dealt with personally. He was in the Communist Party and fought for other things, while my mother, for her it was as if the whole thing came from another galaxy." Susan is pointing to the apolitical stance of many German Jews before the war, a depoliticization that on the one hand enabled them to assimilate into German cultural life (perhaps even a precondition for the assimilation) around the turn of the century and to rise to the top in many fields; on the other hand, it blinded them to the precariousness of their position, to the actual racism around them. The outsider status of her father—coming from an orthodox Jewish family in Ukraine, and then growing up in Austria—enabled him to see the Germans more dispassionately, neither bitterly remembering a rejection nor anticipating full acceptance.

When the Nazis finally achieved power in 1932, their radical antisemitic program still seemed unbelievable to many well integrated Jews. Yet inscribed on the body of Susan's grandmother was a history of difference that her mother inherited, though no longer merely as a physical difference but also as a historical-psychological perception. "She wasn't big, blond, and blue-eyed, nor a brunette," Susan describes her grandmother, "[but] a classical Jewish type, with black hair. And because of that [my mother] felt herself to be different; she always felt inferior." A physical distinction, inscribed in her mother's body, formed the basis for an exclusion, a historical inheritance to be carried around. "My mother can develop an incredible hate. And she developed this hate for the Germans, directing it against West Germany: there is that state that never stopped, never broke [with the Nazis]." In this she shared a sentiment with many leftists, especially Communists, who returned to the GDR after the war. For them, West Germany, which incorporated many leading Nazis into its administrative ranks and judicial system and was tied to the same capitalist structure as the Third Reich, was the bastard child of Hitler. East Germany, on the other hand, did not identify itself with German tradition (at least not until the 1980s); additionally, a clean sweep was made of the bureaucracy and judicial system, with, for example, eighty-five percent of all Nazi judges being fired.[8]

For Susan's parents, this distrust, or hate in the case of her mother, of all things German extended even to a refusal to identify as victims of the Germans. They wanted nothing more to do with official German systems of classification; in fact, they delayed for twenty-eight years the decision to become GDR citizens. And her mother hesitated for years before applying for *Wiedergutmachung*, recognition as a victim of fascism. In order to obtain that recognition, one had to offer proof of persecution, something many actual victims viewed as humiliation before old German authorities. Her father, Austrian by birth, had to file his claims in Austria. He also refused to apply, but eventually a friend did it for him—not for reasons of conscience or historical reckoning, emphasizes Susan, but because it was available and he needed the money. "Western currency is short here," he reportedly said. Succumbing to his needs and the pressures of a friend, he obtained official status as a victim of fascism from the Austria government.

The process of obtaining and maintaining citizenship had a perverse meaning for the "R." family, because, Susan stresses, they were "vagabond types, who never were interested in having a fixed home and a position. I was always for that. I always wanted to leave and experience something else. [When we discussed moving] it was mostly to countries where they had to build something." Yet this building—termed the *Aufbau* in the GDR—was finished by the time Susan reached adulthood. By the mid-1970s the economy had stagnated, and the leadership sought merely to protect its past accomplishments rather than risk proposing new changes. Indeed Susan had the paradoxical *Schicksal* of being exiled in a country that presented itself as future-oriented but romanticized its past (see Borneman 1992b: 74–82). She enjoyed neither the protections of East German citizenship nor a sense of belonging there, although she did share with its residents the experience of being contained.

Entering into Susan's homelessness is another dimension of experience and membership from which she was estranged but which, paradoxically, also had a hold on her: religion. Much like in the case of her citizenship and loyalty to a state, Susan was estranged from religion, having only formal ties through her genealogy. Her subjectivity was elsewhere: she identified herself as atheist. Yet even this belief, seemingly in agreement with official state doctrine, did not facilitate finding a home in the officially called "worker and farmer state," for that state practiced a particular interpretation of Marxism as religion. Atheism functioned as dogma and creed within a holistic system of state-mandated rites and rituals. Therefore, with respect to belief, Susan felt very much on her own.

Susan's Jewishness

"In my family there was constant discussion over Christianity and Judaism, about which is better. My mother," says Susan, "was very much taken by Christianity, my father by Judaism. We [children] were only spectators." In recalling her spectator role in the past, Susan is merely finding earlier forms of the activity, which, as she was talking to us, so dramatically characterized her present situation. It seems as if she is always watching and listening, but never able to arrive at a final standpoint; she assumes positions that are constantly relativized by changing contexts. Her radical reflexivity and readiness "to understand the possibility of a multiplicity of relative viewpoints" (Gadamer 1979: 110) decenters her narrative, enabling her to place herself in the perspective of others, including, as we will see, non-Jewish Germans. This recognition is in fact a precondition of historical consciousness. "Today no one can shield himself from this reflexivity characteristic of the modern spirit," writes Gadamer (1979: 110). As soon as Susan finds a fact or event or story located in her past to which she might cling, and which might be used to frame and interpret her self, it seems to escape from its time sequence and reenter her consciousness as part of a different sequence of events.

How does she deal with the radical indeterminacy of her position? She oscillates between different frames: "But it somehow really

137

made an impression on me that I was living as a German, but felt myself to be Jewish, in the sense that I wasn't somehow guilty of the *Taten* [deeds, implying complicity with the Nazis], that I was one of the persecuted peoples." And then she switches frames: "I somehow had the proud feeling of belonging [to the Jews], but at the same time [that produces] insecurity, because I know so little about it. . . . It's quite the vogue now to live as a Jew in the GDR, and there again I'm a little different." According to Susan, the desire of so many contemporary Germans to meet a Jew or their interest in Jewish things "is like observing foreign, exotic animals. . . . I also always see it from the other side"—she emphasizes her relativity, her Jewish and German positions, but then takes a stand, at least on this issue—"I'm not a religious person, and I'll never be. It's simply too late for that." Susan is only too aware of how "late" it is, as she talks to us in the waning months of the Cold War, on the abyss of a new, unforeseeable era that she suspects will totally destroy the old. The descent into her-story painfully deconstructs the illusions and myths that might make her life seem linear and coherent. However, this descent is also a way to finding a voice, an enabling predicate for narrativity and historical consciousness. It makes more transparent the coming devastation of her parent's political ideology and the collapse of the state, as well as her own situatedness in the present contexts framed by this ideology and this state.

Unable to find a fixed frame located either in the past or the future, Susan expresses a basic ambivalence about commitment and hesitance about moving out of her present. Nietzsche, in his essay "On the Advantage and Disadvantage of History for Life," characterized positions of radical historicality, like Susan's, as lacking "the strength of being able to *forget* and enclose oneself in a limited *horizon*" (1980: 62). Indeed, her stark honesty in remembering opens, instead of delimiting, her horizon, making her vulnerable, as Nietzsche says, in "an endless-unlimited light-wave-sea of known becoming" (1980: 62). Moreover, her ambivalence about claiming an essential otherness is prefigured by an unbridgeable sense of apartness from any group. "I always see some danger there," she avers, referring to practicing Judaism in Germany, which "holds me back" from entering the Jewish community as a member. Where precisely does she locate this danger?

Susan points to an answer in response to our question as to whether she was raising her children to be conscious of their Jewish background. "They don't even know it. There's always the question: Is it a religion or a race? When it's a religion, then it's really the case that it doesn't make sense, because I'm not religious. Thomas [her husband] also actually is somewhat afraid, because there's always some antisemitism. And why should you put this burden on the children? Otherwise," she repeats, "they don't even know about it," stressing the obvious fact that no identity is out there to be found, but rather, all identities are constructed by selection among alternatives and learning the rites and behaviors that go with group membership. For Susan, Jewishness is not an essential identity waiting to be confirmed, but a learned story that would frame her experience in a particular way. Furthermore, it is a dangerous identity when affirmed in Germany. She addresses this question by choosing not to affirm a Jewish identity; her decision is not a matter of finding the really real, a truth outside of history. It is not, Nietzsche would say, like art or religion, which reaches for a truth independent of context. Her Jewishness is contingent on and inseparable from her present situation.

One might ask if her rejection of Judaism isn't derived from a fear of antisemitism. She can recall only one incident in her past: "I was with my school class in a village, and we were quite loud. Someone said, 'That's just like a Jewish school.' Otherwise, I never experienced anything of the sort." Vastly unlike the conditions under which her parents constructed their identities, Susan's own experience of antisemitism is limited to one retold as humor: Jewish children are less disciplined than German children—certainly not a pernicious comparison.

This is not to say, however, that Susan is wholly unconcerned about the resurfacing of antisemitism in the virulent forms experienced by her parents. She has reservations and fears, as stated above, about informing her children about Jewishness. Regarding her marriage to Thomas, who is not Jewish, her parents were unconcerned about his ethnic or religious background, only "they were quite relieved that Thomas' family didn't do anything in the Third Reich. My stepmother was an opponent of the regime." Yet Thomas resists her constructing any Jewish identity for herself. "I

139

do not decide alone; the decision rests with my husband. I myself would go to the Jewish community, I think, I would, if it were up to me. But I know for sure that he wouldn't like it, because he doesn't even accept [it]; he would ask what kind of sense it made [to go there]." And she concludes forcefully, "I think that antisemitism is still there.

"In the school I always had problems because I was raised to be so critical," she continues. "I always spoke up about what I found unfair. Thomas [whom she met at age seventeen] saw the problems I had. He thinks that I'm naive. I am naive, but I'm not so political that I'd . . ." And Susan reverses gears, imputing to herself more agency. She did go to the Jewish community once, but says "I can't say that I felt comfortable there. I rationalize my time: I am studying English; I exercise to keep a bit fit. That's already two days. And [as a medical doctor] I often have to work nights. To be an atheist takes a lot of energy, even in Germany." Whatever Jewishness means for Susan, it is not religion and it is not race. Her connection to Jewishness is historical, one that can be traced genealogically, that can be experienced in the present but affirmed only in a particular social space, specifically in Israel and America.

Susan, America, and Israel

Susan's personal relationship to America parallels, in an extreme form, hers to Austria and the GDR: All three are partial, truncated, subject-object relations, with seemingly overdetermined histories that permit little dialogue and no agency for herself. With respect to America, she has in fact no history of her own. "In any case, I have had absolutely no connection to America. We fled while I was still small." The United States took her father's citizenship away, and her mother "gave her [passport] back, on moral grounds." Her father then reassumed his Austrian citizenship, through which her mother, as wife, and the three children automatically obtained citizenship also. (It is striking how her mother's identity is taken completely out of her hands by states and men: first, by the Nazi state, then by her legal marriage to a man disliked by his state (the USA) and to whom she is bound.) The family entered the GDR with

140

Austrian citizenship, which set them apart from other East Germans. "We were somewhat different," explains Susan about family status in East Germany. "Anyway, [this fact] certainly made an impression on me."

Her parents "were completely into the rituals of the GDR, . . . immediately joined the ruling Socialist Unity Party (SED), [though] they weren't GDR citizens." European socialist parties had traditionally defined membership in non-national terms, but following the end of World War II, most of these parties became more national-focused and -based. The SED, in particular, was selective about its foreign national members, given the Cold War context and its fear of spies in the ranks. For Susan, even though she "felt [herself] somewhat different" from other GDR citizens, there was "no confrontation in the political domain," because her parents, being in basic agreement with the regime, were strong supporters of the state at home. "Back then that was all no problem; I don't know," she hesitates, "how that is today." She joined the Young Pioneers, for children up to the age of twelve, and later the Free German Youth, for those aged twelve to thirty, even though, she emphasizes, "I do not have GDR citizenship."

And then Susan reflects, "I can only say that I've lived my conscious life (*bewußtes Leben*) here"—emphasizing that she is constituted by those personal experience of which she is conscious—"my conscious life has taken place only in the GDR. For that reason, I am bound to the GDR. In upbringing, we [in the family] were not raised as Germans. We had Austrian citizenship; therefore we travelled on vacation to Austria or England. My parents never allowed these limits to subjugate them after 1961—she elliptically refers to the building of the Wall.

For Susan, whose conscious life (*bewußtes Leben*) is intimately "bound to the GDR," being Jewish is not part of living there, but rather only possible for her in two other territories: Israel and the United States. She begins answering a question about her own relation to Jewishness as follows: "About the topic of Jewishness. I basically did not know that I was American"—she slides from identity to topography, bringing in America and Israel—"not until I visited a cousin of mine, whose father lives in Israel." Her father's sister had resettled in Israel in 1934, married, and had two sons,

141

one of whom resettled in New York. This son, Susan's cousin, got married in 1971 and invited Susan to his wedding. She went to the American embassy in West Berlin to get a visa on her Austrian passport. But she needed no visa, the embassy officials explained, since she was already an American citizen. She need only apply for a passport, which would take six weeks to obtain. Since the wedding was in four weeks, and a visa took only three, she applied for the visa instead. When she returned to pick it up, the embassy surprised her, however, with a passport. "I needed only a pass photo and I would get a passport!"

Susan did actually attend that Jewish wedding in the United States, traveling on an American passport, making her relatives "insufferably proud" of her—a Jew from East Germany with an American passport. But she found it all somewhat embarrassing. "Since I wasn't really raised a Jew, it presented me with certain problems. On the other hand," she turns back on herself again, "I didn't make the attempt to know about it in its details." Therefore, during the trip, she "always felt uncertain," which did not detract from her most important memory, of "a fantastic belonging, what you don't at all know here [in the GDR]. Naturally," says Susan about the Americans, "I told them only [about] their merits." Much as the size and wealth of America impressed her, so did the "fear of the Americans, the [general] fear of blacks," the racism, and the fact "that I was forbidden to travel alone in the subway in New York." Moreover, she found it odd that later, when she decided to marry Thomas, she had to justify to her American relatives her decision not to have a Jewish marriage.

In narrating her life, Susan counterbalanced her genealogy of kin, along with its entire affective and experiential import, with genealogies of other memberships, particularly those of citizen and nation. Her perspective is informed by cross-cutting and overlapping genealogies, each of which positions her differently with respect to culture, nation, and state. Through a process that selects, foregrounds, highlights, sequences, and periodizes, she creatively narrativized each descent out of heterodox events and happenings. No single membership necessarily takes priority over the others. "It's quite clear," she asserts about the relativity of citizenship and political membership, "that you don't feel yourself bound to a country just because you have a passport from there."

Susan even goes so far as to maintain that she feels bound to countries from which she has no passport. Like many German Jews who still live in some part of Germany, Susan shares a special relationship with the state of Israel. "I did go alone to Israel once. I happened onto the idea that I'd go and see how things are there. My parents agreed." She could stay with her father's sister, who had settled in Palestine in the early 1930s. "Then came the war," meaning the 1967 war, "and my parents thought it was too dangerous and uncertain." Several years later, the opportunity presented itself again. She finds most memorable about the trip an event that marked her sense of Jewishness: the experience on the airplane from Bucharest to Israel. "That was like a big family. You had the feeling that it wasn't important where you came from. Talking with one another, somehow I was taken by that." The trip seemed more meaningful than either the departure or arrival. Susan was "taken by" the unconcern for "where you came from," the disregard for ultimate kin and citizen origins. Israel was a topos on which she could place her dreams of belonging to a community of vagabonds (see the interviews by Ostow 1989).

Susan and Historical Consciousness

With no fixed tradition—neither Jewish nor German, communist nor capitalist—to which she could claim any primordial belonging, Susan felt stranded in an ethereal, disintegrating present. The mass exodus to West Germany of her fellow GDR residents—all citizens, unlike her—left her feeling, she tells us, even more like a beached whale. The formal documents—Austrian and American passports, East German visa—granting her freedom to go where she wants meant very little to her. "Now even more [of the people] with whom I work are gone, more [of those] from my circle of friends have gone over there [to West Germany]. I have a permanent visa, so I have the possibility to travel to West Berlin, and I've kept contact with those who have left. But it's like this: I don't make myself an exception from the other GDR citizens. In this respect, I feel as if I am

143

fully GDR. It's a fact that I could always travel. It's a fact that other citizens of the GDR could also travel when they have relatives. But it's somewhat different to travel alone and not with a partner or with your family. Since I married, I've nearly quit travelling.

"I can still travel to West Berlin, and I go shopping and visit someone, but it's different. Basically, I'm just as imprisoned as the other GDR citizens. I feel pretty much identical to them in this respect." Susan is, then, technically free to move around as she wishes. The restrictive laws of the GDR do not apply to her, an Austrian citizen. Yet she feels "just as imprisoned as other GDR citizens." Why? Because, for Susan, reaching adulthood entailed finding "a partner," marriage, and having children. It is her commitment to these individuals, to domestic life, that positions her in their world and hence imprisons her.

Though technically registered as an American citizen, her American passport has since lapsed, and Susan laments her failure to get her it renewed in 1976. By that time, the Americans had an embassy representative in East Berlin. She went in and applied, but the man behind the counter couldn't give her any direct answers. "Later I found out that he was a GDR citizen working there, not an American. I found that unfair." American embassies in Eastern Europe, which were forced to hire a certain number of native personnel, were notorious for their lax security. Susan asks herself, "Why [didn't I get it renewed]? I guess out of laziness. I would have had to go to someplace, and. . . ." Anyone with experience in Eastern Europe before 1989 knows what a labyrinth the bureaucracy presented when one sought to obtain things that the state didn't want to distribute—but which the state reserved for itself to distribute. Rather than complain about these obstacles, Susan criticizes herself for laziness. In her struggle to find a voice to articulate her own needs, she always returns to self-critique—in a fashion that became the norm in the waning months of the existence of East Germany—about her own shortcomings, her own lack of initiative, her own inability to stand alone. Paradoxically, her search for belonging is compounded, not facilitated, by the fact that she is a full member of no group and therefore not bound formally to, nor privileged by, the rules and traditions of any particular group.

144

She sees herself as a mediator between sets of interests and constraints: her German husband and Jewish descent, East and West, career and children. Although she is a very capable doctor, as capable as her two brothers, whom she views as geniuses, she cannot commit herself to her work and career at the cost of others. Her parents exhort her to study for an advanced degree and become a head doctor at the Charitee. But she is torn between the "huge responsibilities [of the head doctor], responsibilities that you can't push onto others, that you have to decide for yourself," and being a "simple doctor." Susan equivocates: "Actually, whether that is what I want, I don't know." She has three children, one of whom is "somewhat handicapped," requiring special daily attention. The service shifts for head doctors "are so long. These are all things that you have to consider. Either you do this, or you do that." Indeterminacy tropes Susan's story, as she searches for a definition of "what [I] want to do, what [I] want to be." Her past, reconstructed genealogically, has imprisoned her in one corner of the present, yet an awareness of this present swings her back to a reflection on beginnings. Reflection on beginnings, in turn, presents the past as arbitrary, as possible paths taken and not taken. Hence, it opens up a painfully indeterminate future, not fixed by history but nonetheless articulated through it.

Here Gadamer's reflections on the nature of experience are relevant, "The truth of experience always contains an orientation towards new experience. That is why a person who is called 'experienced' has become such not only through experiences, but is also open to new experiences. The perfection of experience . . . does not consist in the fact that someone already knows everything and knows better than anyone else. Rather, the experienced person proves to be, on the contrary, someone who is radically undogmatic; who, because of the many experiences he has had and the knowledge he has drawn from them is particularly well equipped to have new experiences and to learn from them" (1982: 319). Rather than confuse Susan's basic indeterminacy with a lack of clarity or will, we should commend it as a result of knowledge obtained from experience properly reflected upon.

Conclusion

Through this examination of Susan R.'s narrative autobiography, I hope to have demonstrated the necessary relationship between genealogy, narrative, and historical consciousness. If genealogy is an essential method of reconstruction, and narrative the form by which that reconstruction obtains meaning, then historical consciousness is the way one situates and evaluates that meaning in time and space. Each performs a job that predicates the others in reaching the common goal of cultural understanding. Susan's story affirms Foucault's statement about genealogy: "The forces operating in history are not controlled by destiny or regulative mechanisms, but respond to haphazard conflict. They do not manifest the successive forms of a primordial intention and their attraction is not that of a conclusion, for they always appear through the singular randomness of events" (Foucault 1977: 154–155). Indeed, Susan's narration of her story in the waning days of the Cold War dramatized the "single randomness of events," making her often painful choices more sober, more reasoned. Her acceptance of indeterminacy in culture, nationality, and citizenship, of ambiguity and conflict within identity, bespeaks a contemporary heroism, one less of the ritual leader than the everyday survivor.

Drawing on Susan's genealogy of "effective historical kin," we uncovered what Nietzsche called an "effective history," meaning one that inverts the relationship that traditional history establishes between proximity and distance. We began by focusing on things nearest to us, on personal events rather than political history and theoretical models of how Susan's kin should be represented. Her telling was perspectival, inseparable from and indeed informed by the moment of its inscription. Despite his equivocations about hermeneutics, Foucault supports Gadamer's conception of historical consciousness when he writes that a "final trait of effective history is its affirmation of knowledge as perspective" (1977: 156).

Anthropologists have often evaded acknowledging the historicity of their own productions. While priding themselves on knowledge of place, they often deny their special grounding in time (see Fabian 1983). By striving toward a fuller historical consciousness, we anthropologists are doing much more than merely acknowledging

146

the historicity of our productions. For method and context are not merely constraints that might be bracketed or overcome, or in some way understood as dependent variables. They might also be seen as the necessary and enabling space in which narrative is made to work. Our understanding of historical space is more than a prelude to knowledge of the objective world; it is also a form of knowledge about events of cultural significance necessary for a self-articulation and definition in the present.

This articulation proceeds genealogically and is given form by narrative. But narratives do not contain within them a measure for their truth-value. They are fictions of events, representations of what happened, one no more true than the other. It is historical consciousness that redeems this endeavor by "affirming knowledge as perspective," by restoring truth-value to the articulation of form. A mature narrative obtains truth-value only and insofar as it is conscious of the conditions of its production, aware of and capable of learning from its own beginnings. In much the same way that Susan's telling through genealogy is tied to a presentness that she cannot—and should not try to—mask, that, in fact, situates her knowledge, we anthropologists are also, if we remain faithful to our method of intensive fieldwork, bound to a present from which we cannot—and should not try to—flee. Indeed, it is in this space where form is (per)formed that one finds the articulation of narrativity, genealogy, and historical consciousness. Hence, the inescapable embeddedness of the fieldwork situation in the present should not be seen as a problem to overcome, but as a fundamental and specifically anthropological source of knowledge.

NOTES

1. In an article by Scott Long and myself (1991: 285–314), we were interested in demonstrating how a dialogue between practitioners in the disciplines of literary study and anthropology could generate a mutual practice of textual criticism. My project in this essay is to demonstrate a *necessary* conceptual relationship between anthropology and literature. I wish to thank Andy Wallace and Jeanette Mageo for their insightful comments in helping me clarify the relationships discussed in this paper.

2. The usual distinction made between ethnographer and anthropologist is that the former merely engages in fieldwork, that is, in data collection at the site where "the native" or subject studied lives, whereas the latter goes beyond fieldwork to fit data into forms that facilitate comparison cross-culturally. In this essay, I compare anthropologists to literary critics who deal with narrative, both of whom depend upon some sort of ethnographer or kind of ethnographic activity to construct the texts to be analyzed.

3. In a foundational essay on social action as a text, Paul Ricoeur (1981: 197–221) argued for the autonomy of text from author after its initial inscription in writing. I would maintain, following Edward Said, that this distinction is overdrawn, for the initial event of production is "incorporated in the text, an infrangible part of its capacity for conveying and producing meaning" (1983: 39). The understanding of texts has already commenced upon reading, argues Said, and "is already constrained by, and constraining, their interpretation" (1983: 39). Indeed, many anthropologists have experienced the situation of inscription itself—that means the fieldwork setting and the moment of authorship—as a revealing source of anthropological knowledge.

4. I am aware that anthropologists and literary critics also concern themselves with texts that do not take narrative form, such as some fragments, poems, and chronicles. However, I would argue for the cultural primacy of the narrative document. As "a primary and irreducible form of human comprehension, an article in the constitution of common sense" (Mink 1978: 132), which fashions diverse experiences into a form assimilable to structures of meaning that are generally human rather than culture-specific (White 1984), narrative is central to the disciplines of anthropology and literature. "Narrative in fact seems to hold a special place among literary forms," maintains Peter Brooks (1984: 4), "because of its potential for summary and retransmission: the fact that we can still recognize 'the story' even when its medium has been considerably changed."

5. Susan R. is one of twenty-three German-Jews whom Jeffrey Peck and I interviewed during the Summer of 1989. We interviewed eleven in West Berlin and twelve in East Berlin; twelve who reached adulthood before WWII, eleven who reached adulthood after WWII. All participants in our project had been in exile (or their parents had been in exile) in one of the countries of the Allied Forces, and all had returned to either East or West Berlin. Our criteria of selection was not random, but designed to illustrate a range of comparative historical contexts. Drawing on twelve other autobiographical interviews from this project, we completed a book, "Sojourners: The Return of German Jews and the Question of Identity"

(Peck and Borneman 1996) as well as a film by the same name of those who returned to East Germany. This interview with Susan R. was conducted in German; the translation and interpretation are mine.

6. See the discussion of Nietzsche's use of these terms by Foucault (1977: 140–142).

7. Foucault and Nietzsche nearly always used the genealogical approach to take apart and deconstruct some putative unitary whole. I follow both of them in insisting that genealogy does both deconstructive and reconstructive work.

8. On denazification, see Weber (1985: 107–109) Dotterweich (1979), and Niethammer (1988: 115–131). For a comparative discussion of the meaning of postwar reform in East and West Germany, see Borneman (1992a; 1992b).

REFERENCES

Borneman, John
  1993. "Uniting the German Nation: Law, Narrative, and Historicity." *American Ethnologist* 20(2): 218–311
  1992a. "State, Territory, and Identity Formation in the Postwar Berlins, 1945–1989." *Cultural Anthropology* 7(1): 44–61.
  1992b. *Belonging in the Two Berlins: Kin, State, Nation.* Cambridge: Cambridge University Press
  1991. *After the Wall: East Meets West in the New Berlin.* New York: Basic Books
Borneman, John and Jeffrey M. Peck
  1996. *Sojourners: The Return of German Jews and the Question of Identity.* Lincoln: University of Nebraska Press
Brooks, Peter
  1984. *Reading for the Plot: Design and Intention in Narrative.* New York: Alfred A. Knopf
Bruner, Edward
  1986. Ethnography as Narrative. In *The Anthropology of Experience.* E. Bruner and V. Turner, eds. Pp. 139–158. Urbana: University of Illinois Press
Bruner, Edward, ed.
  1984. *Text, Play and Story: The Construction and Reconstruction of Self and Society.* Washington D.C.: American Ethnological Society

Clifford, James
>1988. *The Predicament of Culture.* Cambridge: Harvard University Press

Clifford, James and George Marcus, eds.
>1986. *Writing Culture.* Berkeley: University of California Press

Fabian, Johannes
>1983. *Time and the Other: How Anthropology Makes its Object.* New York: Columbia University Press

Foucault, Michel
>1977. *Language, Counter-memory, Practice.* Donald F. Bouchard, ed. and intro. Ithaca: Cornell University Press

Gadamer, Hans-Georg
>1982. *Truth and Method.* New York: Crossroad Publishing Company
>1979. The Problem of Historical Consciousness. In *A Social Science Reader.* Paul Rabinow and William Sullivan, eds. Pp. 103–160. Berkeley: University of California Press

Herzfeld, Michael
>1985. *The Poetics of Manhood: Contest and Identity in a Cretan Mountain Village.* Princeton: Princeton University Press

Long, Scott, and John Borneman
>1991. "Power, Objectivity, and the Other: Studies in the Creation of Sexual Species in Anglo-American Discourse." *Dialectical Anthropology* 15 (4): 285–314

Marcus, George, and Michael Fischer
>1986. *Anthropology as Cultural Critique.* Chicago: University of Chicago Press

Mink, Louis O.
>1978. Narrative Form as Cognitive Instrument. In *The Writing of History. Literary Form and Historical Understanding.* Robert H. Canaray and Henry Kozecki, eds. Pp. 129–149. Madison: University of Wisconsin Press

Mitchell, W.J.T., ed.
>1981. *On Narrative.* Chicago: University of Chicago Press

Niethammer, Lutz
>1988. Entnazifizierung: Nachfragen eines Historikers. In *Von der Gnade der geschenkten Nation.* Hago Funke and W.-D. Narr, eds. Pp. 115–131. Berlin: Rotbuch Verlag

Nietzsche, Friedrich
>1980. *On the Advantage and Disadvantage of History for Life.* Transl. with Intro. by Peter Preuss. Indianapolis: Hackettt Publishing Company

1964. The Wanderer and His Shadow. In *Human, All too Human II, The Complete Works of Friedrich Nietzsche,* Vol. VII. Oscar Levy, ed. New York: Russell and Russell

Ostow, Robin
1989. *Jews in Contemporary East Germany: The children of Moses in the land of Marx.* New York: St. Martin's Press

Ricoeur, Paul
1984. *Time and Narrative,* Vol. 1. Chicago: University of Chicago Press
1981. *Hermeneutics and the Human Sciences.* Cambridge: Cambridge University Press

Said, Edward
1983. *The World, the Text, and the Critic.* Cambridge: Harvard University Press

Weber, Hermann
1985. *Geschichte der DDR.* München: C.H. Beck

White, Hayden
1984. "The Question of Narrative in Contemporary Historical Theory." *History Theory* 23 (1):1–33
1978. The Historical Text as Literary Artifact. In *The Writing of History: Literary Form and Historical Understanding.* Robert Canary and Henry Kozicki, eds. Pp. 41–62. Madison: University of Wisconsin Press
1973. *Metahistory. The Historical Imagination in Nineteenth-Century Europe.* Baltimore: Johns Hopkins University Press

6

Grenzregime *(Border Regime):*
The Wall and Its Aftermath

Heidi

Heidi recently turned fifty. She is beginning a new life, in a re-united Germany, in a "Europe without borders." Born in 1944, in Cottbus, eastern Germany, she is an unplanned child of the former German Democratic Republic (GDR), one of those women on whose labor the socialist state had staked its future. Already in 1949, the year of the founding of the East German state, GDR leaders concluded that it was in the state's interest to take seriously the socialist ideology of *Gleichberechtigung,* equal rights for men and women. They included an equal rights guarantee in the constitution. They opened the educational system to women a generation before the West German regime did. They engaged in a kind of affirmative action for women, not only encouraging them to take part in *Aufbau,* the rebuilding of the economy and society, but also making it difficult for women to remain, in the language of the time, "only housewives." The regime suspected that that there would be much resistance from older women like Heidi's mother, who had never worked outside the home before the war, as well as from adult men, who were unaccustomed to treating women as equals. Indeed, throughout the 1950s, the promise of higher pay, a better standard of living, and more freedoms enticed large numbers of skilled East German men (and some women) to the capitalist markets of the West, which, at that time, favored labor by men (and housework by women)—with the result that the GDR's future was increasingly tied to its women.

Under these circumstances, Heidi and her mother and her brother stayed in the East. Heidi would be educated in the new schools. She and her brother would benefit from being children of proletarian parents, members of the class that, according to official propaganda, was to take over leadership—sometime in the future. This would make them loyal to the state, so the new state thought. And, indeed, her brother remained loyal, making a stellar career as a me ber of the socialist party and manager of a state-owned Kombinat, trust company. Soon after completion of her studies, Heidi began despising this state, and her hatred grew over the years. Her status as a "chosen" person, and her ambivalence about it, distinguished her from all West German women of her generation, who were not "chosen" but had to contend with the officially sanctioned reassertion of patriarchal social conventions and a phallic state ideology after the war, who had to organize a social movement to fight against the state for a personal stake in the future (for a statistical comparison of women's statuses, see Geißler 1992: 236–263).

When Heidi was eighteen months old, her father died. Eleven years later, she left her mother to live in a boarding school and study mathematics, a "male" discipline. Heidi says that her experience in the boarding school was formative. It replaced the nuclear family romance, already impaired by her father's early death, with a peculiar Oedipal triangle of State, mommy, me. In this triangulation, the state differed from all prior forms of phallic authority in that it initially tried to foreground its visibility; it struggled to establish a legitimate authority not in private, behind closed doors, but in public discussions, on a world stage. Heidi knew exactly where her support and where the Law were coming from, and precisely because of this knowledge she experienced no sense of awe or lack with respect to the state.

West German feminists frequently criticize East German women for lacking a critique of patriarchy, for allowing men to "exploit" them by not demanding of men an equal contribution to child care, or for unselfconsciously becoming mothers. But because the East German state initiated the critique of patriarchy, women there were not forced to develop their own movement to oppose it. And even though an extremely large percentage of East German women became "mothers," they were never forced into marriage in order to support their children, as was frequently the case in West Germany. Moreover, for those East Germans who found themselves in an unhappy marriage, divorce had been simplified and largely separated from decisions about the couple's finances or property. For West Germans, legal divorce was expensive and contingent on a property settlement. Heidi took for granted her significance to this state and its laws, to the new order; her critique of it did not grow out of an understanding of gender(ed) oppression.

The GDR was, after all, a revolutionary state. It invoked as the condition of its legitimacy not traditional authority but a future communist order in which Heidi was to be an integral part of the imagined new center. Marx and Engels may have been iconic fathers of the new state, but this was to be no normal nation-state. In contrast to the legitimation strategy of the Federal Republic of Germany (FRG), *Rechtsstaatlichkeit*, rule of law, was never a fundamental principle of the GDR's authority. Instead the GDR appealed to a model of "socialist legality": the conditions of rule were neither fixed nor firm but considered merely a means to achieve a more just, socialist order. The GDR represented itself as a historical alternative to patriarchy, specifically to the patriarchal authority of West Germany, which in turn represented itself as the successor state of the Third Reich—with the accompanying benefits and burdens. The sovereign was not the Verfassung, the constitution, as in the West German Rechtsstaat, but the "dictatorship of the proletariat" as interpreted by the ruling Socialist Unity Party (SED). The GDR constantly drew attention to the contingent and constructed nature of its own powers, emphasizing its newness, denying any continuity with prior German states, rewriting both its civil and criminal code several times, revoking laws within days after passing them, and undermining the power of all mythical origins and all fathers. In an effort to create new forms of authority, the state improvised, continuously redrawing borders and boundaries, renaming persons and things, endowing its laws with an

155

aura of provisionality. Since its dissolution in October 1990, the GDR is often reduced, both colloquially and in formal legal discourse, to its *Grenzregime*, border regime—to the entire system of rules and regulations intended to demarcate East Germany from its West German counterpart, to enclose, bound, and reconstitute its "people."

Heidi remembers her boarding school experience as one of unending debate, discussion, and critical reflection about the present and future. Her best friend at the school, who was preparing for a career in international trade, is still her best friend today. Back then, they talked about everything, Heidi said, until the wee hours of the morning, everything except for the fact that he liked men, something he only told her twenty-nine years later, after he had married and divorced, and changed his career several times, always because his homosexuality got in the way. Although he tried to keep his sexuality secret from his ever-inquisitive state employers, they either suspected or came to know. Up to 1969, the official line was that homosexuality did not exist in the socialist, family-friendly GDR; it was a perverse "condition" and product of capitalism, existing on the other side of the Great Divide, which, of course, one should not, or could not, cross (see Borneman 1991b). Heidi still does not forgive him for not sharing this secret with her, nor does she forgive herself for not having known earlier, for having missed all the conspicuous signs that he had tried to hide from her. "It would have been so much easier with all my men"—she was married twice—"if I could have said to them that he was homosexual. They were very jealous of us and never accepted my friendship with him, that we had such complete confidence and trust in each other." To Heidi, this relationship represented an explicit openness and reciprocity, a transparency that could countenance no boundaries. It was in contrast to her relation with the state, which was built on a series of public secrets. She took private secrets about the past or present to be a violation of trust; everything had to be acknowledged and discussed.

When the Wall was erected, in the early morning hours of August 13, 1961, Heidi knew nothing of her friend's "condition." She was still in boarding school, still filled with a youthful enthusiasm about postwar reconstruction. It took six weeks to complete the

Wall, and, while Heidi watched with concern the political events and controversy surrounding it, she did not experience them as a delimitation on her freedom. As part of a generation designated heirs to the Idea of Communism, Heidi fully identified with the perceived need to secure the border and protect the nascent state. She had already visited West Berlin many times and had witnessed the smuggling of precious East German goods at the border. Therefore, at first she agreed with the leaders of her vulnerable state that the border and its effect of containment was a precondition for her further growth. Yet for the next twenty-seven years, she had to endure the twelve kilometers of 1.25 meter high concrete slabs along with 137 kilometers of barbed wire that encircled West Berlin, with an equally well-policed barricade constructed to separate East from West Germany. As Heidi grew into adulthood, her experience of this encirclement changed.

Containment

No border in the modern period has received more of the world's attention and been the source of more fantasy and fear than *die Mauer*, the Berlin Wall. Leaders of the self-proclaimed "Worker and Farmer State," the GDR, justified its construction as necessary to realize an idea, this-worldly-Communism, and to secure their own rule, in the name of the people. Officially designated an "anti-fascist protection barricade," the Wall had little to do with fascism but a great deal to do with protection. It was supposed to halt the further sabotage of a hemorrhaging East German economy by preventing the workers, who had been fleeing to the West in massive numbers, from leaving. This economy, organized around socialist principles of collective ownership, central planning, and just redistribution, proved unable to keep pace with the general prosperity provided by its West German, capitalist counterpart.

The Wall became the material symbol of the Cold War division of the world into two moieties within a single city and within a formerly unified territorial state. It served mythical ends as a twofold functioning sign—icon and symbol—embodying, enacting, and standing for the opposition between capitalist and communist alliance

157

systems, between "plan" and "market," between "security" and "liberty." It prefigured the memory of the GDR as a Grenzregime.

"Containment" as both concept and practice played a special and ironic role in the life of the Wall. As a concept and strategy, "containment of communism" originated in Britain and the United States in the late 1940s to deal with a Communist enemy thought of as contagious, or irresistible, and likely to set off a chain reaction of ideological and political conversions, similar to falling dominos, in countries that came into contact with it (Gaddis 1982). But events took a cruel twist and the supposedly contained East German state internalized this strategy, constraining itself and its own citizens as well as being confined and isolated by the West. For a variety of reasons ranging from fear of the state to belief in socialism, most GDR citizens initially cooperated with this strategy.

West Germany effectively practised the British and American strategy of "containment of communism" on East Germany, which had the effect of exaggerating and dramatizing the East German citizen's experience of confinement and enclosure. The Hallstein Doctrine, formulated in 1955, established the principle that the Federal Republic was the sole sovereign representative of all of Germany; any state that granted political recognition to or established diplomatic relations with the other Germany would be declared an enemy and penalized with sanctions. Unable to enter into full diplomatic and economic relations with most of the world's states, East Germany remained an economically innocent member of the community as it did not (could not) engage in exploitative relations with countries in the so-called Third World. Instead, its leaders tried to become self-sufficient. Long before the idea of "generic" items became a new form of commodity differentiation in the West, the state's planners distributed products under single names: peas were sold as "Tempo-erbsen," detergent became "Spee," coffee houses were called simply "Espresso." Instead of producing pride in self-sufficiency, the lack of product differentiation and choice in the East came to be associated with uniformity and conformity and tended to reinforce the image of the West as more developed and dynamic, more diverse, more colorful. Only a few intellectuals, who often had limited but coveted access to Western goods, seemed to take a perverse satisfaction in the standardization and lack of choice in commodities.

Despite the protective space that the Wall provided for East German goods, this respite lasted less than a decade. By the 1970s, the mixed economy, which had never been totally socialized, had deteriorated to the point that it needed major injections of capital from the West—which it got during the period of detente. As the younger citizens of the GDR grew increasingly impatient with the experience of containment, including, of course, the inability of the economy to keep pace with Western standards, pressures to cross the border mounted. The 1980s saw a small-scale proliferation of social protest groups under the protection of the Protestant church, organized around issues of environmentalism, sexuality, liberty, and social justice. Late in the evening of November 9, 1989, Günter Schabowski, a member of the ruling Politburo, assured the world press that restrictions on visas to Western countries were in the process of being lifted. On guard against doubletalk, a journalist pounced: Did the new travel law also extend to the West Berlin border? Schabowski wavered. He had received the new regulation just minutes before. "Yes," he said, "it says here Berlin (West)." Within minutes several hundred young citizens had gathered outside a Berlin border crossing. The border guards were taken aback. The Wall was about to open (Borneman 1991a: 1–4). Without *die Mauer*, neither the East German state nor the Cold War could be sustained. Within a couple of months, the so-called "domino effect," which had hypothesized the fall of capitalist countries to communism, worked in reverse, as the governments of the entire East bloc, with the exception of Albania, fell. And a year later, even the Albanian regime capitulated.

Our Relationship

During my initial East Berlin fieldwork in 1986, Heidi's boarding school friend, now a gay man, introduced us. I became acquainted with many women like her, of her generation, of her social situation, women who had professional identities and were not dependent on men. This dependency on men, specifically on fathers and boyfriends/husbands, for money or jobs or emotional completion, or even as an antithesis for self-definition, seemed, by contrast, to

159

mark all West Berlin women whom I knew. Not that Heidi rejected men; only once in her adult life, for several years after the birth of her second daughter, did she live without a man. But I always sensed in Heidi an integrity, or the search for such an integrity, independent of her relationship to a man, to a husband, to a father, to a provider. It was clear to me that the assertion of this integrity had its costs, that Heidi had to struggle without a role model and against social conventions (the status of the law notwithstanding) that defined her solely in terms of other family members. She had to overcome nagging self-doubts about her own worth and her own right to liberty. I suspect (and here I am undoubtedly overly systematic) that I represented to her an intimacy and freedom made possible by three kinds of productive ambiguities: (a) I did not project onto her a *gender* that was the opposite of mine—and, in turn, she did not need this opposition, (b) the erotics of our relationship were not tied to *sexual* expectations, (c) because of my own working-class origins, I was only partially identified by a *nationality* belonging to the First World or the Golden West. Because these ambiguities blurred conventional boundaries, Heidi never identified me with the phallus, as an authority who indexed her own lack of freedom, material goods, education, and taste—"inadequacies" directly tied to nearly every East German's self-esteem.

Moreover, there was a way in which Heidi appealed to and affirmed my desires to challenge the very boundaries that seemed to define me. She also provided me with the opportunity to work through certain idealist projections which she embodied. I had seven siblings in the United States, including six sisters, who, unlike Heidi, had not been able to transcend or even fundamentally alter the role of "woman" as defined by their working-class origins; I was a gay man from the West who had experienced some of the limitations of liberalism's exalted liberties, while Heidi had experienced the limitations of socialism's security. We asserted no essential difference to each other, though in practical terms it was obvious that we lived in radically different worlds and that our worlds were in some fundamental sense closed to each other. What fascinated me was that my lack of access to her experiential world did not translate into my exclusion from it. Although she was a mother, Heidi in no way lived through her daughters when we met, but treated them as special relationships that were also open to me, if I wished to establish relationships with them. She said that, for her, motherhood was initially the pleasure in feeling a child's skin, the sensuousness of a child's touch—hardly experiences that most parents felt comfortable sharing with me. She also understood socialism's fundamental aporia: a celebration of the working-class, which is supposed to transcend its conditions of origin and simultaneously reproduce itself as working-class, to aspire to petty-bourgeois ends without then becoming "bourgeois." And, although I was a graduate student from Harvard University, she did not reduce my identity to matters of my career, which is what many people do when they find out that I am gay—I become, for them, only "an anthropologist." Instead, Heidi seemed to take genuine delight in understanding how I stood with respect to class, sexuality, and profession, and how those structures articulated in me. We sought each other out neither because of a desire for completion nor for domination/submission. We provided access to alternative worlds that were beyond the domain of experiences open to us personally. Our relationship has sustained itself on mutual curiosity.

Heidi's Separation

On November 11, 1989, two days after the opening of the border with West Germany, Heidi moved to Rosenheim, a large but sleepy Bavarian village nestled in the mountains midway between Munich and Salzburg. She refers to this radical move simply as *das Wechsel*, the change. Three years later, she decided to separate from her second husband, Sieghard, a medical doctor with whom she had lived for sixteen years. I arrived at their home two days after Christmas 1993, on the evening that Sieghard moved out.

Sieghard has never had any close friends—one of Heidi's strongest criticisms of him—and therefore he had to rely on "the family," meaning Heidi's two oldest daughters, Peggy and Greta, along with Greta's boyfriend, to help him move the heavy furniture. The youngest daughter, Franzi, who is twelve and Sieghard's only daughter-by-blood, has such a strong aversion to her father that she refused to help in the move. On that evening, Sieghard ran into Franzi in

161

the hallway and asked if she wanted to take a vacation with him sometime the next year. Offended that he would pose this question at this parting moment, as if he had taken no note of the years of coldness on his part and avoidance on hers, Franzi silently turned away and withdrew to her bedroom. The other two daughers remained amiable with Sieghard throughout the move, only too pleased, they told me, to get him out of the house, as well as the family, something they had encouraged Heidi to do for years. Without complaint, they lifted furniture twice their own weight the entire evening. I offered to help, but Peggy said that Sieghard would have problems accepting the help of a male stranger visiting her mother. The oldest daughter, Peggy, is twenty-seven and works as a midwife in Hamburg. The middle daughter, Greta, is twenty-two and in an apprenticeship program to become a potter.

I hid in the kitchen during that part of the evening, reading a book that Heidi had just given me, about the Treuhand, the agency set up to administer and privatize state-owned property in the former GDR, estimated in early 1990 to be worth 650 billion D-Mark. Heidi was impressed by the book's documentation of how this valuable property, instead of being sold and the profits distributed (in 1990, estimated at around 40,000 D-Mark ($25,000) per East German citizen), was either undervalued and sold or given away to Western firms by the Treuhand. Rather than distribute any money to former citizens of the GDR, the Treuhand singlemindedly pursued privatization. This entailed eliminating around thirty percent of all jobs in eastern Germany. The outcome seemed obvious and predictable to me, the outsider with no personal investment in the outcomes of unification. Although Heidi was now an enthusiastic resident of the western part of Germany, she had not become a complete insider, a full Wessi. At some very basic level, she still identified with the fate of Ossis: the former citizens of the former GDR.

As I read, Sieghard moved out. Over the previous eight years, Heidi and I had had regular telephone conversations, but we had been together only twice before, and I had visited her and her family just once prior to this visit, in 1986 in Cottbus. At that time, Heidi seemed to me extremely angry: critical of her neighbors, of her colleagues at the college where she taught mathematics, of the people of Cottbus, and of the state. They all wanted her to keep quiet and uncritically accept her role as a small-town teacher, wife, and mother, according to Heidi. Only some of the students seemed to respond positively to her endless energy and engagement. Sieghard appeared as a shadow of a person, someone to whom Heidi also could not turn for support; he left little, if any, impression on me.

Like many of her compatriots, Heidi experienced the final years of the GDR as a social death. Her professional life was blocked, and worse for her, she was asked to teach lies in her job at the local community college—about the market, the economy, the health of the state. She clearly saw the state going bankrupt, the economy getting worse, but material wealth had never been that important to Heidi. She wanted something else. Although the state had propagated a "unity of career and motherhood," Heidi had never been able to realize that unity to her satisfaction in her own life. The state's pronatal and pro-women policies had produced mixed results. To be sure, Heidi had been able to give birth to and raise three daughters without consistent support from any of the particular men she had lived with, and without giving up her career. For that she was thankful. And many women, unlike their male counterparts, stayed in the GDR, unwilling to leave their mothers behind and appreciative of the training and education they could not have obtained in the West. Yet the demands of raising three girls, a task of which Heidi is proud and in no way regrets, consistently placed restrictions on her occupational advancement, leading her ultimately to settle for a minor teaching post. By the mid 1980, her marriage had become merely a habit and stymied her personal development, though Heidi admitted this to me and to her daughters, and perhaps to herself, only recently. Her daughters had not experienced the enthusiasm and intensity that Heidi had had in the boarding school in the *Aufbau* years; they lacked any sense of attachment to Cottbus or to their friends.

By 1988, Heidi had made up her mind to leave the GDR, it was only a matter of when and how. Sieghard went along with her decision, but, disturbed by the specter of unemployment and financial insecurity in West Germany, he would have preferred to stay in the East. The obvious way to leave was to obtain approval to visit a relative in the West: *Familienangelegenheiten* (family occasions) were one of the priority grounds listed by the state for travel. Heidi selected her aunt's eightieth birthday in 1989. The date for the planned trip was November 11. After about a year of paper-shuffling through the labyrinth of bureaucracies, both she and Sieghard obtained permission, first from their employers, then from the state and the state's security apparatus, to travel with the entire family to Rosenheim. Heidi told only one person, her gay friend from the boarding school, that she did not intend to return. She and her family told none of their neighbors, nor any of their colleagues at work or school. Silently, working conspiratorially as a family unit, they discreetly sold a few large items of furniture and the automobile but planned to leave all the rest behind—photo albums, clothes, china, their entire material history—for fear that the approval to travel would be denied if it appeared that they were leaving for good.

From the time of the building of the Wall to 1964, travel of East Germans to the West was restricted to prominent persons or to *Reisekader*, those officially approved as trustworthy. An agreement reached in 1964 allowed retired persons to visit West Berlin or West Germany once a year. Not until the late 1960s, when former Social Democratic Chancellor Willy Brandt initiated *Ostpolitik*, did the GDR begin expanding the limited opportunities available for some of its citizens to travel to the West. His strategy of *Annäherung durch Wandel,* Change through Rapprochement, contrasted sharply with the prior Christian Democratic strategy of *Abgrenzungspolitik*, Politics of Demarcation. The category of visits regulated by an agreement between West Berlin and the GDR, signed on December 20, 1971, referred to *dringende Familienangelegenheiten*, pressing family events. Possible grounds for visits included baptisms, marriages, life-threatening illnesses, death of parents, siblings, and children, wedding anniversaries, and birthdays. These familial categories created an entirely new dynamic between citizens and the state, as well as constituting a form in which the desire to cross the Wall was legal.

In the following decade, however, pressure to travel or, alternately, to leave, grew so intense that the GDR expanded its system of selling disgruntled citizens to the Federal Republic. In

1974, for example, it doubled the number of ransomed political prisoners, to 1,100, from the 630 ransomed the year before. By 1984, it again came up with a new strategy, not only of doubling the number of ransomed political prisoners (from 1,105 in 1983 to 2,236 in 1984) but also authorizing a mass release of would-be migrants (from 7,729 in 1983 to 37,323 in 1984) (Wendt 1991: 390). This emigration (including isolated cases of coerced exile) did not, however, function as the state intended, as a so-called "social safety valve." Ridding itself of its most unhappy citizens did not relieve the state of the pressure to make its borders more permeable. Instead, each successive exodus created visible absences in friendship circles and work units within the GDR, and thus generated dissatisfaction among those who remained. This pressure for expanded movement was also not relieved by increasing the number of permissible visits per year, nor by enlarging the category of people permitted to travel to the West and to return. These permissible visits did not exceed 60,000 until 1986, when, in the liberalization coinciding with Erich Honecker's first visit to the West, 573,000 visits were allowed. The number of visits increased to 900,000 in 1987, with the category "family" often broadly and arbitrarily extended by officials to friends and acquaintances (Borneman 1992a: 142–146, 305–310). Under the rubric "family," Heidi applied to visit her mother's only sister on her birthday. Although they had exchanged letters over the years, they had never met before. Not attaching any particular importance to blood ties, Heidi had no idea what to expect.

I held these visits and this travel policy to be cruel jokes. It was the ultimate absurdity that the GDR, a state founded on socialist principles of universal brotherhood, would attempt to "liberalize" policy in this way to meet both the rising expectations of its own citizens to travel as well as to comply with provisions of international agreements on "bringing families together" that it had signed in return for international recognition, culminating in the Helsinki Accords of 1975. This "liberalization" was not only a betrayal of its earlier principles of fairness and inclusion based on need and performance, but also an affirmation of the principle of *jus sanguinis*, blood-based descent, a racist categorization that had served the National Socialist government particularly well in its extermination policies, and remained the legal principle of FRG citizenship (Senders 1996: 147–176). It was also the legal rationale behind West Germany's insistence that all GDR citizens had an automatic right to FRG citizenship, since they, too, were Germans by blood. Heidi knew all this, but, despite her moral reservations, she also knew that her blood-based membership was the only legal category available that might make it possible for her to leave.

Two weeks before the scheduled trip, Heidi's mother died.

The trip to my aunt then took on added significance. I don't know how I made it through that week. I also had to do everything for Sieghard, I knew he wouldn't have the strength to organize the move himself. And I had to arrange for the funeral of my mother, her death hit me real hard, I'm still working through this loss. I swear I didn't sleep the whole last week before leaving. On the day after the Wall opened I was teaching. A few of the students took the day off to go to West Berlin, but most were still there. We had a marvellous, open discussion about the future. Suddenly all the barriers were gone. And my colleagues! Those who had been most ideological were suddenly very insecure, as if overnight they could see their futures change.

Heidi's aunt lived alone, widowed and childless. Yet she feared the visit of Heidi and her family, or at least that is what Heidi sensed. She feared that this visit would change something. "What do they want from us?" was the refrain that Heidi suspected played repeatedly in her aunt's mind. "We didn't accept a single thing from her," Heidi told me.

And now I'm her best friend. She relies on me for everything—she has no one else. And it is *so* hard for her to accept help from me, from an East German relative. But I'll make her take it, she has no choice. She has no one else to turn to.

For Heidi and her family, then, the opening of the Wall came unexpectedly and suddenly, in the very middle of an exodus that they had planned for over a year. It did not, however, make this planning superfluous.

When we arrived in the West, I said we would do it all ourselves. We got 250 D-Mark from the state and that's it. We
didn't stay in a camp. We didn't ask for anything. And things
were tight. We barely got by. A friend gave us a small loan
that we paid back as soon as we got work. I was so ashamed
by the behavior of the other East Germans, in the camps and
before the authorities who were trying to assist us. They
demanded, "Where are the cigarettes?" "I want some beer!" As
if it was their right! They hadn't earned those things. They
were gifts. It was Bavarian money, not theirs!

And then, how they would always insist they were Ossis—in
order to get special privileges, or to explain away their ignorance! If they wanted to travel somewhere, they'd just get on
the train, and when caught without a ticket, they'd say, "I'm
from the East." I never ever said that, and nobody, not once,
has ever suspected that I come from the East. The same holds
true for my daughters. If someone asks me something and I
don't know, I don't say, "I'm from the East." I just say, "I don't
know."

I asked Heidi if people assumed that Sieghard comes from the
East.

He's a wonderful doctor, you cannot fault him there. But, oh
yes, they know he's from the East. And he's not done with that
history yet. It's very hard for him here. He emphasizes his
East Germanness, his helplessness. I think he longs for the
security he had in the East, but that's no real option for him,
he won't return. He had no friends there either. I was everything for him: cook, bedpartner, maid, I bought his clothes.
But he never knew me, and what he knew he didn't like. I
waited until he received a secure job contract before asking
him for a separation. And his reaction? Nothing. I gave him
a chance to change. Nothing affects him. He's totally closed.
Now he's got a good job, a permanent one, and he's planning
his retirement, waiting for death. He wanted to plan my retirement, too, but I want to live, finally, for myself, to find out
what I really want.

The decision to move West was easy for Heidi. The only question she still asked herself was why she had waited so long. As with all things in her life, she takes time, she thinks things over, and over, and over. She talks things through in a kind of self-therapy, and then talks through them again, and again, and again. Sieghard hated this thinking and he hated this talking. He told her he hated the way she used her hands when talking. "That's me," she told me.

He didn't like me. How could I live all those years under that pressure? He functioned like a black cloud when he entered a room! Franzi would run when she saw him coming. I finally moved out of the bedroom into the basement. He told me something was wrong with me sexually. Something was wrong with *me*! But I knew my problems with him had started long ago, right at the beginning of our relationship. Very early on something just wasn't right. Still, I held out, because of the children, I couldn't just leave.

I remember Heidi telling me eight years earlier about what initially attracted her to Sieghard. They were both attending a Kur, a quasi state-sponsored health spa, and in that atmosphere of health and recovery, they became sexually involved. Heidi said that sex there with Sieghard was novel in that, for the first time, she had sex standing up. He lifted and held her so she could sit on him, and that, she explained, was an experience she had never had. It was also another kind of border-crossing, a violation of norms, an expression of liberty, and one that did not repeat itself once they got married.

During breakfast on the morning after Sieghard left, Heidi said she wanted to say something. I thought it was private, and got up to leave, but she said, "Stay, you can use it for your research." Surprised and somewhat embarrassed, I sat back down. There we were, the three daughters, myself, Heidi, and Klaus, Heidi's West German business partner of the last several years and lover as of the last six months. She had not told Sieghard about him. "It would have been too much for him," she explained, "and if he'd known he would never have separated from me. Besides, I'd made up my mind long before Klaus and I got involved. It took me a long time to convince myself that Klaus was really interested in me"—he is 17 years younger than she, married, and has two children.

I just wanted to wait until Sieghard had job security so that leaving him wouldn't harm him. When I told him I wanted to divorce, his reaction was, "Well, are you sure you can survive alone?" No emotion whatsoever.

What Heidi wanted to say that morning at breakfast was that there were problems with Sieghard's leaving that were not yet, in her words, *bewältigt* (reckoned with/come to terms with). She told us how, at this point in her life, she desired above all freedom for herself. She also wanted the girls to be independent of her, and, she said, she wanted to talk about the consequences of this divorce, its effects on the girls. She had new projects that she was pursuing, one of which is to help Russian and Ukrainian artists who write children's books and draw comics. The disintegration of the Soviet Union has resulted in the collapse of these particular state-supported industries. Rather than see them employed as street cleaners, Heidi is now employing some in her business, as well as subsidizing them in their free time. She is doing this out of conviction and does not expect to make any money from it. Her long soliloquy lasted about a half an hour. At the end, Franzi got up and quietly walked out. Peggy, her oldest daughter, began crying. And Greta, the middle daughter, sat in the middle, mediating rather unsuccessfully between the fronts.

Heidi's Daughters

At that breakfast, Peggy complained that Heidi was admonishing her for not getting involved in the divorce and separation. She insisted that the divorce was Heidi's affair and not hers, that Heidi should have separated from Sieghard long ago. Peggy supported Heidi in whatever she did, but, she added, she would never have put up with seventeen years of marriage to Sieghard. She also felt that her mother was too strong for her, that Heidi's strength was overwhelming, and therefore she had to distance herself from Heidi's affairs. The same, she said, was true of her birth-father, a doctor and former high official in the Socialist party, who insisted that Peggy's affairs were always of concern to him—and this, despite having dumped her and Greta on her mother after their divorce. For six years Peggy had had no contact with her father; yet when Peggy turned eighteen and suggested that she wanted to leave the GDR, her father told her not to go because it would endanger his career. "In early 1989," said Peggy bitterly, "he was the first one [of us] to go to the West when he obtained the privilege [as Reisekader]."

Heidi felt wounded by what she understood as Peggy's withdrawal. She thought that Peggy was drawing the wrong conclusions from her own marital failures. Peggy said her conclusion was that she would never get in a situation where someone could use and demean her like Heidi's two husbands had done to Heidi.

I have known Peggy since she began her education as a midwife. She is giving that career up now to return to school to study ethnology. She explains her fascination with other cultures as partly due to her years of being unable to travel outside the GDR, but also she had always sought out international friends, whom she finds more interesting than fellow Germans. She does not plan on marrying, nor on making the same mistakes with men that her mother did but instead likes to think of herself as open to experiments in life style. Upon resettling to the West at the same time as the rest of her family, Peggy initially found work in Heidelberg; but she found the city too small and provincial and has since moved to Hamburg. All of her friends are now people born and raised in the West, and Peggy never tells people that she was raised in the East. "Why tell them?" she explained to me. "It would only provide certain stereotypes for them to think about me. They never suspect that I come from the East, and I don't offer the information."

Both Greta and Heidi accuse Peggy of thinking herself superior to them. Greta has been involved with a man from Rosenheim several years older than her for the last three years. She broke off the relationship once, though, because she doubted his commitment to her. Within a couple of months he begged to get together again, insisting that she was the one for him. Greta admitted to me that she dominates the relationship, does all the initiating and planning, which, she said, is true of all the women she knows well. She and her boyfriend plan on staying in Rosenheim. "It's not an

170

exciting place," Greta explained, "but we're happy here. It's beautiful. There's work." Peggy accused Greta of remaining with this friend only because she could not find someone better, not because she really wanted to be with him. Greta responded by accusing Peggy of arrogance, and ultimately, said Greta, addressing Peggy's criticism, "that is why people get and remain together anyway."

I, along with Klaus, sat in silence during the accusations and counter-accusations, the tears, the pain. At times we were asked to intervene, which we staunchly refused. Later, I tried to sort out the influence of division and unification on this family, the limitations and possibilities opened for them due to their peculiar positioning. Certainly, division initially worked to Heidi's benefit, in that she had access to and support for education unavailable to most women in the West. But was Heidi's divorce a necessary consequence of not just the move, but of German unification? Did the dissolution of the two-state structure create the possibility for more diverse personal trajectories among the East Germans, including separate developments within and not merely between families? Should one view this divorce, therefore, not only as a loss for Sieghard, but also as a rare opportunity for a middle-aged woman? And what were the reasons, other than birth order, behind Heidi's passions, Peggy's need for autonomy, Greta's accommodations, and Franzi's obliviousness?

Security and Liberty

The Berlin Wall and the border between East and West created a modern historical anomaly: two moieties out of a single city, two political-economic-cultural systems out of one. Anthropologists have been slow to recognize that the creation of systems of difference and opposition was a basic generative principle of the Cold War, a product of modernism and not a phenomenon found only among vanishing or "traditional" societies. Before I went to study the divided Berlin, several generations of ethnographers had been studying non-Western moieties during moments of their disintegration, with no access to a historical explanation of their genesis. After three years of research, however, I realized that I had been witnessing a similar situation, though larger in scale: I, too, was documenting not the construction but the final collapse of a global "dual organization." I had been living through the implosion of a matching, asymmetrical classification of the universe.

Like all boundaries, this border divided, contained, restricted, and limited. It was also extremely productive of desire: it created monsters, heroes, traitors, yearnings, love, and hate. The territorial borders of the state were the most powerful of both the delimiting and productive boundaries that emanated from the Cold War, but they were not the only borders created by the state. The state's delimitations created novel and unanticipated conditions for envy of those who could cross, and for fear of those who had crossed. Once a *drüben*, an other side, was created, someone had to represent this other side. But who was to represent it and how, since few were allowed to see it? Having seen the other side, would someone be content to return to live among the contained? In propaganda and reportage of competing East and West media available on the evening news, this other was always represented not as a wayward child of Germanness but as something that must be abjected or exorcised from the character and organization of Germany. East Germans had to weigh personally the official media images against the stories told by people who had actually been "there." The confusion of images, I would argue, worked to the benefit of the East German state until the 1980s. At that time, the West German television programs became more widely available in the East, and, by the late 1980s, the GDR began granting large numbers of people the opportunity to travel and experience personally the other side. As the West's version of Germanness became authoritative, it came to dominate the perceptions of East Germans, including the idea that their own experiences could better be represented by the West Germans than by themselves. The authoritativeness of the West German media also enhanced its influence, through selective coverage, on the sequencing of the 1989 demonstrations in Leipzig, as well as on consequences of the opening of the Berlin Wall. The GDR's own coverage of these events was never taken very seriously as a set of legitimate counter-representations.

Cradle-to-grave security is what the regime in the East had promised. In order to provide this security, it had built the Wall. But this security state was increasingly experienced in terms Heidi would describe as suffocation, as the antithesis of freedom. While most citizens made their peace with confinement, a few tried to escape. These escapes were well publicized in the West as heroic flights to freedom. In November 1989, most published accounts stated that 197 East Germans died or were shot in attempts to cross one of GDR's borders (what the GDR had criminalized as *Republikflucht*, flight from the republic). By 1992 this number rose to 372. Recently released documents indicate that 588 people died while escaping East Germany. The number of dead will likely increase to around 600 as future accounts begin to include, for example, more of those who drowned in the Baltic Sea swimming to Denmark, or Soviet soldiers shot defecting to West Berlin. Currently the victims include 290 East Germans who were killed while trying to cross land borders into West Germany, 172 who were killed trying to cross the Berlin Wall, 81 who perished in boat attempts to escape across the Baltic, and 20 who were killed while fleeing into Hungary, Czechoslovakia, or Bulgaria. An additional 25 East German border guards were killed by their fellow guards as they sought to flee to the West.

Death was only the most dramatic and tragic of the effects of the deployment of the Wall to provide the bliss of security. Another major effect of the Wall was that large numbers of citizens, especially youths, increasingly measured happiness largely in terms of what they most lacked: liberty. And this liberty was measured by one's ability to travel "abroad," of experiencing what was beyond the Wall and the borders of the state. This experience found its most common expression in "tourism," as it does in the West, and was less a search for something new, for adventure, than a method of distancing oneself from the weighty present, of shedding one's skin. The desire to travel abroad has not been clearly articulated as a right or a liberty by social theorists or social protest movements, which instead, especially with regard to the former East bloc, have focused on free speech, freedom from arbitrary government, and rights to organize. By 1989, a clear majority of citizens, Heidi and her family included, expressed a desire for more of this sort of liberty, articulated in terms of the right to travel to the other side, wherever that site may be located, even at the cost of personal security.

173

The Aftermath

The collapse of the Wall has perhaps permanently changed the terms in which the historical tension between liberty and security are perceived and experienced. While removal of the border has indeed created more liberty for nearly all East Germans, it has also introduced tremendous insecurity into the world of work and the personal lives of many people, which in turn has exacerbated many of the old divisions among former East Germans as well as spawned many new ones. These divisions go beyond the well-publicized stories of *Stasi* complicity and personal betrayals, of family spy scandals where the spy alternately protected someone and limited their advancement (see Chapter 7, this volume; Segert 1993). To "come to terms with history," as Heidi proposed to her daughters, would mean pausing and reflecting on ways in which complicity, betrayal, and opposition were lived as part of a hierarchical system of role allocation, to clarify the personal gains and losses incurred living in the Cold War system of national (in)security states. On the other hand, the new opportunities opened to Heidi and her daughters are available to the extent that they have distanced themselves from their histories and place in the former GDR, to the extent that others no longer identify them with their pasts. Given their own alienation from the East as a home, a place, a culture, this distancing was easier for Heidi and her daughters than for most others, like Sieghard, and it explains to some degree their success. Indeed, they have never returned to Cottbus for a visit, and even refuse to visit West Berlin. The adjustments are also made easier in that their yearning for liberty was never very cleanly mapped onto a desire to travel abroad, and their disdain for boundaries extended well beyond those of the territorial state. Also, their relative unconcern for security is in accord with the demands of the enlarged Federal Republic of Germany, which, freed of the competitive pressure from the socialist East, is now limiting and even dismantling many welfare state policies, especially those necessary for internal national security, which were enacted during the Cold War (cf. Lemke and Marks 1992).

When I asked Franzi, who is now sixteen, what she plans on doing after finishing school, she replied that she would go to the university, perhaps in Bavaria, or Switzerland. She, too, is already looking away from her past, to the West and South instead of East and North. I asked her if she still had contact with any old friends in Cottbus. "No," she replied. Did she miss anyone or anything there, I asked. "No," she said, with a kind of nonchalance that seemed to me unstrained.

Perhaps her generation's sentiment was best expressed in the outcome of a meeting in Naumberg, eastern Germany, of 120 students between the ages of eleven and eighteen from eastern and western Germany in the spring of 1994. They attended what was heralded as the first "German-German Student Meeting." The central question posed by the organizers was, "We were foreign to one another—are we still?" Students responded in a variety of forms, writing newsclips and speeches, making videos and collages, staging musical or theatrical performances. According to the *Frankfurter Rundschau*, the fundamental message was reflected in the observation of one of the fourteen-year-old participants, "I believe that the mental Wall is thicker among adults than us." Indeed, the Cold War experiences that divided the two Germanies are no longer a part of the world of these students. But perhaps more revealing of the state of mind of this generation is the statement of one student, "We were desperate to come up with something so we could discuss how we are still foreign to one another or are supposed to be" (TWIG, 17 May 1994: 7). In other words, how these young people come to terms with division will largely depend on how they react to the framing of current expectations by their elders. Lacking any direct experience with either the early passions behind Cold War division, the disillusionment at its end, or the euphoria turned to bitterness and cynicism at unification, they are at a loss for a framework that might account for their differences. They are, much like all children, left to work with the passions and disillusionment of other generations (see Borneman 1992b).

Some of these elders are now frequently displacing the fantasies and fears provoked by Cold War borders onto an empty space of a shared, amorphous Germanness that is counterposed sharply to asylum seekers, Turks, and would-be immigrants. What ties these particular groups together is their function as a counterconcept to a new nativism. For some Germans, the foreign is no longer the other Germany, but the non-native. This pan-Germanism does not, however, eliminate the use of distinctions between East and West; it merely makes them more difficult to foreground and in some contexts makes them taboo. Many others reject altogether a space of Germanness as opposed to the non-native, and instead try to identify with "Europe," or "the West," or even "the world." Since many former West Germans, being well-travelled and cosmopolitan, are much more capable of representing themselves as European or West or even world citizens than are their East German compatriots, this kind of Euro-gloss often works to accentuate East-West differences. And even if West German cosmopolitanism is a thin veneer that, under the competitive global pressures resulting from unification, is often transformed into an arrogant neo-nationalism shared by those in the East, this arrogance is something that the East Germans cannot (yet) afford to display. Moreover, most East Germans valorize this West German identity by desiring to occupy the space of Westernness, however that may be defined, whether cosmopolitan or nationalist. For now, the operative definition of foreignness is unstable as the significance of borders is increasingly defined less territorially than economically, politically, or culturally, with no clear locations of, or demarcation between, any of these domains.

Gender, Sexuality, Nationality

The dynamics of gender, sexuality, and nation in former socialist countries, like East Germany, are frequently oversimplified by observers from countries in the West, who think that they recognize prior versions of themselves in the East. One popular version of these dynamics is that while time generally stood still in the East, women did change some, men not at all. The logic goes that while Western Europe promoted positive nation building and cultural change during the Cold War, socialist regimes suppressed nationalist sentiment and all forms of social movements. Therefore, according to this version, the eruption of suppressed nationalist sentiment, or the re-assertion of traditional gender norms and behaviours, or the proliferation of sexualities, was to be expected

176

once the Iron Curtain came up (for a refutation of this thesis as regards Romania, see Verdery 1991). We might begin correcting this version by taking into account the complex and changing nature of differentiation during the Cold War, the interplay of gender, sex, and nation as three loosely articulated systems of difference. This interplay was by no means the same in each of the East European countries. Certainly, the socialist "bloc" existed at the state level, but within that bloc the dialectic between security and liberty was inflected by divergent lived histories. For example, socialist ideology did not have the same impact on the radically different gender systems in the north (for example, Poland) and the south (for example, Serbia); sexual practices changed significantly in East Germany but the whole subject remained relatively taboo in Romania; nationality was a very difficult and schizophrenic identity in East Germany but obtained added coherence in state policy in Poland and Bulgaria. In the case of the divided Germany, Cold War oppositions worked to exacerbate all three systems of difference.

The German-German border influenced both men and women, neither was left standing still in time. Oppositional nation-building processes provided a meta-framework in which social identities unfolded. Arguably, with the death of Hitler and the "unconditional surrender of the nation" (or, the "collapse," as it is still frequently designated), the Law of the Father no longer held. (One might even date this authority shift to the death of Hindenburg.) But to lose this father-function did not necessarily harm "men." Many men also fought for women's rights, especially in the 1950s in certain social classes in the East, and in the 1970s as part of a generation conflict in the West. Many men also either had lost their fathers in the war or grew up hating them, and therefore worked just as hard as women did to kill the Father, to eliminate vestiges of the authorial system that traced power from *Gottvater* to *Landesvater* to *Familienvater*. On the other hand, loss of the father-function did alter fundamentally what it means to be a "man," as it also changed the conditions under which "women," like Heidi, developed. Heidi's first husband tried to preserve his father-function and the power inherent in that position. Whatever gains this may have meant to his career were counterbalanced by his loss of a relationship not only with his wife but also with his daughters. Heidi's second

177

husband, Sieghard, had a more ambivalent, if not passive, relationship to the Father; but he, too, failed to construct a positive alternative for himself to pre-war notions of German masculinity and sexuality, and he, too, paid dearly for his lack of imagination.

For both men, notions of male (and female) sexuality seem to have changed even less than notions of gender. With respect to the relation of the loss/death of the Father to the experiencing of alternative sexualities, East and West differed considerably. The intense generation conflict of West German men and women in the 1960s often revolved explicitly around a "reckoning with the past," meaning the death of the Father, and around sexual experimentation as social provocation (Borneman 1992a: 237–283). In the East, sexual experimentation was primarily a private and relatively depoliticized activity and did not become part of a generational confrontation as in the West. Heidi explains her attraction to a young West German man who has benefited from this sexual experimentation as part of a historical dynamic largely in terms of his refusal to assert traditional forms of "male" authority.

Memory of the Wall

"1989" marked the end of a period that began in 1945 and was characterized in double-speak as both a "postwar" and a "Cold War" era. It was indeed a "cold" rather than "hot" struggle in that it was fought—despite both sides' rhetoric of progress toward MAD (Mutually Assured Destruction)—over quotidian life, as a war of attrition, less to destroy the other than to lame it and to fix the terms of its future. This drama of reaching the final historical form of human society— in the case of the GDR, a scientifically driven utopia—concluded, according to some, not with the collapse of the East bloc but with the spread of liberalism to that traditionally illiberal region. As predicted, capitalist markets and parliamentary democracy were immediately exported to the East. But contrary to many early prognoses, these key symbolic systems of the victorious West have not provided an end to history, for the meaning of "markets" and "democracy" has changed steadily, as do all export models when they come into contact with actual consumers. It is

increasingly clear that liberalism functions much like other utopias, including GDR Marxism: in the name of a universal humanism, it functions more to reproduce a particular regime of tolerance
and property distribution than to support any abstract group interests or humanity taken a whole. Instead of the end of history and
the crowning of Liberalism, we have the end of belief in a universal
"man," with the result that the meaning of 1989 and of the Wall
(our most recent past) remains open to multiple interpretations
and rereadings, depending on the position and interests of the
observer.

The Berlin Wall itself continues to exert pressure on history, no
longer as a border—with their usual thoroughness, German officials have nearly totally removed remnants of the Wall from around
Berlin—but as a trinket, a museum piece, a global commodity. In
these forms the Wall now has a fixed, "free world" meaning: any
part can substitute for the former whole Cold War and bring forth
a memory of freedom and its denial. Land along the eastern side
of the Wall, which had been expropriated by the GDR, has either
been returned to its last owner or is being fought over in court. One
can now buy from Turkish dealers throughout Berlin stones painted
to look like chips of the graffiti-signed, western side of the Wall, to
wear around the neck, or to hang on the ears, or to display on a
living room mantel. Some sections of the original Wall have been
preserved and repainted in scenes symbolizing freedom, or its con-
verse, oppression, and then sold or donated to groups and individuals in at least seventeen countries. Several slabs that were repainted
by self-proclaimed international artists in 1990 still rest in their
old spots in what is now called "East Side Gallery." One section
stands near the demilitarized zone that separates North and South
Korea, several stand in front of the United States presidential li-
braries honoring J.F.K., Ronald Reagan, and George Bush. Even
the C.I.A. headquarters in Langley, Virginia, has adorned itself
with a panel from the Wall— no doubt less to evoke "freedom" than
to reinforce a view lacking any historical evidence, a memory that
claims the CIA—despite its endless blunders—contributed to the
final victory over Communism. The one association completely
missing in any of these material commemorations is the relation of
Cold War borders to "tourism"—that peculiar interpretation given

liberty by most of those East German border crossers who prompted the opening of the Wall on November 9, 1989.

Within two years of the border's demolition, people in several places in Germany began rebuilding it. For example, a 130 meter (426 foot) part of the fence between the eastern town of Geisa in Thuringia and the western town of Rasdorf in Hessen has been reconstructed. Although the entire border was torn down in 1990, three years later mayors of both communities wanted the fence as a memorial to the decades-long compulsory division. Originally, two kilometers of the border fence were to remain standing as part of an artistic project that would include reclaiming Point Alpha, a former American base at this site. By 1987, the Rainbow Association, which was founded to build bridges between East and West, had proposed to the government of the GDR the construction of an international meeting site, complete with a rainbow spanning the former border crossing to serve as a visible sign of reconciliation— but the GDR rejected the idea. But in July 1993, artists from the former East and West finally met at Point Alpha to address the theme "Living Without Borders." Presently the accommodations at Point Alpha are being used to shelter asylum seekers, whose number in Germany increased dramatically with the opening of the Wall. Needless to say, asylum seekers have become a prototype for post–Cold War international border crossers. The category includes an extremely heterogeneous group of people, impossible to classify according to a single geographic, political, cultural, or economic criterion. Most seek both liberty and security; all want a "better" life (or in some cases, simply a life) elsewhere.

Rebuilding the Wall to keep certain memories of division alive has not prevented former Communists whom one still associated with Cold War borders from returning to power in most of the former East bloc states, including in some of (the new) eastern Germany's provinces. It must be noted, however, that none of these former Communists promise a return to Cold War borders, though many appeal to a redrawing and reassertion of borders, mostly along nationalist or economic lines (for the position of former East German Communists, see Bisky *et. al.* 1993). The opposition politicians who initially replaced the Communists also contributed to their own demise; most have been unable to maintain popular support by offering liberty and free markets alone, nor have they been able to project their problems onto an external enemy, as was the case with both sides during the Cold War. Where this externalization of problems has been tried, as in Chechnya or Yugoslavia, xenophobic and genocidal nationalism has been the accessory deployed by politicians to stay in power. Indications that something has been learned from the experience of the Wall's division are isolated, and those few politicians who dare to acknowledge the simultaneity of people's needs for security and liberty, variously interpreted and balanced, have frequently been isolated within their own political parties.

Grenzregime

In explanations of "1989" and events leading to the collapse of East European Communist regimes, including the dissolution of the GDR, two basic approaches in the social sciences prevail: either one begins with a theory or model and finds examples to prove or disprove it, or one begins with specific histories and looks for ways to account for them. I have chosen the latter approach, preferring the richness and complexity of experiential history to the parsimony and elegance of a model. In this choice I have followed a long anthropological tradition of explanation that, as Clifford Geertz has written, "substitutes complex pictures for simple ones while striving somehow to retain the persuasive clarity that went with the simple ones" (1973:33). The question for me, as an anthropologist, is not whether certain experiences or events lend themselves to serve a particular model (to prove or disprove) but from what perspectives one might account for and do justice to particular experiences and events. In other words, social science is put less in the service of itself than of the objects it seeks to constitute and explain.

The authoritative account on which most social scientists tend to do their modelling of Eastern European revolutions has been that of Timothy Garton Ash (1989, 1990). For the East German revolution, Ash listed a compendium of factors, including the development of an opposition that provoked repression, a lack of will on the part of Egon Krenz (Honecker's replacement as head of party and state), the influence of West German television, and Gorbachev's warning. The attempt to weigh these factors has produced a wide variety of models, such as Karl-Dieter Opp's sociological proposal for "a micro-model specifying a broad set of individual incentives to participate; then we contend that political events and changes in the social context together with existing coordinating mechanisms produced the large-scale demonstrations of 1989" (1993: 659); or Sidney Tarrow's political science model, which suggests that the "rebellions" were a result of an "opportunity for ordinary citizens to express and expand [their] demands" (1991: 15); yet others attribute events to intellectual dissent and the peace movement (Allen 1991), or "the element of surprise" (Kuran 1991). These factors are all undoubtedly important, but importance says little about significance, and significance is always relative to the perspective from which one wishes to explain. Yet this perspective from which one speaks is rarely itself examined and made a part of the analysis. A reflexive sociology that would include in a description of the object examined the measures by which value and significance are attributed is all too frequently preached but not practised.

Perhaps the most popular model used to explain the monumental event in the history depicted in this essay—what Heidi calls simply "the change"—has been "exit, voice, and loyalty," initially formulated and applied to the life of firms by Albert Hirschman in 1970. The question often asked is which East Germans were exhibiting "voice": those who demonstrated to stay (and thereby also could be classified as "loyal") or those who opted for "exit" by fleeing to other East European embassies. Since the original model posits the three behaviors as mutually exclusive and leading to different behaviors on the part of the firm, application of the model to East German events, and the collapse of the GDR, has reduced the behavior of actors to a single choice between three categories. The inability to acknowledge multiple (and often contradictory) actions of individuals and the state has resulted in confusion. But who or what is confusing, one must ask, the actions and events or the model? In subsequent work, Hirschman has consistently complicated his own model and warned against overextending his original elegant framework to other contexts. He has done the same in a recent article accounting for the "fate of the German Democratic Republic," warning of "the risk of making too much of a theoretical construct," admonishing us against the search for "mysterious, if preordained, processes that dissolve all contrasts and reconcile all opposites" (1993: 202). After deftly sketching the events leading up to November 1989, he concludes that "exit can cooperate with voice, voice can emerge from exit, and exit can reinforce voice" (1993: 202). So much for simple cause and effect.

In this spirit of theoretical modesty, I have offered a description of one woman, Heidi, and of those close to her, hoping that her story might act as a lens to reveal new patterns and connections in the construction and collapse of borders. I have also fashioned Heidi's story to address the peculiarities of balancing liberty and security while living in a Grenzregime during the Cold War and its aftermath. Any explanation of Heidi's "change" after 1989 must substitute a more complex understanding for a simpler one, since this change cannot be explained in terms of a parsimoniously defined set of isolable factors such as voice, exit, lack of the ruler's will, increased citizen opportunity, dissent and spontaneous cooperation, or surprise. If we disentangle these factors and assign them significance as dependent and independent variables, we are forced a priori to ignore the majority of facts, the excess, that make Heidi's abstract case into a human story. Through this reduction, we necessarily lose in this modelling the historical specificity and complexity of what is to be explained, the singularity of the object. Borders, even an overdetermined one like the Berlin Wall, are the products of ambivalent and multiple inputs; they are fortuitously constructed and dismantled because of contradictory processes that simultaneously support and undermine their continued existence. To focus on the life of one person, and someone marginal to the processes one usually labels History (as in fact we all are), can shed light on only some parts of the story of the Wall and its aftermath. Yet Heidi's life, precisely because of its fundamentally indeterminate nature and marginality, reveals to us a decentered perspective on some of the particularities of the patterned unfolding of the history of a Grenzregime: this series of events at this time in this place. That I have used social theory only insofar as it advances the understanding of her story, rather than made her story serve theory, reflects my preference for keeping method and theory sensitive to the historical exactness and density of human life.

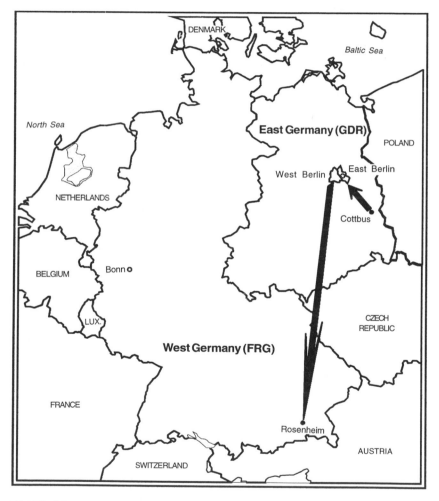

Heidi's Movement, 1989

REFERENCES

Allen, Bruce
>1991. *Germany East*. Montreal: Black Rose Publishing

Ash, Timothy Garton
>1990. *The Magic Lantern: The Revolution of '89 Witnessed in Warsaw, Budapest, Berlin, and Prague*. New York: Random House
>
>1989. "The German Revolution." *New York Review of Books* XXXVI, 20 (12/21/89) 3–14

Bisky, Lothar, Uwe-Jens Heuer, Michael Schumann, eds.
>1993. *Rücksichten: Politische und juristische Aspekete der DDR-Geschichte*. Hamburg: VSA Verlag

Borneman, John
>1992a. *Belonging in the Two Berlins: Kin, State, Nation*. Cambridge: Cambridge University Press
>
>1992b. "State, Territory, and Identity Formation in the Postwar Berlins." *Cultural Anthropology* 7(1): 44–61
>
>1991a. *After the Wall: East Meets West in the New Berlin*. New York: Basic Books
>
>1991b. *Gay Voices From East Germany*, edited and with introduction. Bloomington: Indiana University Press

Gaddis, John Lewis
>1982. *Strategies of Containment: A Critical Appraisal of Postwar American National Security Policy*. New York: Oxford University Press

Geertz, Clifford
>1973. *The Interpretation of Cultures*. New York: Basic Books

Geißler, Rainer
>1992. *Die Sozialstruktur Deutschlands*. Opladen: Westdeutscher Verlag

Hirschman, Albert O.
>1993. "Exit, Voice, and the Fate of the German Democratic Republic: An Essay in Conceptual History." *World Politics* 45 (1):173–202

Kuran, Timur
>1991. "Now out of Never: The element of surprise in the East European Revolution of 1989." *World Politics* 44 (1):7–49

Lemke, Christiane, and Gary Marks
>1992. *The Crisis of Socialism in Europe*. Durham: Duke University Press

185

Opp, Karl-Dieter

    1993. "Dissident groups, personal networks and spontaneous cooperation: the East German revolution of 1989." *American Sociological Review* 58 (October):659–680

Segert, Dieter

    1993. "The State, the Stasi and the People: The Debate about the Past and the difficulties in Reformulating Collective Identities." *The Journal of Communist Studies* 9 (3): 202–215

Senders, Stefan

    1996. "Laws of Belonging: Legal Dimensions of National Inclusion in Germany." *New German Critique* 67 (Winter):147–176

Steiner, Susan, Megan Ratner, Thomas Hofmann, eds.

    1994. *The Week in Germany (TWIG)*, 17 May, p. 4

Tarrow, Sidney

    1991. "Aiming at a moving target: Social science and the recent rebellions in Eastern Europe." *Political Science and Politics* (March 1991) XXIV, (1): 12–20

Verdery, Katherine

    1991. *National Ideology Under Socialism: Identity and Cultural Politics in Ceausescu's Romania*. Berkeley: University of California Press

Wendt, Hartmut

    1991. "Die deutsch-deutsche Wanderungen." *Deutschland-Archiv* 24 (April): 390

PART III

Resistance and Opposition to Authority

7

Trouble in the Kitchen: Totalitarianism, Love, and Resistance To Authority

Love and Politics

In December 1989, the newly empowered parliament in East Berlin called Erich Mielke, the ostensible father of the East German State Security, or Stasi, to answer questions ostensibly about his role in creating a regime of fear, but more likely, to elicit a confession and apology. Mielke surprised and angered the representatives as he unrepentantly defended himself, claiming, "Ich liebe euch doch alle!" (But I love you all!). Afterward, members of parliament and the press concentrated on Mielke's putative insincerity. How could he claim to have loved us, they asked, after so many years of incarceration, intimidation, torture, and even murder? Yet Mielke was not, I would argue, being disingenuous. Indeed, he really did love these people, and he couldn't understand how they had the audacity to claim, after thirty intimate—oh, so very intimate—years of living together, that they were not one, a natural unity like a family, motivated by love.[1] His exclamation of love follows in a long Christian tradition, where the basic modal relationship of self and other is the romantic genre: love thy neighbor as thyself. The problem with such a formulation is twofold: first, that only a narcissistic

189

love, a love of self, enables love of the other, thus narcissism itself often becomes the project and one never gets to a relationship with the other; and second, that this love, based neither on a notion of reciprocity nor exchange, is purely monologic and anti-social. I want to name this relationship after Beaver Cleaver's mother, from the American TV sitcom *Leave it to Beaver*; I will call it the June Cleaver genre.

In this chapter, I intend to illustrate how romance was the dominant genre in which authority was represented and legitimated in relations between state and citizen in East Germany, and contrast this with satire as the dominant genre in the West. Then I will show how use of one or the other genre created different generational dynamics in the two states. And finally, I will identify three dissidents and examine the efficacy of their different forms of resistance. Before I do this, I want to offer another example of what I mean by the June Cleaver genre.

June Cleaver has been an important figure in the development of American conceptions of the romantic form during the Cold War, despite her lack of consciousness about it, or perhaps made possible precisely because she was always so delightfully unaware. Her conception of love receives its paradigmatic political representation in George Orwell's *1984*, a book that perhaps more faithfully than any other recapitulated the image of local and international order shared by the postwar non-Communist world. Here, he defines love as opposed to instrumentality, much as private is opposed to public, and freedom to totalitarianism. Published in 1949 as the Cold War got underway, Orwell's *1984* pits the totalitarian experience against the resistance and experience of freedom of Winston Smith and Julia (No Surname). Orwell is quite explicit about his belief that totalitarianism is less about love than sex.[2] The goal of the Party was "to remove all pleasure from the sexual act. . . . The Party was trying to kill the sex instinct, or, if it could not be killed, then to distort it and divert it" (1983: 57). "The sex instinct," he expounds, "created a world of its own which was outside the Party's control and which therefore had to be destroyed if possible. . . . They [the Party] had played a similar trick with the instinct of parenthood. . . . The children were turned systematically against their parents and taught to spy on them and report their

190

deviations. The family had become in effect an extension of the Thought Police" (1983: 111). Thus, in order to get outside of and resist Big Brother, Winston had to get in touch with his "sex instinct," as well as perhaps his "instinct of parenthood." Accordingly, waiting for Winston is Julia, whom Orwell describes as "not clever" but nonetheless "fond of using her hands and [she] felt at home with machinery" (1983: 107). In fact, "everything came back to her own sexuality" (1983: 110). (Julia's sexuality is defined in opposition to that of Katherine, Winston's wife, whose body stiffened "as soon as he touched her," and who "had long ceased to be a painful memory and [had] become merely a distasteful one" [1983:110].)[3]

Second, Winston must have sex with Julia, not in public but in private, in Nature, "inside [a] ring of saplings," amidst "an occasional crackle of twigs" (1983:104). Orwell leaves nothing to the imagination about what kind of sexuality he meant. Describing the hostel where Julia lives with thirty other girls, she states, "Always in the stink of women! How I hate women!" (1983: 108). Indeed, the "stink of women," thirty of them alone together, with the unnamed possibility of lesbian sex as resistance, is maloderous enough to make any despondent freedom fighter, like Orwell, properly nauseous, and Julia responds appropriately by finding our hero, Winston. For Orwell, hetero sex is an "animal instinct, [a] simple undifferentiated desire, . . . [a] force that would tear the Party to pieces" (1983: 105). This sex, because it is governed by instinct, will occur spontaneously—"it was hard to say by whose act"—by which is meant, as Winston pulls Julia "down on to the ground, she was utterly unresisting, he could do what he liked with her" (1983: 100). Winston simultaneously honors her by revealing his true feelings, what he calls a "love offering": "I wanted to rape you and murder you afterwards." "The girl," writes Orwell, "laughed delightedly" in response (1983: 101). After orgasm, described as "a sort of pleasant helplessness," Julia and Winston "fell apart," and then "almost immediately they fell asleep" (1983: 105). Orwell seems confused for a moment: is this "animal instinct," this sex, a stimulant or a sedative? But no, he quickly recovers his plot and decisively summarizes this entire scene: "Their embrace had been a battle, the climax a victory. It was a blow struck against the Party. It was a political act" (1983: 105).

191

A political act it was indeed, and, as Orwell says, despite its similarity to love or romance, it was, above all, an act of sex—and, let us add, sex from a satirical perspective. But was it an act of opposition, of resistance to order, to authority, to totalitarianism? Orwell's inversion of the private and the political, and his elevation of private, heterosexual acts to the status of political virtue, was in fact a characteristic move in the Western, free world portrayal of everyday life during the Cold War, as was his projection of the lack of this virtue onto the communist world as a form of critique. This particular maneuver is the grounding of authority in the satiric mode. So what on the surface appears to be a June Cleaver story, structured like that of Erich Mielke's, of naiveté, love, idealism, is in fact a cynical portrayal, or a particular type of satire.

Let me turn now to a consummate and unrepentant satirist, Jeane Kirkpatrick, political talk show celebrity, professor, and former Ambassador to the UN. The distinction I am making between satire and romance is a reformulation of the difference she attributed to authoritarian and totalitarian regimes. Her purpose was to legitimate the relation of ruler to ruled in non-communist countries ("right-wing autocracies") that nonetheless had repressive regimes. Kirkpatrick's point was that authoritarian regimes do not have the totalizing intentions of communist regimes, that they still respect the liberal distinction between private life, or, let's say, the kitchen (where the state is morally prohibited from intervening), and public life, or, let's say, the university (where the state has a right to intervene). Furthermore, she maintains that because communist regimes efface this basic distinction between public and private, they can be equated with fascist regimes, both of which are considered subsets of the general category "totalitarian" (Kirkpatrick 1979b).[4] Totalitarian regimes, then, because of their totalizing intentions to intervene in private life, are not reformable, whereas authoritarian regimes, because of their more limited intentions, are reformable—and therefore we must oppose the former but may decide to support the latter.

Kirkpatrick's thesis has not proven particularly useful historically. Most socialist regimes of the totalitarian type gave up power in 1989 (contrary to their ideology), whereas most of the authoritarian regimes have found new methods to perpetuate their rule

192

(thus proving unreformable). Thus, to compare Poland or Czechoslovakia before and after 1989, for example, is to compare radically different modes of authority relations, but the structure of authority in Brazil or Pakistan has remained remarkably consistent even after the displacement of more extreme forms of right-wing regimes. Although her distinction is not without some validity, she makes the error of defining her units, "states," in terms of a set of discrete categories or characteristics, rather than looking at them both in terms of their relationships and as parts of larger wholes. Kirkpatrick defines the essence of state legitimacy in terms of the intention of the rulers, whereas it is the actual relation of ruler to ruled in a specific international context that structures and legitimates Cold War authority. Thus, what distinguishes East and West Germany, as Cold War prototypes of Kirkpatrick's distinction, is not any set of essential characteristics specifying ruler's intentions, but rather, the structure of citizen and state relations within the dual, oppositional structures of post–World War II international order. In the socialist East, the state structured its relations to citizens as a romance; in the capitalist West, the state structured its relations to citizens as a satire (more on this later, but briefly, as a critique of vice from a position of authority grounded in the past).[5]

That said, I do not want to obscure, as both Orwell and Kirkpatrick do, the differences within the totalitarian and authoritarian types.[6] Comparing any two objects with one another does not necessarily entail equating them; indeed, comparison is a method by which one also establishes differences. But Orwell and Kirkpatrick do not compare—they equate in order to blur the distinctiveness of regimes. They do this by means of a series of displacements, inversions, and projections that are worthy of a brief digression. As I have indicated above, Orwell derives his Big Brother model of totalitarianism by conflating communism and fascism, which are said to be antagonistic to the private, unsocial ("instinctual") freedom that is supposedly protected by liberal democracies, the unnamed, unmarked opposite. Then he displaces political (public) conflict onto sexual (private) practice: fascism's hostility to private life is projected onto communist ideology, and liberalism's hostility to promiscuity is understood as opposed to communism's support. These projections enable Orwell to invert certain ideological positions of liberals, fascists, and communists. His reasoning goes as follows: Freedom is not equal to totalitarianism ("the Party"). Moreover, totalitarianism negates freedom through repression of hetero sex ("the sex instinct," "animal instinct," "the instinct of parenthood"). Freedom can be affirmed, however, by resistance to totalitarianism (free hetero sex). What is repressed (homo sex: "distort[ed]" and "divert[ed]" sex, "the stink of women [together]") not only survives in Orwell's political unconscious but asserts itself as prior to and dominant over freedom. Thus, emancipation must equal the affirmation of hetero sex ("the sex instinct," "animal instinct," "the instinct of parenthood").

Kirkpatrick, on the other hand, comes to assume the truth of Orwell's inversions and projections, in particular, the cohence of the Big Brother type (a conflation of fascist and communist regimes). By the 1970s, in a period of international detente and a warming in the Cold War, she takes up the task of re-constructing the endangered free willed self. Her immediate goal in this reconstruction was to delegitimate former President Jimmy Carter's universal human rights policy. In order to do this, she had both to negate all connections between freedom and community and to establish a fraternity between "right-wing autocracies" and liberal democratic regimes. In other words, as I shall explain later, she must construct the self-interested individual as the epitome of freedom, prior to and independent of any social whole. Her siblingship between authoritarian regimes is based on how they share a privileging of self-interested individuals. But this similarity obscures the differences between, and denies Kirkpatrick the ability to critique, authoritarian regimes like Pinochet's Chile and Reagan's America. The significant difference between these two is not merely one of degree, nor does it revolve around the ruler's intent. Rather, the distinctiveness of each grows out of the relationship of community to individual, or ruler to ruled: Pinochet's authority rested primarily on his individual will, or, as Kirkpatrick (1973: 60) would have it, "on force as well as consent," whereas Reagan's rested less on the force of his will than on the consent, however misguided, of the community of the governed.[7]

Let me now move the discussion away from typologizing and look at the situation going into German unification, where the romantic relationship of citizen to state in the East is being reemplotted in satiric form. My assumption is, in other words, that when June Cleaver meets Jeane Kirkpatrick there is trouble in the kitchen.

Romance and Satire in East and West Germany

What did it mean to use romance and satire in East and West Germany between 1949 and 1989? A romantic relationship is characterized by a utopian fantasy (the projection of self-fulfillment onto an idealized other) aimed at the transfiguration of the everyday. It implies a total commitment that can bring about great sacrifice, a transcendent personal identity that thrives on fantasy, and the construction of "an illusory world of absolute happiness and fulfillment" (see Lindholm 1988: 6, 28–34; Frye 1957: 193). In socialist East Germany, the relation between state and citizen was imagined and structured as utopian or future-looking, as reality-denying, and as total.

Satire, on the other hand, is a form of authority based not on fantasy but on critique. It is lapsarian or backward-looking, reality-affirming, and partial. Rather than transfiguring the everyday, as is the goal of romance, it aims to substitute for the everyday a superior version of its present form. Thus it presupposes homogeneous, transcendental moral standards in order to ridicule vice in a supposedly stable society. Though satire represents itself as "on the crest of progress," it never forsakes its assumption of a superior moral virtue, which tends to come from its alliance with authority placed in the past (see Adorno 1984: 210–212). This authority is grounded in a critique of corruption and decadence, a fall from grace or a deviation from an original charter, such as a constitution.

Thus, satire becomes more backward-looking over time in order to maintain its vision of humanity as invariant. Contrariwise, romance, tied to a vision of humanity as variant, has the problem of sustaining and legitimating its present over time given that its goal is constant transformation (elimination or abnegation of self) on the way to a utopia. In short, satire critiques the reality of the present as a fallen version of some past, whereas romance denies the present in order to idealize an unattained future. In authoritarian states (including those of the liberal kind) the constitution often functions as the holy document used to measure the legitimacy of the present. In communist states, the Five Year Plan serves the function of projecting authority onto an illusory future.

Here, I will be brief and sketchy about how this genre worked to structure state-citizen relations in East and West. It is necessary to keep in mind that radical changes in content were accompanied by a remarkable continuity in form during the history of this relationship (see Borneman 1992: 74–118). Up until approximately 1965, the East German state had two goals: first, it was concerned about restructuring specific types of relationships (such as mother-child, husband-wife, married couple-community, employee-employer, religious communities-state) and integrating them into societal processes in the public sphere. Second, it sought to reformulate the ethics of human communication in general, what Kligman calls an exercise in the secular cosmology-making of the atheist state (1988: 249–279). For example, in 1958, Walter Ulbricht's declaration of a socialist *Menschengemeinschaft* included ten Commandments of Socialist Morality and Ethics. These included admonishments, e.g., to "lead a clean and respectable life," "to raise children in the spirit of peace and socialism" (see Borneman 1992: 74–118). Educational, legal, and economic reforms placed the child, in accord with the state's future orientation, at the center of a strategy of kinship reconstruction and desentimentalized the family as well as partnership forms. By the mid-sixties, though, the regime had completed most of this legal reconstruction, called the *Aufbau* phase; yet it had still failed to reach the satisfaction and happiness that were the anticipated result of the socialist utopia. Thus, in order to remain true to the romantic genre, since demarcation in form from the West was equally if not more crucial than consistency in content, the East German regime began to idealize its past accomplishments, culminating in the present. This relation to the past remains romantic rather than satirical, since it *idealizes* the past's contributions to the present, whereas satire would use the past to engage in *critique*. After 1965, love and sentiment were brought back into family law, and by the mid-eighties, partnership in the form of a state-sanctioned marriage had become the legal focus of family policy.

The West German regime followed an opposite pattern. It sentimentalized the family, promulgating a policy of restoration, centered around the "housewife marriage," that favored continuity over change and elders over youth—until approximately 1968. Prodded by social protests at that time, it gradually enacted educational, economic, and legal reforms that shifted the kinship focus from love and a particular partnership form to economics and child-centered families. In effect, the two states reversed themselves with regard to content, adopting foci which their opponent had earlier embraced, while remaining consistent and oppositional in both form of self-representation and explicit nexus to kin policy.

These shifts in policy content, which, I would argue, were necessary in order to maintain the particular form of authority (satiric or romantic) adopted in 1949, affected different generations of citizens. Thus, if looked at as they unfold over time, these two forms of authority have different consequences for the construction of age-grading systems, they exert alternate influences on the formation of generations. Because East Germany—and here this argument might be extended to all socialist and fascist, or romantic, regimes—looked to the future, it sided with the youth over the elders, but only of its first generation of youth, those born between approximately 1930 and 1955. West Germany, as in other constitutional republics, sided with traditional authority against youth, and thus experienced three oppositional youth movements in the first three decades of its history (the Halbstarke [half strong], the Achtundsechziger [68ers], and the Rote Armee Fraktion [Red Army Faction]).[8] In late summer 1989, a new generation of East German youth fled the state, initially across the Hungarian border, in an apparent total repudiation of the legitimacy of the state's romantic vision of its relationship with them. The satiric mode in West Germany, on the other hand, seemed to have produced a stable situation as well as universalizing itself, as some members of all three youth movements have been incorporated into the state apparatus itself. As unification with the East unfolded, many West Germans across the political spectrum and of different ages united together around the superiority of their constitution, with some, like Jürgen Habermas, even appealing to a formal *Verfassungspatriotismus* as a base for the relation of citizen to state that is superior to all others.

197

One of the major reasons why satire is a more effective form of authority than romance lies in its particularism and roots in the local, in contrast to romanticism which is abstract and universalistic. As a consequence of its ties to the concrete, satire must first recognize or acknowledge difference before undermining it. Romance, on the other hand, due to its basically monologic and narcissistic idealism, is rooted in a denial of reality. Thus satire, in order to be effective, must know the other, while the effectiveness of romance lies precisely in its misrecognition, in its ability to create illusion and foster fantasy.[9]

Modernist and Postmodernist Resistance

Thus far, I have dealt mainly with the genres of authority in which relationships between state and citizen were constructed, and not with a comparison of perceptions of these relations by the various actors. The perspective I have taken does not attribute this genre to the willed construction of either the state or the citizen. Rather, genre is both product and precursor of this symbiotic relationship.[10] A genre, either romance à la June Cleaver or satire à la Jeane Kirkpatrick, encodes facts in a particular plot structure that, in turn, authorizes the account. The authority of a genre is derived from the morality attached to its form, which, when employed, legitimates the relationship (see White 1987: 13). I could further delineate how each genre was, and is now in retrospect, separately perceived by state and citizen in East and West over time. Indeed, the new German state—supported by some citizens, resisted by others—is developing two new areas of morality: *Regierungskriminalität,* governmental criminality, to prosecute acts ranging from shooting at the border, government-organized smuggling, and financial frauds similar to the U.S. savings and loan scandal, committed before 1989, as opposed to *Vereinigungskriminalität,* economic illegalities committed during the "transition" to a "free market" and "democratic state" (see Borneman 1991). A discussion of these themes, however, would divert us too far from our discussion of Orwell's and Kirkpatrick's models of the "totalitarian" state and effective resistance to it. For the remainder of this chapter, the question I will

198

focus on is: how does the loved one assert difference in a romantic relationship?

We can examine three responses to the romantic state: first, the June Cleaver (or romantic) response of hetero sex or withdrawal into a private niche, which we might evaluate by looking at the East German Christian Democratic politician Günther Krause; second, the Jeane Kirkpatrick (or satiric) response of modernist resistance, for which I will use the example of poet/singer Wolf Biermann; third, the postmodernist response, for which I will use the example of poet/artist Sascha Anderson.

Our June Cleaver figure's inspiration might be George Orwell's Winston or Julia, who thought they were resisting totalitarianism by leaving the politically contentious world aside and retreating to the putatively instinctual, private domain of romance and hetero sex. Did their private domain actually function as a retreat or resistance to the political world, or should we see it as an extension of, a necessary complement to, this type of political gestalt? Of our three responses, the politician and married man Günther Krause was the most compliant to authority, the most appropriate for the totalitarian regime, as he also was in serving as transportation minister for the Helmut Kohl–led government. Orwell's cynical positing of an inherent opposition between (private) romance and (public) totalitarian rule is directly contradicted by the example of Krause, whose instrumental calculations and opportunistic nose for power meshed harmoniously with his private hetero sex life in the former GDR, and likewise, serves him well in the new Federal Republic. Krause joined the East German Christian Democratic Party in 1975, rose in the ranks, and was integrated into the West CDU in 1990. He became the East German representative in negotiations over the Unity Treaty, for which he was rewarded the post of Minister of Transportation in the first pan-German government following the October 3, 1990, elections. In this new post, he has aggressively pushed for expansion of freeways and increased use of private automobiles in the East. But he is perhaps best known for his loyal service to his family and to Helmut Kohl, specifically in the generous care he provides for his family's future (primarily by securing private real estate and using his ministry to direct highway expansion near property owned by his family). Yet he has represented himself as a resister to the old regime, pointing to three acts: in 1987, the writing of a paper for the GDR computer giant, Robotron, encouraging the use of English in instruction and more personal freedom for engineers in the company; in 1988, encouraging youth at an official youth club to work toward changing the society as well as discussing taboo topics with them; in the fall of 1989, co-writing a position paper for the CDU condemning socialism. Needless to say, he suffered no penalties for these acts of "courage"; in fact, for some of them he received praise ("Leere Hülse" 1991: 25–28).

Can we conclude that in East Germany, individuals who invested in private love, hetero sex, and "instinctual parenthood" were either in opposition or neutral to the interests of the state? Or does the illusion of a private world, the "sort of pleasant helplessness," have a sedative effect in contributing to stabilize both totalitarian and authoritarian regimes—with the possible exception of the fascist type?[11] Contrary to Orwell's predictions, it was not the affirmation of desire in private that constituted resistance to communist states, but the expression of passion in any social or public domain. States can make their peace with any sexual act or everyday practice so long as it remains private and does not arouse public passion about the contestability of the social and political order. Accordingly, sexual emancipatory movements, for example, are engaged in resistance to authority only when private acts are brought into the public domain, where they act to problematize the very frontier between private and public. This questioning then produces dangerous knowledge which arouses public passion and politicizes by making power relations transparent and thus knowable. In other words, resistance means to disturb Orwell's post-orgasm scene, it means the alternate movement from his ideal state of "pleasant helplessness" into public life, and from public back to private.[12]

What I mean by a dialectic between public and private is explicated persuasively by Louis Dumont in his analysis of holism and individualism in German ideology.[13] Dumont's analysis of the basis of Nazi authority offers insight into the basis of authority in other ideologies. In his analysis, Dumont clarifies the fallacy of a logic in which Kirkpatrick also engages, namely, misunderstanding the relation of, on the one hand, holism to totalitarianism, and on the other, individualism to freedom. First, he posits that German cultural particularism, as explicated by Herder, was a reaction to the universalism of the French. Herder's notion that all cultures (Volk) are unique and equally meritorious (though in different ways) was, a century later, read by many in the scientific community in biologistic and Darwinistic terms, namely, that cultures are like species: unique and hierarchically ranked. This ideological move was not a communitarian or holistic one, but one of projecting the (modern) categories of the individual, now biologically understood, onto the social whole. Thus, in Nazi ideology the community (Volksgemeinschaft) was not seen as an independent social whole as Herder would have had it, but as a biological individual writ large.

Dumont contrasts this kind of German methodological individualism with Durkheim's holism, where the social is prior to and independent of the individuals. Further, he claims that Durkheim's distinction between mechanical and organic society parallels Tönnies's distinction between Gemeinschaft and Gesellschaft. Viewed empirically and comparatively in France and Germany, France made this transition to "modernity" by imagining itself in terms of the universalistic concept of "nation," while Germany stuck with the particularistic concept of "Volk." Nazi ideology, then, represented community in social Darwinistic terms, as "the struggle of all against all," in other words, as a game of power with no transcendent social whole independent of this game of will to power. Since the real struggle, for Hitler, is one of biological individuals, Dumont concludes that "individualism is enshrined at the heart of Adolf Hitler's worldview" (1986: 172). By extension, Hitler understood the Volk as a natural or racial category, as "the only valid foundation of the global society and virtually the only cause in history" (1986: 175).[14]

What race does for Hitler's theory of nature and history, the hetero "sex instinct" does for Orwell, and self-interest does for Kirkpatrick. All three ideologists reject holism, and elevate to a virtue biologistic or naturalistic explanations of the individual, which then becomes the base of their authority.[15] Community, in turn, is viewed as an "antinatural factor that deflected history from its normal course" (Dumont 1986: 176). And although both Orwell and

Kirkpatrick appear to be fighting totalitarianism, they are, much as Hitler was, "infected with the poison [they] pretend to be fighting" (Dumont 1986: 176). For Kirkpatrick, any holistic representation of public good disintegrates in the confrontation with her misrecognized individualism. "Politics is based on self-interest," she writes, maintaining that "the pursuit of individual purpose is socially beneficial"(1973: 60).[16] Her conclusion is telling: we must above all "protect our national interests" (1986:11), whose "authority rests on force as well as consent." When she asserts that "patriotism is a social virtue" (1973: 60), she has effectively effaced the distinction between community and individual, so that instead of a dialectical movement between the two we have an isomorphic and essentialist (mis)identification of one with the other. A naturalized "self-interest" or greed is both cause and effect of "national interest." Although her ideology of self and national interest is not foregrounded in race, neither was Germany's ideology of the Volk before 1918. Thus, the danger of this type of Rational Actor Theory (RAT) model of thought, which is, after all, extremely influential if not the dominant paradigm in the "scientific" social sciences as well as in theories of international relations, lies more in the uses to which this kind of logic lends itself than in the more narrow conclusions any of its proponents may draw in their own work.

We can return now to our other two reactions to the East German regime, both of which have more to say about resistance than the example of Günther Krause, who, like Kirkpatrick, identifies self-interest with national interest with community. Both poet/singer Wolf Biermann and poet/artist Sascha Anderson fashioned themselves as dissidents, and thus were, in temporal succession, darlings of the West German media. Biermann followed in the footsteps of communist and human rights advocate Robert Havemann, who was imprisoned with Erich Honecker in a KZ during the Nazi period and later became the most outspoken dissident in East Germany. In the early '70s Biermann was banned from singing on stage in the East, and in 1976 was exiled to West Germany for singing his oppositional songs (officially called: "enemy propaganda") while there on a tour. He did not confuse his sex acts with resistance, and neither did the Stasi. Nor did he think that they were necessarily about love. Rather, for Biermann music and poetry constituted the form of his resistance. On the other hand, the state, in its romantic relationship with Biermann, thought of sex as an instrument to create love.[17] Thus, as Biermann reports, the Stasi tried constantly to seduce him, sending him beautiful women, even adolescent girls. And if they couldn't entice him, they tried to get his female partner, sending her a tall, dark-haired "lady's type," with the instructions, "You are to develop a real romantic relationship" (Biermann 1992: 184). From the transcript based on a bugged sex act—the bug was apparently under Biermann's bed—we obtain the following Stasi description: "Wolfgang Biermann engaged in sexual intercourse with a woman. Later he asked if she was hungry. The woman explained that she would enjoy a cognac. It is Eva Hagen [Nina Hagen's mother, jb]." The Stasi seemed especially pleased by the result of this sex: "After that the object is quiet (ist Ruhe im Objekt)." Indeed, that is what they wanted, Ruhe im Objekt, and if it took hetero sex to do that, then all the more such sex for Wolf Biermann.[18]

In one of his songs from the mid-seventies, Biermann (1992: 181–182), in turn, articulates his romantic relationship with the Stasi.

Menschlich fühl ich mich verbunden	On a human level I feel connected
Mit den armen Stasi-Hunden	With those poor Stasi guys
Die bei Schnee und Regengüssen	Who in snow and pouring rain
Mühsam auf mich achten müssen	Must painstakingly watch my every move
Die ein Mikrophon einbauten	Who installed a microphone
Um zu hören all die lauten	In order to hear all the loud
Lieder, Witze, leisen Flüche	Songs, jokes, quiet curses
Auf dem Klo und in der Küche	On the john and in the kitchen
Brüder von der Sicherheit	Brothers from security
Ihr allein kennt mein Leid	You alone know what I suffer
Ihr allein könnt Zeugnis geben	You alone could bear witness
Wie mein ganzes Menschenstreben	To all my human strivings

203

Leidenschaftlich, zart und wild	Passionately, tender and wild
. . . Und ich weiß ja: Hin und wieder	And I know full well: Now and then
Singt im Bett ihr meine Lieder	You sing my songs in bed
Dankbar rechne ich euchs an	For which I'm glad to give you credit
Die Stasi ist mein Ecker-	The Stasi is my Ecker-
Die Stasi ist mein Ecker-	The Stasi is my Ecker-
Die Stasi ist mein Eckermann.	The Stasi is my Eckermann.

Johann Peter Eckermann was an assistant and close confidant to Goethe. After Goethe's death, he published their conversations, eulogizing and mythologizing the man. Likewise, Biermann portrays the Stasi to be his confidant/confessor. For him, they are everywhere, recording his every thought and act. Indeed, over the course of Biermann's life in the GDR, the seventy individuals assigned to spy on him wrote more than 100 books, over 40,000 pages worth of reports about him. While still in the GDR, he portrays himself in a romantic relationship with them: "You alone know what I suffer . . . all my human strivings—passionate, tender, [and] wild." But he does not confuse his human strivings with resistance. For Biermann, resistance is his music, where he makes public and transparent the structure of authority.

Nonetheless, the Stasi, also viewing the relationship as a romance, is stung by Biermann's ironic distance from its love. Always trying to record the latest versions of his songs, they project onto Biermann's representations their worst nightmares of themselves. With bugs under his bed and agents following his concerts, the Stasi has numerous transcriptions of his lyrics. And like an expectant but insecure lover, they note every change in semantics, tone, intention, longing for the parapraxis that would be the window to his soul. Yet, instead of understanding themselves as the confessor/ confidant of Biermann—as he understands them—they hear in the last three lines of this song, "Die Stasi ist mein Henkersmann" (my executioner) as well as "Die Stasi ist mein Echomann" (my echo). If Biermann felt forced to flaunt more openly and aggressively his opposition, the Stasi increasingly heard in this expression reinforcement for its own paranoia and anxiety. The Stasi reaction was to engage in "die Zersetzung": a policy of systematic demoralization, subversion, and decay of the lifeworld of those it defined as its other.[19] Divorce followed. Biermann was "ausgebürgert" in 1976. He moved to Hamburg, which distanced him spatially from Berlin and enabled him to continue singing virtuous protest songs untainted by happenings in the East.

This was not the case with poet/artist Sascha Anderson, my first contact in East Germany in 1984. I was referred to Anderson by a West Berlin author who was employed by the Protestant Church and barred from travelling in the East because he had published a book of interviews with East German youth entitled, *Null Bock auf der DDR*, literally, *Fuck the GDR*. Since the early eighties, Anderson had become the leading figure among a group of artists, poets, writers, ceramic artists, potters, and hangers-on in the Prenzlauer Berg section of East Berlin. To the extent that there was an alternative scene and publicized resistance to the regime, it was in Prenzlauer Berg, and Anderson was the leading figure. In 1986, he was arrested and exiled to the Federal Republic for "treason" and for organizing "activities against the state." He resettled in West Berlin. During his last ten years in the GDR, he had been publishing his poetry, along with the work of other artists, in what might be called small-batch, private collector production, without going through the state system of censorship and publishing. For this activity, he was, in the late seventies, apparently beaten by the Stasi, and, in the following years, repeatedly harassed, picked up for interrogation, and threatened with his life. Since the publication of some of the Stasi files in the fall of 1991, it has been revealed that he wrote rather complete reports on his friends and fellow artists for those meetings with the Stasi, that, in fact, the Stasi considered him one of their own, an IM, unofficial co-worker.

In this combination of poetry and espionage, Anderson is part of a long tradition of poets—for example, Geoffrey Chaucer, Christopher Marlowe, Sir Walter Raleigh, William Wordsworth, Whittaker Chambers—whose affinity for the micro-meaning of the word was matched by an equal attraction to the macro plots of politics and power. Anderson's place in this lineage is perhaps singular in that he saw his relation to the state and society in what I would call

205

postmodern terms.[20] Like other Prenzlauer Berg artists at that time, he had read some of the works of French poststructuralists, illegally smuggled into the GDR, and had formulated a new stance, a new relation, to authority, to self, to the possibilities for freedom. In contrast to Anderson's postmodernism, Biermann's stance is decidedly modern. Biermann is celebrated for his originality; Anderson worked with forms of pastiche. Biermann's texts are concerned with semantics or meaning and purpose, determinacy, universalism, ethical questions from a God the Father position of moral authority. Anderson's texts are concerned with rhetoric and play, indeterminacy, particularism, aesthetic problems from a position of pluralistic otherness. Whereas Biermann's concentrated, redemptive writing is also marked by a paranoia about power, Anderson's dispersed, stagey prose is marked by a personal schizophrenia.

Anderson's cultivated schizophrenia is, however, not merely a stance. It also leads him into several contradictions. On the one hand, he realized, as Foucault would put it, that to enter a discourse is to enter a system of domination, to speak is to use words already assigned meaning in a system of power relations. There is no escape from the "prisonhouse of language." Thus, he writes in a recent poem, "DIE EINZIGEN DIE NICHT BEIM STASI SIND SIND DIE DIE DABEI SIND." (The only ones who are not with the Stasi are those who are with the Stasi.) (Steinert 1991: 57). And in the self-introduction to the collection of GDR poets entitled "Bestiarium literaricum," he plays with his duplicitous role, describing himself as "etlicher Spezies Schreiber aus der Fauna der Assoziativen Finalpoesie der blasseren Hälfte Berlins und Umgegend oder Morphosophistische Travestie . . ." (Some species of writer from the fauna of associative final poesy of the paler half of Berlin and vicinity or morphosophistic travesty.) Since the revelation that he worked for the Stasi, Anderson has argued that he spoke occlusively, in an aesthetic or poetic mode that made the information less capable of being instrumentalized.

On the other hand, Anderson admits that he was so uncomfortable working within this system that his foremost thought was of getting out: "aus dieser Scheiße rauskam" (get out of this shit). "Das ist vor allem das Gefühl: nur raus. Man will einfach nur raus aus der Sache" (More than anything else it's the feeling: just get

206

out. You just simply want to get out of the thing). "Die haben mit ihre Schlüsseln geklappert, und ich wollte nur noch raus" (They would jangle with their keys, and I just wanted to get out). At times he even goes so far as to describe himself as actually outside the system: "Wir waren doch damals an der Peripherie des Staates, frei von allen staatlichen Institutionen" (After all, back then we were on the periphery of the state, free of all state institutions). He insists, in a Foucauldian style: "I tried not to live in this system. Perhaps that was false. But it was a kind of self-defense. I thought, if I enter in to any particular system, in the system of the political lyric, in the system of the opposition, then I'll be faßbar (comprehensible/tangible)." "I worked against this state, in so far as I sang in public, for example, Biermann songs. But more important and more anti-state was to circumvent the censorship system. We weren't a union of authors, we weren't an indictable group. We had an infrastructure, a communication system that was against the state (staatsfeindlich). I hold to that. That's one of the few things in my life in which I've been successful" (cited in Radisch 1991: 17, 18).

Love and Difference

Indeed, that is our final question. Was he successful in resisting the state's "love offerings" and in creating a domain of autonomous action, and if not, who was? To be sure, we do not live in a heroic age; there are limits to the demands we can make on people to resist harassment or persecution. I can name on one hand the men or women of my acquaintance with Biermann's strength and integrity, who maintained a virtuous, completely oppositional stance. About one thing, however, we can be sure. The one type who in fact supported the system was the modernist accomodator, the romantic couple of the June Cleaver genre, the Winston Smith and Julia (No Surname), the Günther Krauses of the GDR. By pretending that a depoliticized private life and instinctual hetero sex were acts of opposition, and by reinforcing the public/private distinction, they in fact were the most complicitous group in a regime that relied on their quiescence.

The debate about what actually constituted resistance in the GDR has thus far consisted of acrimonious attacks not against the quiescent masses but the self-styled postmodernist resisters. Leading an attack against Anderson for his role of double agent for both the opposition and the state has been the dissident of another generation, Wolfgang Biermann.[21] In November 1991, Biermann attacked Anderson as "Sascha Arschloch," Sascha Asshole, in his speech accepting a prestigious literary prize. From a position of uncompromising moral integrity and unrelenting opposition to the regime, Biermann could see only betrayal in Anderson's complicity. Certainly Biermann is right in insisting that Anderson need not have submitted to working with the Stasi, and that in submitting, he undermined work of the opposition. But we must ask: was Anderson's opposition any less effective because the state helped to construct it? Or was it less effective because he betrayed his own theoretical premise of occlusion in writing succinct descriptions of his friends' activities for the Stasi. From the state's romantic perspective, creating an opposition was a necessary aspect of its form of authority: because it merely loved and projected that love onto its citizens without being able to register the reception, it needed a real opposition within precisely to articulate the difference between lover and loved which, in the imaginary, it in fact denied. The state also, of course, wanted a voice within that opposition.[22] Anderson's detractors would likely point out that his reports were often so detailed that they enabled the Stasi to subvert and divide the opposition. Anderson might respond that the opposition would have had no voice if they had only worked outside of, rather than also within, the state.

Furthermore, wasn't Biermann, the modernist resister, deluding himself that he operated outside "the system"? Didn't he obtain his shape, his integrity, only as a mirror-image, in contrast to and in negation of the authority of the state? Moreover, after he was forced into exile, not only did the society he so sought to change lose access to his voice, but his own music lost its mission and seemed a limp exercise in a nostalgic search for his old alter-ego, the East German state, which now denied his existence. I attended a concert of his in West Berlin in late 1988, approximately a year before the collapse of the regime, where I felt myself in a time warp. To be sure, Anderson, the postmodernist resister, was also forced to leave, in 1986, ten years after Biermann's exit. Yet even after his deportation, he continued undermining the distiction between outside and inside, working for the Stasi (and, presumably, for the opposition) in West Berlin—change of geography did not lead to a total loss of social context. Despite these important differences, I do not want to detract from an appreciation of the similar social role both men played as dissidents during their particular histories in East Germany. We should not lose sight of the way in which they both provoked reactions and repressions by the state. They forced the state to show that it relied on coercion for its legitimacy, which, in turn, revealed dangerous knowledge about the limitations of its control—and, I would argue, accelerated its loss of legitimacy.

We must also seriously question whether modernist resistance of the Biermann type would have been possible in the GDR of the eighties, for this period of High Detente was characterized by cooperation and increased interdependence between governments in the East and the West. Indeed, Thatcher and Reagan were not more receptive to their own dissidents than were Honecker and Ceausescu. And the strategy behind West German Ostpolitik, initially formulated by the Social Democrats in the late sixties but continued in the eighties by the ruling Christian Democrats, was to stabilize the East German regime in the expectation (correct, in hindsight) that it would lead to rapprochement and official liberalization in the East. Thus the "dissident" was neither an emic nor etic invention, neither merely a result of some autonomous free will nor merely a reaction to the dominant authority, but a complicitous category, a supranational product of Cold War competition between states and their nationals over the legitimacy of political representation. The same might be said about the Cold War internationalist origins of Orwell's hetero sex and Kirkpatrick's self-interest models, both of which, while intending to legitimate a parochial image of reality, were constructed with an inter-national audience in mind.

The end of the Cold War is likely to mean a universalization of forms of satiric authority, as well as an end to romantic authority and to forms of resistance tied to it, such as those of revolutionary action (see Touraine 1991: 121–141). With regard to resistance to romantic authority, we might conclude that if the modernist strategist reified the opposition and discreteness between official authority and dissidence, the postmodernist strategist fudged an important distinction. Reification by the former resulted in virtuous critique but ineffectual exile, ambivalence by the latter in staged opposition but cowardly complicity. It is unlikely that we will transcend these issues of morality in our present satiric state. And the dialectic of simultaneous complicity in and opposition to official authority, much as it engulfed the poet Sascha Anderson, will probably trouble us all, in the kitchen and in the university.

NOTES

I conducted the fieldwork on which this chapter is based between June 1984 and January 1992. It was funded in part by grants from Fulbright-Hays, the Krupp Foundation, the International Research-Exchange Board, the Social Science Research Council - Berlin Program for Advanced German and European Studies, and the MacArthur Foundation Peace Studies Program at Cornell University. I want to thank Jim Steakley for a close reading of the manuscript. All translations in the text are mine.

1. Mielke is not alone among East German leaders who reacted uncomprehendingly to the series of events removing them from power. Deposed leader Erich Honecker, for example, in interviews consistently expressed his sense of being betrayed (by the people he loved and served) rather than showing any signs of contrition. Also, see the interview with Alexander Schalck-Golodkowski, identified as Public Enemy Number One in the first six months after the opening of the Wall because of his role in creating wealth for the regime through international black market exchange, where he appeals to his "dream of a just society" and talks in romantic terms of his service to the people (Krause-Burger 1992: 3).

2. Here Orwell is undoubtedly relying on the folk theory of Nazi totalitarianism, which, it was assumed, was anti-sex except for procreative purposes. In the history of European communist states, Ceausescu's Romania comes closest to the Nazi model. But the other communist states, with few exceptions, were *initially* quite liberal with regard to sexuality, certainly more liberal than their "democratic, free" counterparts in the West. With the heating of the Cold War, they, including East Germany, became more pronatal, though not always antisex. For the East German regime, sex of all forms except that between adults and minors was accepted, if not openly encouraged, so long as it was either procreative,

remained private, contributed to a general depoliticization of public life, or reinforced public morals as defined by the state itself (See Sinakowski 1991; Borneman 1987; Obertreis 1985; Steakley 1977). Orwell's basic model was propagated by most other popularizers writing freedom stories during the Cold War. Perhaps the most successful of those who followed was Milan Kundera, writing from his safe exile in Paris (see especially his *The Unbearable Lightness of Being*).

3. To establish Katherine as lesbian is unnecessary for Orwell's argument. The key for his argument is her lack of an instinctual receptivity to men: that she "stiffens" when "touched" by a man. Representing the "frigid woman" as totalitarianism, unfreedom, and even treason, is of course, a cynical inversion of the usual representation of reality, for the "communist" type was associated most often with free love whereas the June Cleaver type was assumed most often to be chaste, if not cold, to men. In fact, Cleaver was also not always sexually *receptive* to her husband Ward in the TV series, but her affinity with Orwell's Julia, and distance from Katherine, lies in the fact that she is always sexually *compliant*. Julia is Orwell's ideal woman because of her nymphomania: she desires generic hetero sex, not merely with Winston, but with all men at all times.

4. Empirical studies do not support the other side of the equation, the claim that Western liberal republics have created and nurtured a protected "private" domain immune from official ideology and policy. The pattern in liberal states has been exactly the opposite: massive state intervention in the reproduction of the economy and direct links between state policies and the formation of preferred individuals and preferred family structures (see, for example, Balibar 1991: 86–105; Borneman 1992; Hobsbawm 1990; P. Sahlins 1989; E. Weber 1986).

5. The transition in Europe from a feudal to a liberal order mandated that political regimes find new ways of legitimating themselves. Replacing the ideology that certain rulers had the inherited right to rule over certain subjects, even to kill these subjects, was an ideology that the ruled had a right to determine their rulers in a relationship between themselves as citizen-nationals and their state. Thus, since the latter part of the eighteenth century, a new vision of a moral order of republican nation-states has supplanted the old feudal one, with the demand on rulers that they explicitly represent their legitimacy by regularly proving that they have "the consent of the governed" (see Giddens 1985: 201ff.; Skinner 1978). In the intervening 200 years, many variant forms of representing and legitimating this new link between nation and state have developed. But since 1945, these variant forms have been incorporated

into the two great modernist mythologies, structured roughly around an ethos of production (capitalism) and an ethos of egalitarian distribution (socialism), both of which have been concerned with the regulation of life. With the collapse of the bipolar world order in 1989, a clear victor has emerged in the competition over mythologies that legitimate rule. The productivist paradigm peculiar to liberal-capitalist has "won" over communism, the "free" over the "totalitarian" states, as the Cold War duality was represented—but precisely at a moment when the modernist paradigm of production and accumulation is being refigured around a postmodernist one of consumption and debt (see Harvey 1989).

6. Here, it is important to compare more concretely citizen-state relations as they were lived over time in the two types of totalitarian regimes, fascist and socialist (see Jäckel 1983: 39–43). In the German case, the argument is often made that East Germans were victims of a double dictatorship, and thus have lived a continuous history. This misleading claim ignores the following differences:

1. Hitler did not need a wall to keep Germans in, whereas, by 1952, East German head of state Walter Ulbricht had already lost much of his legitimacy, and the building of the Wall in 1961 seems, in hindsight, while not foreordained, certainly necessary at that time to save the regime.

2. Although Nazism, Stalinism, and East German socialism were all dictatorships (without free elections and public spheres) that transgressed human rights, minimally after the death of Stalin in 1953, the state terror associated with Stalin and Hitler (e.g., show trials, murders, sudden disappearances) was, with very few exceptions, absent in the GDR.

3. Nazi ideology is based on a thoroughly discredited race theory, whereas Marxism is a theory of political economy, written in support of socialist values of egalitarianism that are still respected today. To the extent that socialism was separated from democratic values (in other words, adoption of Leninism and rejection of the Rosa Luxembourg thesis), it increasingly resembled fascism.

4. Hitler and Stalin engaged in genocide, imperialism, and war to secure internal legitimation; the GDR did not resort to any of these means. In general, communist and fascist regimes seem to correspond to the contrast made by Todorov (1984: 143–145) between two types of civilization—sacrifice and massacre. The communist systems are of the sacrifice type, with a tendency to sacrifice the Other (i.e., class enemies) within themselves, therefore reli-

gious murder (of the heretical Other within) in the name of the official ideology. The Nazis are of the massacre type, with racial genocide against the foreign-identified (i.e., the Jew and gypsy), along with externally oriented imperialist tendencies.

Furthermore, current attempts to substantiate the totalitarian (continuity) thesis by equating East German socialism with fascism must also find ways of explaining away the continuities between West German liberal democracy and fascism. The West German state has consistently claimed continuity with the past in so far as it tied its legitimacy to carrying on the fight against communism that the Nazis had begun. At the same time, West German political leaders have sought, much as did the Nazis, to link the socialists to a generalized "evil Other." Thus, for example, in 1982 Chancellor Kohl and Ronald Reagan met at the Bitburg cemetery to honor the victims of the war. These victims included soldiers of the Third Reich along with members of the resistance and Jews. Were the dead in this cemetery victims of Nazism or communism? Later, Kohl went even further, comparing Gorbachev to Goebbels, a comparison he was then forced to retract. The fact that the West Germans never engaged in a thorough prosecution of Nazi crimes also is part of an explanation for why they are so vehement about dealing severely with the Stasi and Stasi co-workers (having let most Gestapo agents off the hook), and why they pursued Honecker in Moscow like they did not pursue Eichmann or Mengele in Argentina. Having failed in the first attempt at historical reckoning, they will do it right the second time around.

7. On this point, a Gramsci-inspired analysis would be allied with Kirkpatrick's. Gramsci's notion of hegemony would lead one to conclude that force and consent are simply two modes of the unstable relation between ruler and ruled used to obtain compliance to authority. True enough. As Coronil and Skurski (1991: 289–336) demonstrate in an analysis of political violence in Venezuela, force and consent ("violence" and "reason" in their text) are neither opposed nor do they chronologically follow one another, but are used simultaneously to construct the nation. My point, however, would be to stress that theories of hegemony ignore the consequences of prioritizing one mode over the other, distinctions that are extremely important for theories of agency, as well as for relations of rulers to the ruled. The individual would conceptualize a different sort of agency for him/herself depending on whether the regime assumed that force or consent was its *primary means of legitimating domination*. This alternative conception of self would in turn lead to possible restructuring of forms of authority. However problematic the notion of consent, a theory of democ-

213

racy becomes impossible if one conflates, as does Kirkpatrick, consent with force. Politics is thereby reduced to the notion of raw power.

8. Thus, the dichotomies Orwell and Kirkpatrick posit between public and private, state and citizen, freedom and totalitarianism, considered as essential intentions and identities of states and citizens, and not as relationships within the Cold War context, obscure more than they explain. In fact, their function is not in the first instance to describe or explain, but to engage in a present moral critique grounded in a past (traditional) authority. They are both satirists. The West German state resisted change until the early seventies, and throughout this period represented its youth as an ultimate source of decline. This youth, in turn, embraced experimentation, a trope that positioned it in opposition to the regime's emphasis on restoration. Slowly, the positions of both youth and regime changed in response to each other.

9. I am following Walter Benjamin here. He describes satire as "the only legitimate form of regional art" (1978: 260). Although satire represents itself as transcendental, unchanging, and in command of virtue, it actually adjusts constantly to the new—without ever acknowledging the shifts. Romance represents itself as materialist and changing, but ultimately pretends dynamism where there is none. Under the rubric of a virtuous critique, the West German state incorporated all difference into its very apparatus, assimilating the opposition ostensibly against its will. The East German state constantly rejected what it could not integrate, thus exiling its dissidents to West Germany. Under these conditions it became increasingly difficult to sustain its utopian illusions over time, yet, it could not turn to the West German strategy of affirming the moral superiority of the past. Even when, after 1965, the GDR began to sentimentalize marriage and the family, it idealized not a past version but what it had already achieved, culminating in its present. Proclaiming that the golden age had arrived only increased citizen dissatisfaction. Contrariwise, when the FRG finally began adopting infrastructural change after 1968, it did so under a grand coalition government with no admission of a break from its high moral grounds.

10. The circular logic of this argument—a genre that both structures relations and is structured by them—is similar to the socio-logic Bourdieu (1984; 1977) posits concerning the relation of the structures of the habitus to structuring dispositions. One caveat: I do not mean to imply that a single genre, used as an ideal type, is exclusively at work in any instance or in every domain. Rather, one genre assumes a priority over the others.

214

11. See notes 2 and 6.

12. Since unity, the new Federal Republic has shown consistency in its moral authority stemming from a satiric relation to its citizens by reinforcing the distinction between private (romance) and public (instrumentality). To date, the most severe sentence given to an East German spy has been to Gabriele Gast, a woman who infiltrated the West German domestic spy division, the Bundesnachrichtendienst (BND). She received a sentence of 6 years 9 months, whereas her superior received a sentence of 18 months with probation pending good behavior. Why? Her superior, Stasi Major Karl-Heinz Schneider' spied merely for instrumental reasons, as a paid employee in his service to the state. Ms. Gast, on the other hand, did not spy for reasons of finance or career—so the court concluded—but out of love for her superior. It was this confusion of categories that were supposed to be kept separate and pure—mix of instrumentality and love, public and private—that, for the West German justice system, proved so objectionable (see Sechs Jahre . . . 1991: 5).

13. Dumont's brilliant analysis of individualism stops short of critiquing what he calls "the fundamental distinctions of the modern world," in which he includes the public/private distinction. He accuses those who undermine this distinction of "barbarity" and being "totalitarian in spirit" (1986: 177). Mea culpa.

14. We can now also begin to understand a basic difference between Nazi and communist ideology in the relation of individual to community. The Nazis understood the community as the sum total of biological individuals; the communists saw community as constituted by, though not reducible to, different generations and occupationally defined selves. This difference is apparent in the prototypical art of the two ideologies: Nazi art reduced community to an exaggeratedly muscular and gendered individual, unsmiling, often stripped of clothing and standing alone; Socialist Realist art sought to represent a stylized, harmonized, happily working, fully clothed community (see Golomstock 1990). Current American predispositions to the cult of the body—such as aerobics and body building—draw directly on the same strain within modernist ideology as did the Nazis.

15. In defining the natural individual, each author comes up with a different version of the "other." For Hitler, the abstract idea of "Aryan race" is given content with the Jew as other; for Orwell, the abstract idea of "instinctual sex" and "instinctual parenthood" is given content with the socialist "Party" and homo sex as other; for Kirkpatrick the abstract idea of "self-interest" and "national interest" is given content with "Marxist

215

revolutionaries" as other. In each case, what they designate as alien and prior obtains its coherence only by means of a repression/denigration of the marginal or deviant term. To paraphrase two of the insights of deconstruction: the other is always already there, and understanding this deviant other is a condition of understanding the supposedly prior center.

16. In all fairness, I must note some movement in Kirkpatrick's ideology over time. In a 1979 article, shortly before she switched political parties from Republican to Democrat, she notes that "the Republican Party has not articulated any inclusive vision of the public good that reflects concern for the well-being of the whole community" (1979a: 34). She admonishes Republicans to go "beyond espousing private virtues" (1979a: 35). Yet, in her later work (1986; 1979b) she drops this demand altogether.

17. While the East German state and society clearly encouraged hetero sex, its relation with forms of sexual alterity was indeed ambivalent. GDR law in fact, when compared to law in West Germany or the United States, was consistently as or more tolerant about all forms of sexual expression. Yet social attitudes, which also found expression in public institutions (e.g., sex education, schools, television, film production, licensing of bars), most often resisted a liberal interpretation of the law (see Borneman 1991; Steakley 1977). The East German Stasi, often considered a state within the state, actually used the social stigma of and discrimination against homosexuality to its benefit. It recruited gay men as co-workers, convincing them that, in the words of Andreas Sinakowski, who was recruited at the age of nineteen and worked with the Stasi for five years, they were "human beings, just like anyone else, only perhaps more attention was paid to them." Sinakowski, who carried the double stigma of Jew and homosexual, actually gained a positive identity denied to him by the wider society by informing for the secret police. "I felt assured," he states. "[But] by 24, I was so nuts, so schizophrenic, I thought I'd never get myself together again" (cited in Tagliabue 1992: A4).

18. Among the interlocutors to whom I am addressing this chapter, I would like to particularly point out the misleading, ideologically motivated coverage of Germany by *The New York Times*. In a recent article by Stephen Kinzer (1992: 24–52), the Bonn bureau chief of *The New York Times*, that summarizes published German accounts of these events, Stasi stories are renarrated as Orwellian nightmares—thus obscuring, as do Orwell, Kirkpatrick, et al. public and private, hetero sex and resistance. Big Brother ("[a] frightening pathology [sic] of the men who led East Germany" [1992: 27]) is portrayed as anti-family and anti-hetero sex: it "sought to break up their marriage and turn their friends and even their

216

young son, Jonas, against them" (1992: 42). One seemingly minor example that illustrates the theoretical consequences of this emplotment: To skew the American reception of Biermann's files, Kinzer translates the phrase cited above, "ist Ruhe im Objekt," as "Then it was quiet inside" (1992: 27). This translation presents the reader with a set of misleading associations. The "Objekt" to be quieted is not an outside opposed to inside but Biermann himself in his "private life" in order that he not act in "public life." Kinzer leads one to conclude that the Stasi wanted to destroy the family and hetero sex life of East Germans, whereas Stasi intrusions into domestic life were not an end in themselves, but meant to discourage involvement in public life.

19. "Die Zersetzung" was a popular term during the Nazi period, used to denigrate Jews. For example, the Jewish Geist was "zersetzend": nihilistic, degenerate, critical without contributing to harmony.

20. Anderson is one of many prominent "dissidents" who were discovered to have worked both in opposition to and with the Stasi. Among the more well-publicized figures: Heinrich Fink (a theologian and peace movement leader who was elected rector of Humboldt University in 1989; widely respected as an independent spirit in the East, Fink had apparently for many years written reports for the Stasi; he was fired in December 1992); Knud Wollenberger (who had spied on his wife Vera and other members of the leading independent human rights/ecology movement in the eighties); Manfred Stolpe (a leading figure in the Lutheran church in the East, elected as Minister-President of Brandenburg-Vorpommern in the new FRG; as part of his former job, he had continuous conversations with the Stasi). American media portrayal of these figures has been consistently misleading. For example, Kinzer calls Anderson "ultra-hip", a self-described "anti-political anarchist" (1992: 50), without placing him in the inter-national context of 1980s "dissidents", as he was known during that period.

21. Biermann's attack is reminiscent of Hannah Arendt's (widely criticized) virtuous critique of Jewish authorities for their cooperation with the Nazis in their own extermination. The Nazis regarded this cooperation as the cornerstone of their Jewish policy. They even supported the notion of Jewish "autonomy" in running the concentration camps, so that at Theresienstadt, as Arendt (1964: 123) points out, "even the hangman was a Jew." Under these circumstance, one must question the sense of total resistance, which, though of course always possible, is perhaps not an efficacious strategy.

22. Peter Hohendahl (1992) has suggested that writers and poets like Biermann and Anderson functioned as essential mediators between

the people and the Stasi, giving voice to the people which the Stasi in turn tried to control, direct, transform, tranquilize. Thus, the space in which poets and writers worked in socialist systems was quite different than in liberal democratic republics, and must be understood in its own context.

REFERENCES

Adorno, Theodor
    1984. *Minima Moralia*. E. Jephcott, trans. London: Verso
Arendt, Hannah
    1964. *Eichman in Jerusalem*. New York: Penguin Books
Balibar, Etienne
    1992. The Nation Form. In *Race, Nation, Class*. E. Balibar and
    Immanuel Wallerstein, eds. New York: Verso
Benjamin, Walter
    1978. *Reflections*. E. Jephcott, trans. Peter Demetz, ed. New
    York: Harcourt Brace Jovanovich
Borneman, John
    1992. *Belonging in the Two Berlins: Kin, State, Nation*. Cam-
    bridge: Cambridge University Press
    1987. Sexual Aufklärung and Sexual Practices in the German
    Democratic Republic. In *Homosexuality, Which Homosexuality?
    Conference Papers, Social Science Vol. 2*. Amsterdam: Free
    University
Borneman, John, ed.
    1991. *Gay Voices From East Germany*. Jürgen Lemke, German
    author. Indiana: University of Indiana Press
Bourdieu, Pierre
    1984. *Distinction: A Social Critique of the Judgment of Taste*.
    Cambridge: Harvard University Press
    1977. *Outline of a Theory of Practice*. Cambridge: Cambridge
    University Press
Coronil, Fernando, and Julie Skurski
    1991. "Dismembering and Remembering the Nation: The Se-
    mantics of Political Violence in Venezuela." *Comparative Stud-
    ies in Society and History* 33: 288–337
Doerner, William R.
    1985. "A Dazzling Array of Opportunity." *Time*, June 17, p. 16

Dumont, Louis
    1986. The Totalitarian Disease: Individualism and Racism in Adolf Hitler's Representations. In *Essays on Individualism: Modern Ideology in Anthropological Perspective*. Pp. 149–182. Chicago: University of Chicago Press.
Giddens, Anthony
    1985. *The Nation-State and Violence*. London: Macmillan
Golomstock, Igor
    1990. *Totalitarian Art*. New York: Harper Collins
Harvey, David
    1989. *The Condition of Postmodernity*. London: Basil Blackwell
Hobsbawm, E. J.
    1990. *Nations and Nationalism Since 1780: Programme, Myths, Reality*. New York: Cambridge University Press
Hohendahl, Peter
    1992. Restructuring the Public Sphere: The Politics of Contemporary Germany, Public lecture, Society for the Humanities, Cornell University, March 5.
Jäckel, Eberhard
    1983. "Die doppelte Vergangenheit." *Der Spiegel* 52 (1991): 39–43
Kinzer, Stephen
    1992. "East Germans Face Their Accusers." *The New York Times Magazine*, (April 12): 24–52
Kirkpatrick, Jeane J.
    1986. *The United States and the World: Setting Limits*. The Francis Boyer Lectures on Public Policy. Washington, D.C.: American Enterprise Institute for Public Policy Research
    1979a. "Why We Don't Become Republicans." *Commonsense*: 27–35
    1979b. "Dictatorships and Double Standards." *Commentary* 68 (5): 34–45
    1973. "The Revolt of the Masses." *Commentary* 55 (2): 58–62
Kligman, Gail
    1988. *The Wedding of the Dead*. Berkeley: University of California Press
Krause-Burger, Sibylle
    1991. "Manchmal treibt ihm die russische Seele Tränen in die Augen" (Sometimes his Russian soul puts tears in his eyes). *Der Tagesspiegel*, (December 31): 3
    1991. "Leere Hülse." *Der Spiegel* 51

219

Lindholm, Charles
>1988. "Lovers and Leaders: A Comparison of Social and Psychological Models of Romance and Charisma." *Social Science Information* 27 (1): 3–45

Orwell, George
>1983. *1984*. New York: Harcourt Brace Jovanovich

Radisch, Iris
>1991. "Das ist nicht so einfach." *Die Zeit* 45, 111.8.91

Sahlins, Peter
>1989. *Boundaries: The Making of France and Spain in the Pyrenees*. Berkeley: University of California Press

Skinner, Quentin
>1978. *The Foundation of Modern Political Thought*, 2 vols. Cambridge: Cambridge University Press

Steakley, Jim
>1976. "Gays Under Socialism: Male Homosexuality in the GDR." *The Body Politic* 29: 15–18.

Steinert, Hajo
>1991. "Die Szene und die Stasi." *Die Zeit*, p. 57

Der Tagesspuegel
>1991. "Sechs Jahre und neuen Monate Haft für 'Spionin aus Liebe': Urteil des Bayerischen Obersten Landesgerichts in München." *Der Tagesspiegel* (December 20)

John Tagliabue
>1992. "Game is up, so informers inform on themselves." *The New York Times*, January 30, p. A4

Todorov, Tzvetan
>1984. *The Conquest of America: The Question of the Other*. New York: Harper and Row.

Touraine, Alain
>1991. The Idea of Revolution. In *Global Culture*. Mike Featherstone, ed. New York: Sage

Weber, Eugen
>1976. *Peasants into Frenchmen: The Modernization of Rural France, 1879–1914*. Stanford: Stanford University Press

White, Hayden
>1987. The Value of Narrativity in the Representation of Reality. In *The Content of the Form*. Baltimore: Johns Hopkins Press

8

Education after the Cold War: Remembrance, Repetition, and Right-Wing Violence

Measuring Successful Education

In 1966, Theodor Adorno wrote for German radio a manuscript entitled, "Erziehung nach Auschwitz," education after Auschwitz. In this essay, Adorno maintains that all considerations are secondary to the question about what to do to avoid a repetition of Auschwitz. "The barbarism [which he identifies with "the principle of Auschwitz"] continues," he writes, "as long as the conditions which might produce a relapse continue in their essence to persist." His goal is to isolate the mechanisms that made Auschwitz possible, and in this vein, he concludes, "the climate that is most supportive for a revival . . . is a reawakened nationalism." The role of intellectuals, he maintains, is on the one hand to educate children, and on the other, to engage in a "general enlightenment" that would "create a spiritual, cultural, and social atmosphere that would prevent a repetition. . . . The single, truthful force against the principle of Auschwitz," he continues, "would be autonomy, if I may employ the Kantian expression: the strength for reflection, for self-determination, for not-going-along." In fact, this last element, the willingness to work against the collective interest, is the one that

221

Adorno singles out as most important for the prevention of a repetition of the principle of Auschwitz.

I cite Adorno (1991) here because now, at the end of the Cold War, we are confronted with a problem similar to the one he faced following World War II and the Holocaust: how might one remember without repeating? How might one act so that the mechanisms responsible for particularly barbaric or grotesque episodes in our history do not repeat themselves? "Never again Auschwitz" indeed may ring a bit hollow in light of the kinds of massacres we have seen in Cambodia during the Cold War and the "ethnic cleansing" we recently witnessed in Rwanda and Bosnia. My comparison of the Holocaust with other, more contemporary genocides is not meant to deny its singularity, for, in the words of Saul Friedlander, it marks "some kind of outer limit of state criminality" (Friedländer 1993). But in order to prevent the operation of its "principle," that barbarism Adorno sought to identify, we should not wait until barbarism reaches "some kind of outer limit." And in the spirit of Adorno's conceptualization, the racial violence and genocide in Bosnia is, I think it fair to say without in any way relativizing or trivializing the horror of Nazi annihilation policies, the operation of "the principle of Auschwitz."

In Germany, the birthplace of "the principle," however, something has changed since Auschwitz (see Chapter 10). The argument often made that education in the two Germanies since 1945 has utterly failed is, I think, clearly wrong. I say this not to minimize the significance of the more than 2000 acts of violence perpetrated against foreigners in both 1991 and 1992, including the bombing and burning of homes for asylum seekers and the 17 murders by right-wing groups, of which eight of the victims were foreigners. Indeed, the Office of Constitutional Protection estimated at that time that political parties of the radical right in eastern and western Germany had about 40,000 members, of whom 6,000 were ready to use violence (Steiner *et al.* 1995: 1). Equally, if not more disturbing than these specific acts of murder has been the acceptance, often extending to support, of this violence by a large number of German bystanders.

Does this wave of violence illustrate a repetition compulsion? Ignatz Bubbis, Chairperson of the Central Council of Jews in Germany, recently put this violence into a different framework, concluding that it is an example "[not] of too many right-wing extremists, but [of] too few democrats" (Steiner *et al.* 1995: 2). Here Bubbis is observing from a decidedly West German perspective, which maintains that the proper response to fascism is more democracy. The official position in the German Democratic Republic (GDR) maintained that the proper response to fascism entailed the elimination of capitalism and antifascist education, especially in the schools (Borneman 1993).[1] Neither perspective, we might note, emphasized Adorno's prescription, that autonomy and resistance to "going along" was needed to prevent a repetition. From Adorno's perspective, these violent events and the reactions to them in the unified Germany would be a good test of successful postwar education. In the fall of 1992, several million East and West Germans demonstrated publicly their unwillingness to go along, organizing peaceful marches and demanding that politicians and police take resolute action to stop the violence. Following these demonstrations, politicians and significant numbers of relatively apolitical citizens have been spurred into action against this new wave of right-wing violence. This action alone did not stop the violence, though it did demonstrate an unwillingness to go along. One may criticize the kinds and effectiveness of the various responses, but let us for a moment remain with the mass rallies. If these demonstrations, with participants from the East and West, are indicative of a more autonomous citizenry, then what are they the result of? In what way did either "more democracy" or the "elimination of capitalism and antifascism" contribute to this result?

Today a "repetition compulsion," a further turn to violence in Germany—at its most extreme, like the scenes in Bosnia-Herzegovina —is extremely unlikely. This most recent violence in Germany was not a repetition of old antagonisms suddenly allowed to resurface but a new phenomenon, a product not of fascism and World War II but of the Cold War. Before going on, I want to emphasize that, despite the post-unification growth of neo-nationalist movements in Germany, the accompanying violence is not a product of "nationalism." Adorno had identified nationalism as the single factor most likely to bring about another Auschwitz. For Serbia and Croatia today, as well as for much of the former Soviet

Union, Adorno's analysis seems to hold true, that the resurrection of nationalism prepares the way for the principle of Auschwitz. In Germany, by contrast, unification has provoked a spirited debate on nationalism, its nature and history, its dangers and accomplishments. Nationalism has not become a mass rallying cry that unifies a majority against some externally hypostasized other, partly, I think, because of successful education over the last forty-five years.[2] The question remains, though, where exactly, when, and for what reasons has education been successful? And exactly what is the renewed violence in Germany a result of?

Education Oriented to the Past

If we agree that violence is not an individual psychological pathology but a cultural predisposition dependent on social mechanisms and a particular social milieu for expression, then our analysis of violence must be directed to these social mechanisms and milieu. And that milieu today is not simply post-Auschwitz but also post–Cold War. Hence, "education after Auschwitz" must be regarded as an ongoing historical task to which we must now add "education after the Cold War." My task, then, is considerably more modest than was Adorno's; it presupposes an extension of Adorno's analysis and not its completion.

In order to extend Adorno's analysis, we must first recognize that the origins and functioning of the Cold War cannot be attributed to nationalism, but rather, to three factors: a particular kind of supranational ideological, segmentary, bloc-building, a particular kind of symbiotic relationship between small, dependent client states and superpower, welfare-state needs, and exploitation of the perhaps universal human tendency to create mirror-images by projecting one's own lack or inadequacy onto others. The division of Germany and the "dual organization" resulting from it were not a planned or necessary consequence of losing World War II, and certainly not a penalty for "Auschwitz", which the Allies were only too eager to forget within a few years after the end of the war (Vollnhals 1991; Henke and Woller 1991). Rather, this division was a planned and necessary consequence of the Cold War (Borneman 1992; Staritz

224

1985). Resistance to the Cold War would have entailed, following Adorno's critique, reflecting on these factors and asserting autonomy with regard to the use and abuse of the mechanisms that made them possible (see Chapter 7). For the remainder of this chapter, I would like to focus on Adorno's prescription for behavior—failure to reflect and willingness to go along—among East German intellectuals during the Cold War, and thereby shed light on the conditions that made possible a Cold War, and on how one might educate so as to prevent its repetition. Finally, I will bring this analysis to bear on the Cold War origins of right-wing violence in the newly unified Germany.

I shall begin with the observation that the two arguably most influential postwar writer-intellectuals in Germany, the West German Günter Grass and East German Christa Wolf, have had difficulty reorienting themselves since November 1989. Both Grass and Wolf, we might note, became great writers in their personal confrontation with the mechanisms that made the Holocaust possible. *Die Blechtrommel* (The Tin Drum) by Grass and *Kindheitsmuster* (Patterns of Childhood) by Wolf were undoubtedly essential reorienting texts for several generations of Germans in East and West. They provided a new, critical reading of the German past and thus an opening to a new future. My point is, however, that neither author was able to follow his or her insights of the Nazi past with the same kind of analysis of either the Federal Republic (FRG) or the GDR during the Cold War. Both saw German division following World War II as a result and necessary consequence of German fascism and Auschwitz. Neither was able to see this division as a product of the Cold War, with its own mechanisms, strategies, and socio-logic. Hence, both authors viewed unification through a lens focused on the horrors of the past and the dangers of a repetition; this view simultaneously filtered out the opportunities for the present and future that might result if the Cold War ended.

Moreover, from today's perspective, the datedness of much of their work is attributable to the kind of ideological distancing they engaged in. By ideological, I do not mean loyal to the regime, *Staatsnah*, an accusation often made unfairly against Wolf, who recently admitted to writing reports for the state security in 1959 and 1960 (Wolf 1993). In fact, Wolf devoted much of her writing to a critique of actually existing socialism in the GDR. And Grass was a consistent critic of the Federal Republic. Rather, I mean ideology as thought "organized by a principle of occultation," as Claude Lefort writes, "thereby suppressing all the signs that could destroy the sense of certainty" (1986: 202–203). Grass and Wolf wrote as if they possessed a knowledge of the past—objectifiable, fixable, other—that arose from its own order of things, dependent on a distance between themselves and this history. This distance constantly reinforced a view that their own ideas could supposedly objectify and make intelligible the Nazi past as an isolable period of history. In any case, Grass and Wolf belong to a generation that oriented itself and derived its moral authority from its ability to respond to its collective past, primarily World War II and the Holocaust, as if they were on the side of good and as if this past were the embodiment of evil. Their acute ability to reflect on the past, on 1933–1945, was thus not matched by an equal acumen in reflecting on the present, on 1945–1989, precisely because their generation did not have, and could not create, the "distance" necessary for the same kind of analysis of their present. For the majority of Germans, who are minimally twenty years younger than either Grass or Wolf, the period 1933–1945 no longer remains the point of orientation. For younger Germans, both authors provide few insights for life after 1989.

Cold War Education in the German Democratic Republic

To understand why this is so, one would have to analyze the interaction of West and East German intellectuals as they constructed themselves as separate *Szene*.[3] Here, I will narrow my focus to East German intellectuals and analyze separately three generations who were active in the Cold War. I follow a typology made by Rainer Land and Ralf Possekel in a recent monograph (Land and Possekel 1992). The first generation of intellectuals in the former GDR is presently of Erich Honecker's age or older, in other words, most members are no longer living. This generation of intellectuals—and here I am limiting myself to those in or near positions of

226

power, e.g., Johannes R. Becker, Anna Seghers, Stefan Hermlin—was composed mostly of committed communists. Its members experienced class conflict at the end of the Weimar period, often worked in the antifascist resistance, and suffered under or at least encountered and had to make an arrangement with Stalinist repression either in the USSR or later in East Germany. They returned to the Soviet Zone and contributed to the early building of the state. This generation produced very few dissidents (the most well-known being Robert Havemann, Wolfgang Leonard, Stefan Heym), because most had been trained in the habit of obeying Party discipline, which was assumed to transcend individual or national interests. Those who worked close to Walter Ulbricht, and later Honecker, leaders who themselves were by no means intellectuals, were afflicted by what we might call the Kissinger-effect, of maximizing the principle of proximity to power as an end in itself, irrespective of the content of this power. Those unwilling to serve the repressive apparatuses of the state tended to remain silent rather than disobey the Party. Land and Possekel have referred to this arrangement as one of "'communicative' silence" (Land and Possekel 1992: 18). It was precisely this communicative atmosphere of taboos, marked by agreed-upon silences, that increasingly characterized the behavior of this generation of intellectuals as the GDR and the Cold War took concrete form.

This generation was the last to work in the nineteenth-century tradition of intellectuals. West German sociologist Wolf Lepenies has characterized intellectuals generally—I would restrict his schema to those educated before World War II—as torn between melancholy and utopia. He writes that intellectuals tend to be critical and dissatisfied, constant complainers about present conditions. They tend to "suffer, correctly, on the condition of the world," and thus have a basically melancholic temperament (Lepenies 1992: 14). Alternately, writes Lepenies, in order to escape melancholy, they think up utopias. For this pre-war generation of intellectuals, the melancholy was replaced with hope as they worked to realize a socialist utopia in the GDR. But this utopia had already clearly gone adrift by the early 1950s. What held it on course—in the minds of these intellectuals—was, on the one hand, Party discipline, and on the other, a conviction that they were committed antifascists and thus involved in negating the principle of Auschwitz. Party discipline supposedly steered people in a progressive, future direction. And the halo accompanying the antifascist self, an identification with the Soviet Union as victims of fascism, sealed one off from having to think about the past.[4] Both mechanisms, Party discipline and identification with the antifascist Soviet Union, worked to foreclose consideration of and reflection about the specific nature of German fascism as well as about its further reproduction in the GDR. These mechanisms fostered the illusion that the GDR and its people had been inoculated against potential strains of fascism. The avoidance of this ultimate evil, in the eyes of this generation, was sufficient to ground and justify both self and community. As we know with the benefit of hindsight, Party membership and antifascism tended to reduce *raison d'être* to *raison d'état*.

Moreover, for this generation of East German intellectuals, the Federal Republic served as the alter-ego of the antifascist. Since the FRG never thematized capitalism or antifascism, but instead represented itself as "democratic", the GDR responded by calling it "a merely formal democracy" compared to its own true democracy in the "better Germany." Sigrid Meuschel argues that this view made for a basic anti-Western attitude, resulting in a "symbiosis between antifascism and Stalinism" (Meuschel 1992). Critical intellectuals and the Party never coalesced into a protest movement for democratization in the GDR, as they did in Poland and Hungary in 1956 and in the 1980s, because, as Meuschel argues, the possibilities for social improvement of the disadvantaged classes were coupled to a subaltern position vis-à-vis Party nomenklatura. Hence, the "strength for reflection, for self-determination, for not-going-along," which Adorno had emphasized as the "single, truthful force against the principle of Auschwitz," was displaced onto resistance against an isolable past, making it unnecessary for this generation to reflect on their own postwar behavior or on the present.

A second group, whose members came of age in the 1950s, is commonly called the *Aufbau* [reconstruction] generation. They had experienced neither class conflict nor the communist idealism of their predecessors. Instead, the new state, the GDR, claimed to be founded in the interests of its youth, committed to create a "better Germany" through a reeducation its youth. Some of the members of this generation had graduated from the *Arbeiter und Bauern Fakultät* [worker and farmer faculty] set up to educate children from working-class and peasant families for positions of leadership. Indeed most GDR intellectuals were a new historical class; most came not from bourgeois but from working-class or lower white collar families. Ultimately, however, they exercised minimal power in the GDR, for the old Communists of the first generation continued to rule up to one month before the Wall came down.

Among Politburo members, for example, only Egon Krenz represented the Aufbau generation. A friend of mine who studied existential philosophy in the early 1980s knew the Krenz family well and told me the following story. He had had many conversations with Krenz, on many different topics. Once, in a discussion of Marxism, they reached a point where they were confronted with a direct contradiction between theory and practice in the GDR. Krenz replied to my friend, "When I am confronted with these situations, it is best to sit firmly in the saddle and hold the reins tight." Krenz, who can hardly be called an intellectual, nonetheless shared with intellectuals of this generation inherited taboos on public expression of opinion along with a sense of obligation to praise the Party in a kind of Orwellian Partyspeak in public discourse. The public domain in the GDR shrunk over the years, so that by the 1970s the realm of the social had become smaller and privatized. Günter Gaus coined the term *Nischengesellschaft* to refer to this retreat to and elaboration of the private sphere (Gaus 1985).

This second generation of intellectuals also shared with their elders a moral commitment to the state and to the East German society as a morally superior model and alternative to the Federal Republic. In their service to the state, they frequently employed a naive notion of knowledge equals power. Inspired by the idea of "scientific Marxism," they sought to discover the laws of nature and direct them to the benefit of humanity. Yet the knowledge that they put at the disposal of the state—primarily in economics, demography, education, psychology, administration, and political science—did not so much serve for general enlightenment, as many had hoped, but was often put to use by the state and its security apparatus, the Stasi, to make the exercise of authority more effective. Even for the state, this knowledge did not always lead to more effective administration. For

229

example, economists consistently misled Walter Ulbricht in the 1950s by propounding a theory that socialism would be able to *überholen ohne einzuholen*, overtake capitalism without having to catch up to it. Likewise, political scientists misled leaders of the state by propagating a theory that linked unproblematically capitalism to imperialism, and a theory of state legitimacy that assumed a reconciliation of democracy with the idea of dictatorship by an avant-garde Party. In short, knowledge often did not equal power. Instead, it more frequently served to legitimate faulty theories of order, planning, administration, psychology, education, and the like. And where knowledge was "correct," or *gesichertes Wissen* [secure knowledge], in East German terminology, as in the psychology or medicine employed by the Stasi to create fear or destabilize the personalities of suspected dissidents, it often worked against the long-term interests of East German society and merely in the interests of short-term state stability and a ruling elite from an older generation.

The state's reaction to what the most critical intellectuals of this generation said and wrote was either to isolate them within or exile them to West Germany. In exile, intellectuals like Rudolf Bahro and Wolf Biermann, for example, did not function as diasporic intellectuals waiting to return, widely read or heard in dissident circles in their country of origin (as was the case with many exiled Polish, Czech, Hungarian, and Russian intellectuals). Instead, they were integrated into certain Szene in West Germany and remained largely cut off from their potential audience in the GDR until the opening of the Wall.

In the late summer of 1989, as the consequences of Gorbachev's reforms became increasingly clear to the world, this Aufbau generation, along with a few critical intellectuals of a prior generation, began preparing and organizing itself to take over power from the old leadership. What prompted them to move quickly was the flight across the borders in Hungary and into the embassies in Eastern Europe mostly by members of a third generation of East Germans, intellectuals and non-intellectuals alike, who shared a common disrespect for and total lack of loyalty to the East German "project". The reaction of the different generations of intellectuals to this flight is rather telling.

Most of the generation of old Communists were unable to respond to this crisis. Their disorientation, in my opinion, was the basic reason why they lost their will to rule and continually capitulated to opposition demands in the summer and fall of 1989 without resorting to a "China solution" (Florath, Mitter, and Wolle 1992:238).[5] The writer Stefan Heym, one of the few dissidents among his cohort with an audience in the West and East, became a self-proclaimed spokesman for the East German "masses" in the Western media, in particular for *Der Spiegel*. He reacted to events in the fall of 1989 by calling for a proper education of the masses as to the socialist project, and later criticizing East Germans for their "cannibalistic lust" after consumer goods. For this message, he found only a tiny audience in the East. And in the West, he was criticized pointedly by the ex-GDR author Monika Maron, who had resettled in Hamburg, for intellectual arrogance and "disrespect of the people" (Maron 1993).

Members of the reconstruction generation who had organized the mass demonstration of between 600,000 and one million on November 4, 1989, in Berlin, also called for a reinvigoration of socialism. Like Heym, they also, following this demonstration, had problems finding an audience. Lepenies calls these people "heroes for five days," from November 4 to the opening of the Wall on November 9 (Lepenies 1992a). The real heroes, he concludes, are the thousands who fled into the embassies and across the Hungarian border. They were the ones who totally destabilized the regime and quickened its final collapse, and few among them were intellectuals.

Here we arrive at a controversial question with respect to the role of this third generation in the collapse of the GDR. Were those people who risked their lives and fled the GDR in September and October 1989, and who through 1992 continued to flee the ex-GDR at the rate of approximately 2,000 per week, heroes or victims of a false seduction? In other words, were they heroes for fleeing the GDR and precipitating the end of the Cold War, or was this more a cowardly flight to capitalism, a succumbing to the seduction of the sirens of Western abundance (see Borneman 1991; Chapter 4)? The vast majority of the people who engaged in this flight were, as I mentioned, members of a third generation of GDR citizens. And the intellectuals among them were predominantly children of the new social classes that were constituted by the Aufbau generation. They were without personal memory of the two world wars or the Third Reich. Instead, one might argue, they are complete products not only of the Cold War but also of "education after Auschwitz" in the GDR.

Education after Auschwitz

Land and Possekel divide the intellectuals among this third generation into a group of non-Marxists and a group that they claim is characterized by a mentality of "conspirative avant-gardism" (Land and Possekel 1992: 22–26). The non-Marxists, who formed the basis of what were in the 1980s called "Basisgruppen," attempted to work outside and often in opposition to the state; above all, they tried to "not-go along." They criticized the masses for being totally coopted by the state, the ruling Socialist Unity Party for being incapable of reforming itself, the state-recognized artists and intellectuals for being corrupted (in other words, trading acquiescence in return for travel privileges to the West), and the society in which they lived for being based on lies. Because the GDR's public domain had been so dramatically shrunken in size, the voice of this group of intellectuals and their critique had a small hearing among the people; they remained totally marginalized. Most members of the church and other, one might say, "normal" members (in GDR slang, *Stino*: stink normal) of the society actually disliked social critics. During my initial fieldwork, the GDR stumbled through a series of highly publicized confrontations with "dissidents" from 1987 to 1989. At that time I rarely heard expressions of support for the more radical system critics, such as Bärbel Bohley or Freya Klier. And those few who did express support and solidarity for the more radical opposition often stressed to me that they felt relatively isolated and were not part of a "silent majority" who thought differently. Hence, the younger critics in the GDR often relied on contacts with West German or "Western" intellectuals, myself included, for emotional and moral support, as well as to take their "voice" outside the confines of private gatherings in apartments, artistic happenings, or church-supported events. This

232

group of East Germans, I might add, is the one in which Timothy Garton Ash, who (along with Milan Kundera) was perhaps the "official voice" on Eastern Europe for the free West, cultivated an interest and to whom he gave voice in his reporting on East Germany and East Europe for *Granta* and for the *New York Review of Books* (Ash 1989, 1990). One of the problems with Ash's work is that he so closely identified with these dissidents that during the heady days of the collapse of East European regimes he was not able to put their voices in the larger context of a widespread social disapproval of critical positions and thus understand the weakness of dissident authority claims.[6]

Those intellectuals characterized by conspirative avant-gardism agreed with much of the critique of the non-Marxists, but instead of moving outside the state and Party, they developed a conspirative mentality to work in and around it. (Sascha Anderson, the dissident and Stasi informant, is perhaps the extreme example of such a mentality.) For example, many worked with the Stasi as IM, unofficial co-workers, because the Stasi was one of the few official institutions willing to address the taboo topics and problems of the society. It seemed as if the Stasi was genuinely interested in reform, whereas the Party and the state apparatus were controlled by an aging elite who categorically refused to acknowledge any problems whatsoever. The Protestant church and many of its members were also involved in this conspirative activity. In the 1960s, the leadership of the church made a new, cooperative arrangement with the state, yielding its staunch oppositional role in order to redefine itself as "the church in socialism." From 1990 to 1993, governmental and media investigations of Manfred Stolpe, the current Minister-President of Brandenburg and former representative elected by the church to deal with the state, came to revolve around the question whether his, and the church's, conspirative attitude actually made him, to use Lepenies's phrase, a hero or a betrayer of the people.[7]

To be sure, the flight across the Hungarian border was a heroic act insofar as it quickened the collapse of a non-democratic regime and the end of the Cold War. The fact that most people were motivated for this flight by hopes for a better material life should not, as I've written elsewhere, lead us to condemn them (Borneman 1992: 248–254). They sought what they imagined could be had but what they themselves lacked. How is a people supposed to know the value of political freedoms before they have experienced them? And even when the non-intellectual masses have experienced political freedom, this is no guarantee that they will grant it the value of an absolute. I would be more willing to condemn individuals who had already enjoyed bourgeois freedoms but then were willingly to give them up (a good number of examples in the United States come to mind) than I would be willing to criticize East Germans for not prioritizing freedoms that they had never experienced.

Some German intellectuals of what I have called the first and second generations have criticized this third generation precisely for fleeing the republic and thus in part being responsible for the negative consequences of unification. Certainly unity was rushed and many of the humiliations and actual harm suffered by East Germans could have been avoided. The brain drain from East to West and the takeover or closing of most publishing houses and newspapers, for example, have indeed made "self-realization" more difficult for most East Germans. East German intellectuals have felt singled out by the wholesale delegitimation of entire biographies, often on spurious grounds, such as having been a committed communist. Furthermore, they have been victimized by what many call *Siegerjustiz* [justice of the victors], which has accompanied *die Abwicklung* : the evaluation, closing, and dissolution of academies and research divisions in the universities (on justice, see Borneman 1993; Bisky, Huer, and Schumann 1993; on intellectuals, see Lepenies 1992; on the Truehand, see Christ and Neubauer 1991; Richter 1992).[8] At the same time, this official Abwicklung, this bringing to completion, has strengthened the *Schadenfreude* or *Besserwisserei* of the West German. Current East German intellectual humiliation and loss, however, are not intended results of the desire by the masses for bananas and automobiles and the right to travel in the West. It is not as if only workers and youth had an appetite for bananas and Mercedes; this taste is one they shared with adult intellectuals.

A more interesting question is: in what way did education in the GDR contribute to this flight? Specifically, what might we conclude from the end of the GDR about antifascist education? One must grant that, given the amount of right-wing violence in unified Germany, the success of "education after Auschwitz"—to be autono-

234

mous, to not-go-along—has been a limited one. Studies seem to show an equal percentage of youths in West and East with a positive attitude to the Nazi period, though the reasons for these attitudes are different. The West German political leadership had rejected the notion of "collective guilt," and ties to America and economic strength served as tropes against which one could distance oneself from the Nazi period. In the East, antifascist education became a pillar of identity. In 1988, for example, "resistance fighters" held 36,000 discussions with more than 1.6 million in attendance. In the 1980s, approximately 200,000 eighth graders in schools visited yearly one of three concentration camps, Buchenwald, Ravensbrück, and Sachsenhausen (Schubarth 1992).

Many observers have argued, as does Wilfried Schubarth, that the GDR discredited antifascism because the state "administered, instrumentalized, monopolized, and ritualized" it (Schubarth 1992: 173). But do not these characteristics hold for all formal education? Schooling is always for a purpose and thus administered and instrumentalized. Without denying the need for a more effective pedagogy to educate about fascism, there really is no evidence that this clumsy form of administered antifascism has caused right-wing violence. The cause of this violence is more likely to be found in the events surrounding the terms of unity itself, such as loss of authority due to the end of Cold War ideological props, or dislocations and uncertainties in lifecourse expectancies. And to the extent that millions of people oppose this violence (similar not-going-along was rare in the Nazi period), this also has to be attributed not to lessons of the Nazi period but to achievements of postwar education. I am most inclined to think that the GDR's education system, to the extent one can attribute cause specifically to it, produced not fascist behavior but cynicism and distance from all authority, therefore precipitating the kind of flight that occurred in the fall of 1989.

Education after the Cold War

I would add yet another defense for those who fled the areas of what was called the "East bloc" for what was and is still known as "the West." They reacted, and are reacting, to the finalty of personal destinies mapped out by the conservative regimes in the East and

235

to restrictions on freedom of movement of ideas and peoples—both central structures of the Cold War. The penetration of international borders, by ideas or people or capital, was always—especially by those in the East—an ultimate heretical act during the Cold War phase of the nation-state system. For many people in the West, tourists and businessmen being exemplary cases, this penetration was, of course, a privilege and "right" of living in the "free world." This old world order was an extension of and particular take on the Westphalian system of independent and sovereign, though insecure, nation-states. It was concerned with securing borders and boundaries, with formulating the rule and enforcing the law. In order to represent itself as a paradigm of security and order, the most active of the Cold War regimes actually fostered instability and insecurity elsewhere, among other peoples, as a mirror and justification for their own orderliness. In Europe, the social welfare state and the West-East divide (NATO versus Warsaw Pact) were the pillars of this order of closed societies, of group identities reassembled in a segmentary lineage structure where each side's self-definition presupposed the dangerous and anxious other. These identities were organized as national families in which all nationals enjoyed certain formal rights and predictable futures as legal subjects within a particular territory, joined to other nationals in higher order coalitions. While social welfare states characterized both East and West, the nature of the legal subject and his/her rights privileged those in the West over those in the East. And this West system of rights was able to maintain itself only with a basic asymmetry: all non-nationals or "aliens" who did not have access to these rules, and whose very inability to articulate with and express themselves in terms of the rules reassured Western legal subjects of their own reality and intelligibility, were legitimately excluded from these rights, these territories, and these futures.

The geographical movement of Germans from East to West, constant during the Cold War but accelerated after the summer of 1989, was not largely a response of the poor to their economic plight, nor of the persecuted to their lack of freedom—as a whole slew of American scholars in various disciplines would like to imagine (and as they are now being told by people of the East bloc in radically revised accounts of what life was "really like" before the opening). This movement is a fairly direct and immediate response to the collapsing Cold War order, more specifically to the inherent instability at the core of the West's system of rights and privileges. The new homelessness and dislocation throughout the former East bloc is also indicative of a more generalized condition of the new world order being constructed. This emerging order signifies, I would argue, not the end of the nation-state but of its specific welfare state form and of the East-West divide as structuring principles of the Cold War. The collapse of these two principles—of the welfare state and the East-West divide—has unsettled both domestic order and international relations, as has the dissolution of the Warsaw Pact and the disintegration of the set of alter-egos in the East. The decentering of rules and penetration of borders are no longer isolated or exceptional acts, as they were during the Cold War, for they are becoming new generative principles, acted out not merely by the resettlers from east to west Germany, nor merely by waves of refugees and asylum seekers, but also by national and supranational businesses and legal regimes. I am by no means original in emphasizing that the condition of homelessness, a new nomadism, has been long regarded as an adaptive reaction to Modernity (Deleuze and Gauttari 1977). As both people and capital increasingly resort to this adaptive strategy, homelessness is perhaps now entering a new stage. It is in this light that I see the East German "heroes": not as asserting autonomy in the Kantian sense, nor concerned with reflection or "not-going-along" in the manner that Adorno stressed. They asserted "exit," to employ a term from Albert Hirschman's much-abused framework of "voice, loyalty, exit" (Hirschman 1986). This exit caused a welcome collapse of a particular system of domination. But it also was part of a panic, a massive flight from a reflective self. It was not a "voicing" in Hirschman's sense, for voice formation, he writes, "depends on the potential for collective action" (Hirschman 1986). Unlike most of the participants in the demonstrations in Leipzig and East Berlin who were intent on reformulating the nature of the collective to which they belonged, those who fled were primarily motivated by a desire to assume an already-constituted voice elsewhere, that of the West German.

My intellectual defense of this flight necessarily ends here, for this flight was not only a rejection of fixity and Cold War order, but also a seduction by consumer culture and escape from a confrontation with one's historical self. Nonetheless, I cannot then identify with the critique lodged against these resettlers by some East German intellectuals. Rather, this younger generation of East Germans points intellectuals in a direction we must go in education after the Cold War. First, we must take seriously their critique of what they fled from—from the conditions of confinement, closure, and exclusion on which the welfare state depends, from the immobility imposed on them that was a precondition for the survival of the national insecurity state during the Cold War. And second, we must critique what they fled to—the phantasmic "civic culture" of the liberal West, with its elections, private life, and consumer culture. The creation of civic cultures is hardly a panacea for the world's problems. It solves neither intolerance nor poverty. Francis Fukuyama's prediction of an ideological consensus in favor of secular liberal democracy has proven to be a liberal conceit (Fukuyama 1992). The idea that democracy in its liberal capitalist form has become an ultimate form of governance serves to obscure the different understandings and uses being made of "democracy," "the people," "markets," and "privatization" for illiberal purposes. Many of the liberal regimes that replaced those "actually existing socialist" regimes in 1989 and 1990 have already become footnotes to a continuous history of displacements. Other than the staging of formal elections, some of these regimes no longer even pretend to democratic legitimation. Even in eastern Germany, the future of liberal capitalism and its relation to democracy remains an open question. Indeed, the sanctification of Chancellor Helmut Kohl, his reincarnation as the Bismarckian national father, suggests more a conflation of historical authority structures than a simple displacement of authoritarian into stable democratic form.

Let us return to my original question about right-wing violence and education after the Cold War. My major argument has been that this violence, in both the East and West, must be understood not as a repetition of repressed aggression and traditions rooted in "Auschwitz" but as generated by the disintegration of mechanisms that structured Cold War order. Racist and nationalist thinking in the GDR, which Schubarth identifies with "an accentuated ethnocentric superiority claim coupled with a massive fear and hate of foreigners" (Schubarth 1992: 177), are not "survivals" of the past, but regenerated forms of group belonging. They are being regenerated because of post-unity problems: lost orientation, fear of the future, economic and status insecurities growing out of present concerns.[9] Under these conditions, intellectuals have a responsibility to take insecurities—regardless of their "real" status or origin—seriously instead of demonizing or humiliating Ossis, or trivializing their concerns (Giesen 1993). Since most East German intellectuals have lost much of their authority, if not their jobs, this educational responsibility to provide orientation during a time of increased insecurity falls primarily to the West Germans.

As the mechanisms that structured authority during the Cold War crumble, remembering alone will not—either in locating the cause of violence or its solution—lead to new authority structures. These new authority structures that seek to manage conflictual and multiple identifications, are, in my opinion, being created within a new "regime of the market," with its emphases on mobility and exchangeability, where the local and global often work in tandem instead of in opposition. That this domain is one from which classical German intellectuals (Marx is, of course, an exception) have traditionally distanced themselves accounts in part for why they have had little to contribute. This leads the sociologist Bernard Giesen to argue that the compensatory role of Kultur, as formulated by the intellectuals that have made up German *Bildungsbürgertum* [educated bourgeoisie] for the last 200 years, is no longer necessary in a united Germany. He concludes that in the future "the field of this national identity will be determined by the bureaucracies of the ministries, where plans for the institutional reconstruction are drawn up and the costs of unity calculated, calculated anew and more or less artificially financed" (1993: 253–254). The problem with Giesen's formulation is that he assumes that national identity is solely a product of intra-national forces, whereas national identity has always been an inter-national affair, always constituted partly by (em)migration, inter-national exchange, and wars (Tilly 1990). By this, I do not mean to exaggerate the interconnectedness of the world, nor to minimize the significance of the role of German-identified actors in German affairs.

In my personal encounters with West Berlin intellectuals, as well as in my reading of essays and viewing of television talk shows and documentary and feature films, I have found the most frequent reaction to right-wing violence is one of alarm coupled with Schadenfreude. The joy over the other's harm is, of course, not joy over violence against foreigners, which everyone abhors, but a smugness about where the danger lies—elsewhere, particularly in the East, especially among disaffected non-bourgeois youth. For example, in a book of essays by West Berlin and West German authors entitled *Der rasende Mob. Die Ossis zwischen Selbstmitleid und Barbarei* [The Raging Mob. Ossis between self-pity and barbarism], satire is employed to critique rampant hatred of foreigners and self-pity in the East (Bitterman 1993). Yet one must ask why the authors (intellectuals?) stubbornly refuse to engage in any self-critique, why they cannot define a position for themselves as bourgeois (West) German intellectuals, 1992—except as the empty contrastive (and cool) sign to the abominable (and overheated) Ossis. "The most embarrassing thing about the GDR," writes Michael O.R. Kröher (1992: 12) in the opening essay, "is the people who live there." He of course means to be funny, but the question is: who is laughing at whose expense? Although it is perhaps too much to still expect a non-coercive exchange between East and West intellectuals, a minimal condition of future exchange would be a more reflexive stance than has been evident to date with regard to the mutual constitution of subjects during and since the Cold War. Intellectuals can and should regain a voice in this reconstruction by articulating and by self-reflectively positioning themselves with and against what are often misleadingly called the "common interests of the market."

NOTES

A shorter version of this chapter was initially delivered at a Social Science Research Council conference organized by Susan Gal, "Intellectuals in Political Life," February 12–14, 1993, Rutgers University. All translations from the German are mine unless otherwise noted.

1. This position can no longer be articulated because the terms of unification—e.g., threatened or actual unemployment, loss of audience, attacks on intellectual integrity, projected homogenization of East Ger-

man elites—have involved a great deal of silencing of East German intellectuals who expected to have a career in the unified Germany (see Chapter 4, this volume). For a documentation and analysis of an East German exhibit on the "myth of antifascism," see Kulturamt Prenzlauer Berg, ed. 1992.

2. Michael Geyer (1992: 75–110) has made a similar argument in an essay on "the stigma of violence" in twentieth-century Germany. Geyer writes that because difference in Germany "remained traumatically linked to the violent process of segregation, exclusion and annihilation in the Third Reich, . . . [postwar society was marked by] the inability to distinguish between violent exclusion and the play of difference." The 1980s mark a "moment of rupture" with "the national project as the pursuit of unity and coherence of the nation," by which he means the possibilities for "an opening for [either] a nationalizing expansion of the unitary ideal with its resulting exclusion of the unwanted and unfit [or] a chance for the discovery of the play of difference in German histories."

3. My omission of West German intellectuals from this analysis is in no way meant to infer that East German intellectuals were primarily or more responsible for the Cold War than West German ones. As Wolfgang Haug (1992: 284) has pointed out, criticism since unity has been "an illumination of a dead order of rule by a living one" rather than in how both sides were caught in the net of the Cold War. I have written elsewhere that East and West Germans during the Cold War were part of a "dual organization" formed through the interaction and asymmetrical exchanges between the two halves (Borneman 1992). An analysis of the specific role of West German intellectuals reaches beyond the scope of this chapter. It would differ fundamentally from my account of East German intellectuals. Because both generational conflict and forms of political authority were structured differently in East and West, opportunities for autonomy and mechanisms for change were also dissimilar.

4. I should note here that the West German identification with "America," "the West," and "American democracy" served a similar function, that of granting West Germans the illusion of immunity from fascism through distance from their specifically German national context.

5. See, for example, the analysis by Stefan Wolle (1992: 234–240) of Eric Mielke, former head of the State Security (Stasi), in the period as the regime's authority is disintegrating. Wolle concludes that in August and

September 1989, the documents "show [Mielke to be] a confused and help-less old man who no longer understands the world. He hangs on stub-bornly to his old thought and speech pattern and yet senses that his time has run out."

6. Ash (1990: 21) admits, "[E]ven here my account is largely from inside the opposition movements and from among so-called 'ordinary people' on the streets." Though he may have had a great deal of contact with "ordinary people" before the fall of 1989, his reportage after the fall of 1989 concentrates almost exclusively on public figures, in particular members of the various oppositions. It is the case that in all of the former East-Central European countries except East Germany, many of these very intellectuals whom he knew moved into positions of power in 1990. Yet between 1991 and 1993, most lost these positions.

7. The state security actually listed Stolpe as an IM, and even awarded him a bronze medal for service. Stolpe, however, insists—and is supported on this claim by his colleagues in the church and by his former contacts in the Stasi—that he never worked for the Stasi, and that if he had been an IM, he would have received for his service a gold instead of a silver medal.

8. A very vivid example of this confrontation with freedom is the case of Horst Klinkmann, reported by Rainer Frenkel (1993: 44). Born in 1935 and raised as an orphan, Klinkmann was an internationally ac-claimed researcher in the transplantation of artificial organs. He had been director of the clinic for internal medicine at the University of Rostock in the GDR, as well as guest professor in many foreign countries. In 1990, he was the first democratically elected president of the Academy of Sciences of the GDR, and thus the official discussion partner in the unification of the sciences in the two Germanies. In May 1992, he was dismissed from his post because of unproved suspicions that he had worked for the Stasi, as well as for activities as an SED Party member which supposedly com-promised his scientific work, resulting in "Fehlverhalten" (literally, errone-ous behavior).

9. See a similar explanation of West German violence by Jörg Bergmann and Claus Leggewie (1993: 7–37). They attribute the violence to young, unexceptional, fairly well-to-do bachelors who are motivated by present boredom. As the degree of security increases, the need for risk intensifies and materializes in a search for places "where the action is." This action is done not to achieve an end but merely to prove oneself in risky situations.

REFERENCES

Adorno, Theodor W.
  1993. "Erziehung nach Auschwitz" (repr.). *Die Zeit* 1:1–3
Ash, Timothy Garton
  1989. *The Uses of Adversity: Essays on the Fate of Central Europe.* New York: Random House
  1990. *The Magic Lantern: The Revolution of '89 Witnessed in Warsaw, Budapest, Berlin and Prague.* New York: Random House
Bergmann, Jörg, and Claus Leggewie
  1993. "Die Täter sind unter uns. Beobachtungen aus der Mitte Deutschlands." *Kursbuch* 11:7–37
Bisky, Lothar, Uwe-Jens Heuer, and Michael Schumann, eds.
  1993. *Rücksichten: Politische und juristische Aspekete der DDR-Geschichte.* Hamburg: VSA-Verlag
Borneman, John
  1991. *After the Wall: East Meets West in the New Berlin.* New York: Basic Books
  1992. *Belonging in the Two Berlins: Kin, State, Nation.* Cambridge: Cambridge University Press
  1993. "Uniting the German Nation: Law, Narrative, and Historicity." *American Ethnologist* 20:288–311
Christ, Peter, and Ralf Neubauer
  1991. *Kolonie im eigenen Land: Die Treuhand, Bonn und die Wirtschaftskatastrophe.* Berlin: Rowohlt
Clemens Vollnhals, ed.
  1991. *Entnazifizierung: Politische Säuberung und Rehabilitierung in den vier Besatzungszonen 1945-1949.* Munich: Deutscher Taschenbuch
Deleuze, Gilles, and Félix Guattari
  1977. *Anti-Oedipus: Capitalism and Schizophrenia.* Robert Hurley, Mark Seem, Helen Lane, trans. New York: Viking Press
Frenkel, Rainer
  1993. "Der Riss im Leben des Horst Klinkmann." *Die Zeit,* April 2:44
Friedländer, Saul
  1993. A Conflict of Memories? The New German Debates About the "Final Solution." In *Memory, History, and the Extermination of the Jews in Europe.* Pp. 22–41. Bloomington and Indianapolis: Indiana University Press

Fukuyama, Francis
1992. *The End of History and the Last Man.* New York: Free Press

Gaus, Günter
1983. *Wo Deutschland liegt: Eine Ortsbestimmung.* Hamburg: Hoffmann und Campe

Geyer, Michael
1992. "The Stigma of Violence, Nationalism, and War in Twentieth-Century Germany." *German Studies Review* Special Issue: 75–110

Giesen, Bernhard
1993. *Die Intellektuellen und die Nation: Eine deutsche Achsenzeit.* Frankfurt/Main: Suhrkamp

Haug, Wolfgang Fritz
1992. Die Wiederkehr des Unerwarteten. In *Erinnern, Wiederholen, Durcharbeiten: zur Psycho-Analyse deutscher Wenden.* Brigitte Rauschenbach, ed. Pp. 276–285. Berlin: Aufbau Taschenbuch

Hirschman, Albert O.
1970. *Exit, Voice and Loyalty: Responses to Declines in Firms, Organizations, and States.* Cambridge: Harvard University Press
1986. *Rival View of Market Society and Other Recent Essays.* Cambridge: Harvard University Press

Henke, Klaus-Dietmar, and Hans Woller.
1991. *Politische Säuberung in Europa: die Abrechnung mit Faschismus und Kollaboration nach dem Zweiten Weltkrieg.* Munich: Deutscher Taschenbuch

Kröher, Michael O.R.
1993. Nichts gegen die da drüben. In *Der rasende Mob: die Ossis zwischen Selbstmitleid und Barbarei.* Klaus Bittermann, ed. Pp 12–30. Berlin: Edition Tiamat

Kulturamt Prenzlauer Berg, ed.
1992. *Mythos Antifaschismus: Ein Traditionskabinett wird kommentiert.* Berlin: Ch. Links

Land, Rainer, and Ralf Possekel
1992. *Intellektuelle aus der DDR: Diskurs und Identität.* Berlin: Gesellschaft für sozialwissenschaftliche Forschung und Publizistik

Lefort, Claude
1986. *The Political Forms of Modern Society: Bureaucracy, Democracy, Totalitarianism.* Cambridge: MIT Press

244

Lepenies, Wolf
   1992a. *Aufstieg und Fall der Intellektuellen in Europa.* Frankfurt/M: Campus
   1992b. "Alles rechtens—nichts mit rechten Dingen." *Die Zeit,* December 11:87–88.
Maron, Monika
   1993. Das neue Elend der Intellektuellen. In *Nach Maßgabe meiner Begreifungskraft: Artikel und Essays.* Pp. 80–90. Frankfurt/Main: S. Fischer
Meuschel, Sigrid
   1992. Antifaschistischer Stalinismus. In *Erinnern, Wiederholen, Durcharbeiten: zur Psycho-Analyse deutscher Wenden.* Brigitte Rauschenbach, ed. Pp. 163–171. Berlin: Aufbau Taschenbuch
Richter, Wolfgang
   1992. *Weissbuch: Unfrieden in Deutschland: Diskriminierung in den neuen Bundesländern.* Berlin: Gesellschaft zum Schutz vom Bürgerrecht und Menschenwürde
Schubarth, Winfried
   1992. Antifaschismus in der DDR—Mythos oder Realität. In *Erinnern, Wiederholen, Durcharbeiten: zur Psycho-Analyse deutscher Wenden.* Brigitte Rauschenbach, ed. Pp. 172–179. Berlin: Aufbau Taschenbuch
Staritz, Dietrich
   1985. *Geschichte der DDR 1949–1985.* Frankfurt: Suhrkamp
Steiner, Susan, Megan Ratner, Thomas Hofmann, eds.
   1992. *The Week in Germany,* 12 November 1
   1995. *The Week in Germany,* 1 May 2
Charles Tilly
   1990. *Coercion, Capital, and European States, AD 990–1992.* Cambridge, Mass.: B. Blackwell
Wolf, Christa
   1993. *Akteneinsicht Christa Wolf: Zerspiegel und Dialog einer Dokumentation.* Hamburg: Luchterhand
Wolle, Stefan
   1992. Operativer Vorgang "Herbstrevolution." War die Wende des Jahres 1989 eine Verschwörung der Stasi? In *Die Ohnmacht der Allmächtigen. Geheimdienste und politische Polizei in der modernen Gesellschaft.* Bernd Florath, Armin Mitter, Stefan Wolle, eds. Pp. 234–240. Berlin: Ch. Links

PART IV

Territorial Sovereignty and Its Violation

9

Emigrees as Bullets /
Immigration as Penetration:
Perceptions of the Marielitos

On April 14, 1980, Fidel Castro removed the guards from the gates of the Peruvian embassy and Radio Havana encouraged those Cubans desiring to leave the island to do so through the embassy. This action initiated an unexpected exodus of 125,000 Cubans in the following four months to the United States. At its peak in May and June, more than 5,000 persons a day made the crossing to Key West, Florida. The United States had acted previously as a country of first asylum for a large number of Cuban refugees, receiving up to 1,700 refugees a week in November 1960, reaching a total of 750,000 Cubans by 1980.[1] The pre-1980 refugees were regarded as political escapees fleeing from Castro's communism and, accordingly, welcomed with open arms. No serious attempt was made to question the motives of these individuals for leaving, and they were readily defined as "political refugees" in the American setting. Anyone leaving a communist country was welcomed by the American government and media for propagandistic purposes, among others, in the American anti-communist zeal characteristic of this century.

The refugees in the 1980 Cuban boatlift, distinguished by the label "Marielitos," provoked an ambivalent response in the United

States, producing an expanded discourse out of previously limited conceptual tools and out of a restricted normative repertoire. The *categorical confusion* resulting from the reception of the Marielitos is the subject of this chapter. I hope to show that this event signifies a discontinuity in American conceptualization of immigration, and thus bespeaks a possible transformation *in practice* of the relationship between the categories used in perception of events of this sort.

I will proceed by first explicating the native categories of Americans, which I derive from official public discourse on the Marielitos. Three levels of reception are separately examined: 1) public statements of then-President Jimmy Carter and of State Department bulletins, 2) the response of popular periodicals (those listed in the *Reader's Guide to Periodical Literature*), 3) the characterizations of those actually involved in the resettlement of the Marielitos, based upon personal interviews conducted by this writer. No attempt is made to explicate Marielito perceptions of themselves. Second, I will seek to uncover the organizing scheme from which the representations for this event were appropriated. What makes possible this set of definitions? Third, I will offer an explanation as to why this particular representation was chosen.[2]

Discourse on the Marielitos

1. The Executive: from "refugees from persecution" to "bullets aimed at this country"

Five days after the opening of the Peruvian embassy gates, President Jimmy Carter characterized those Cubans seeking asylum as hungry "to escape political deprivation of freedom and also economic adversity. Our heart goes out to almost 10,000 . . ."[3] As this initial group of 10,000 grew to 85,000 during the month of May, the statements of both the President and his bureaucracy vacillated between an "open heart and open arms to refugees seeking freedom from communist domination and from economic deprivation" policy, and an attempt to restrict the number of refugees by strictly "enforcing all immigration law" (by seizure of illegal boats) and by verbal admonitions to those private individuals facilitating the boatlift.[4]

The statements of executive officials were constrained at the time by a new set of official definitions embodied in the two-month-old *Refugee Act of 1980*. The *Act* attempted to set new standards for the validity of particular claims of asylum. No longer was automatic asylum to be granted to those individuals fleeing communism. The additional justification of a "well-founded fear of persecution based on race, religion, nationality, social class or political opinion" was now needed.[5] While the specificity of the *Act* might have clarified asylum-seeker status, it did not decrease the number of people who qualified for admission as refugees. One author claims it actually increased the number eligible from three million to thirteen million persons, while the government simultaneously cut back on the number of legal entrants to be admitted, from 217,000 to fewer than 100,000.[6] The Carter administration was not unaware of these ambiguities, as revealed by its muddled attempts to apply the new standards to a refugee situation that lay outside the purview of situations which the legal standards were intended to address.

When defining the Marielitos, the Carter administration's initially external-hostile definitions gave way to increasingly internally differentiated ones. Carter's May 14 statement listed four categories of Cubans, in order of priority to be admitted to the United States: 1) those in the U.S. Interest Section in Havana; 2) political prisoners; 3) those in the Peruvian Embassy in Havana; and 4) "close family members of Cuban-Americans."[7] While the motivation for leaving Cuba was often alluded to in the official statements, the boatlift was characterized more as a "deliberate decision of the Cuban government . . . to force the departure" than as a result of "separate decisions by private individuals."[8] On the one hand, an attempt was made to characterize the Marielitos as "individual refugees from persecution and tyranny," while on the other hand the administration wanted to discourage "Cuba from unleashing a new human wave against this country."[9] In the words of Carter aide Jack Watson, "Castro, in a way, is using people like bullets aimed at this country."[10]

The tendency to see the refugees as bullets rather than "huddled masses yearning to breathe free" resulted from an increased awareness of the nature of the heterogenous composition of the Marielitos, who were unlike previous groups of Cuban refugees. The White House characterized them on June 7 as "of wide age range and [with] a wide range of reasons for coming to the United States . . . (listing) political prisoners, reunifications with families, greater economic opportunities, personal freedoms (as reasons for leaving)." The statement continues, "Fidel Castro has very cynically thrown in several hundred criminals from Cuban jails."[11] This several hundred was soon to grow to estimates of up to 20,000.

2. American Periodicals: "single men," "criminal dregs," "homosexuals"

In a survey of twenty-five American periodicals in the eighteen-month period from May 1980 through December 1981, one finds a fairly narrow range of categorization of the Marielitos, and a characterization lacking in the circumspection of the Carter administration. In fact, the one characteristic they seem to share is their anti-Carter perspective. Journals of the political center-left, such as *Dissent, The Progressive, The New Republic, Nation,* and *Atlantic Monthly* labelled administration efforts "slow and awkward,"[12] lacking "in courage and vision," or as "humanitarianism carefully rationed,"[13] a "policy in shambles, conflicted, this day humane another day insensitive."[14] Journals of the political center-right, such as *National Review, Business Week, Time, Newsweek, Reader's Digest* and *U.S. News & World Report* criticized Carter for missing "a splendid opportunity to focus world attention on a subjugated populace fleeing Communist masters,"[15] for seizing 200 boats instead of focusing on the "traditional role of America as haven . . . (for) freedom-seeking Cubans,"[16] and in general, for not emphasizing that "Cuba under Castro is a nation in lockstep, in which vigilance committees monitor every citizen."[17]

Many of the journals concentrated upon the difficulty in assimilating so many refugees during a recession, and of the threat posed generally by these refugees to Americans. They often passed quickly over the composition of the refugees, and talked instead of competition with poor blacks for jobs,[18] and how the "integrity of the immigration system is being threatened."[19] Says Lance Morrow of *Time,* "The Latin renaissance has left blacks in a unhappy third place . . . . Promises inside the house need to be redeemed."[20] While at times this response seems clearly xenophobic, many writers did not themselves comment on slamming the door to refugees; rather, they focused coverage on those groups like the Ku Klux Klan (with posters proclaiming: "American for Americans" and "We do not support Communist Criminals") or spotlighted other anti-foreign sentiment.[21]

The manner in which the periodicals dealt with the internal composition of the Marielitos differed markedly from that of the Carter administration, partly because they were more intent upon emphasizing the internal makeup of the Cubans, and partly because the news media—both electronic and print—rarely concerns itself with the policy implications of what they peg as newsworthy, whereas that is normally the major concern of the government. What one finds in this regard is a concentration upon the non-family and non-professional element. On the one hand, one finds the labels "single men, criminals, and the mentally-retarded."[22] On the other hand, one finds "poor low-level government workers, some criminals, and the very young" contrasted with the professional upper-middle class composition of earlier emigre groups.[23]

The discourse created on this element of the Marielitos is of several persuasions. There are perspectives hostile to these "gusanos"— Cuba's worms, as Castro put it—while other perspectives try to minimize the significance of the non-family element and of the crimes of those labeled "criminal." Yet the structuring of the immigrants into these particular discrete categories is more significant for a full understanding of how the Marielitos were seen than is the surface heterogenity of representations. In other words, the fact that the "undesirable elements" comprise only 15–20,000 of the 135,000 total is on the surface often ignored when representing the Marielitos. Yet their significance in coloring the perception of the whole far outweighs their numerical strength. This particular representation became increasingly prominent as reporters had opportunities to interview those not yet resettled, and after nearly 110,000 refugees had already been resettled, or removed from the public gaze.

Rarely do journals use identical words to classify the non-family group, yet the representations fall within a definite range, of which

I will offer a sample. James Conway, in *The Atlantic,* initially labels the Marielitos a "dispossessed mass of humanity," then refers to Carter's refusal to "permit our country to be used as a dumping ground for criminals," and then talks of a KKK protest. He listed the non-family group as "violent, anarchic, debased," of which 1774 were guilty of "murder, rape, armed robbery, sodomy, or violent misbehavior," and another 400 were "undergoing psychiatric evaluation." Nearly a third of the article is devoted to the homosexual element, and Conway criticizes media coverage of this group, mentioning three incidents: 1) a photo in the *S.W. Times Record* (Arkansas) of "two flagrantly homosexual Cubans smirking in an open window"; 2) his defense of homosexuals when his bilingual Cuban-American interpreter makes derogatory remarks, that homosexuals are "counter to the spirit of machismo"; and 3) his disapproval of a cameraman for KFSM-TV, whose "lens (was) drawn inexorably toward the si-sis."[24]

J.S. Fuerst, in *Commonwealth,* distinguishes four groups of Marielitos (contrasted with the upwardly mobile earlier emigres): 1) "social misfits: petty thieves, anti-social criminals," 2) "psychoneurotics, and perhaps psychotics"; 3) "a good sprinkling of homosexuals"; and 4) "political dissidents . . . relatives of Cubans in the U.S. . . . the majority."[25] Contrary to Conway's claim that the media concentrated on the homosexual element, only half of the periodicals I examined even mentioned homosexuals. Only Conway and Michael Massing in *Columbia Journalism Review* gave homosexuals prominent coverage;[26] in both cases, it was to decry the kind of coverage given this group. In other words, it is second-order coverage. Of those who balked at the use of the word "homosexual," they uniformly mentioned the disproportionate number of single men, with no speculation as to why they were single.

Only Howard Hunt, for *National Review,* and R.Y. Tomlinson, for *Reader's Digest,* initially wrote wholeheartedly enthusiastic responses to the emigres. Hunt compared them to "the inspired Germans who used to breach the Berlin Wall."[27] Tomlinson concentrated on the oppression in Cuba: his monthly ration of "five pounds of rice per person—usually late, and seldom the full amount—lasted less than two weeks"; "at home he was secretly teaching his children the forbidden principles of freedom and religion." Also mentioned are particular examples of the barbarity of Cuban authorities: forcing "women to strip naked before they were allowed to depart," and grinding "the eyeglasses of Francisco's eldest child . . . into dirt."[28]

As resettlement progressed, the blander tabloids (*Time, U.S. News & World Report, Newsweek*) pandered more to prurient interests as their focus remained on the harder-to-resettle Marielitos left in the internment camps. Thus, they "repeated reports of homosexual and heterosexual rape"[29] and speculated about the "presence of Communist agitators."[30] Yet this kind of characterization is not absent from the earliest reportage (of April and May 1980); it simply isn't always so emphasized. From the beginning, the American media had in the background the Marielito characterization by Castro's official newspaper of "delinquents, homosexuals, lumpenproletarians, anti-social and parasitic elements and bums."[31] Immigrants coded with these kind of messages are not easily re-characterized as desirable gifts from foreign lands.

Progressive writer Milton Mayer comments from a more ironical perspective, one critical of the media. He concludes, "The majority of the Free-World kissers are relatively young males and not all of them lily-white. Fidel was sending us his criminal dregs . . . God's country (is being) used as a sanitary land fill, a dump."[32] His commentary acts as meta-commentary for, while he refuses to categorize the refugees in a mode similar to the other media, he still uses the same categories. In this fashion his article feeds into the burgeoning discourse on the Marielitos.

3. Resettlement workers: "regular people"

This third level reception is inferred from a distillation of interviews with individuals involved in the transportation and resettlement of the Marielitos from Cuba to the United States.[33] Their face-to-face experiences with the Marielitos ranged from initial work with the boatlift of 1980 to resettlement efforts of the last group of interned refugees through 1982. While those individuals interviewed were from only two cities, and while their experiences were diverse, there are no factual or perceptual contradictions in the information they shared with me.

Those individuals directly involved in resettlement of the Marielitos speak with a certain reticence, an experience-wisened lack of confidence in their ability to tell the whole, or even an accurate, story. Clearly, their experiences with a final group of forty hard-to-resettle refugees in Boston struck deep emotional chords and had a far greater personal impact than their previous contact with hundreds or thousands (depending upon the worker) of refugees in their work.

When Hermann (pseudonyms are used in these accounts), a 1973 refugee from Cuba and now resettlement worker, heard that Castro had opened the gates to the Peruvian embassy and was allowing emigration, he immediately gathered $50,000, most of which he had saved in the six years since he had rafted from Cuba to the United States, flew to Florida from Boston and bought a 72-foot shrimp boat. His own initial exodus from Cuba in 1973, with a friend who drowned on the way, was brought to mind when he heard of a massive boat flotilla bringing Cubans to the United States. His initial idea was only to "rescue" a sister and two brothers. However, his involvement extended to two months of illegal transportation of Cubans on his shrimp boat.

According to several other informants, this was not an atypical reaction within the Cuban-American community. "To many this was an anti-Castro statement by the Cuban community. Initially. Then they were confused, had conflicting reactions. They were dealing with Third World people with lots of problems, not middle-class Cubans. There was later lots of resistance to these people within the community." What turned the family—and patriotic-inspired boatlift—into "a nightmare," as one caseworker described it? "It was horrible, hysterical. We had a phenomenally difficult time. They had a phenomenally difficult time adjusting."

"The majority of those who came were regular people—working class, students—who tried to lead a regular life. If there were only 15,000 of those [non-regular Cubans] in the U.S. we'd have a civil war here. I'm not kidding," commented Hermann. While the American press reported the majority of refugees as nonprofessional and unskilled, the Cuban-Americans involved in the resettlement characterized the majority as "regular people." The terminological discrepancy results from cross-cultural transfer of categories, without being cognizant of changed meanings over time. Previous groups of Cuban emigres had upper-middle-class roots in a pre-socialist Cuba. Many came to the United States with money. Those who came with nothing had an entrepreneurial network which most often allowed them to enter a comparable class in America. Today, except for a few army generals and upper-echelon party members, Cubans are mostly "regular people." The majority of Marielitos were skilled, but hadn't the upperclass air of those earlier Cuban emigrants who had been raised in a more stratified society.

This distinction cut across family lines, as many Cuban-Americans disparaged the sacrifices they had made in the flotilla to "rescue" their younger siblings, who did not share the same capitalist ethic as themselves. According to Hermann, "Our worst enemy (in terms of negatively stereotyping the Marielitos) was the Cuban people. They'd say, 'Oh my God, what did I bring here?' In the rescue, we thought in terms of our family first, then of the other Cubans. But once here, many Cubans would say, 'I brought my brother and he's a lazy one. I didn't know.' "

Although many Cuban-Americans became quickly disenchanted with the Marielitos, the majority of Americans had little contact with the group of "regular people," either first hand or from the media coverage. "In the beginning," said Roberto, "it was beautiful. Americans called offering money, shoes. Other stories changed this. It started to roll. It started before they went to the streets. . . . Nothing is heard anymore. Now they are surviving, working, paying rent." The stories he refers to are press characterizations of the non-family element. It was not this element that shook the ardor of the Cuban-American community; they had lost their enthusiasm before the extensive media coverage. But ultimately, it was the non-family element that shaped the characterization of the Marielito in the minds of most Americans.

And how is the select group of 15,000 "troublemakers" portrayed by the resettlement workers? "My first day (in Boston working with them) I was called to get a Cuban out of jail who was trying to hang himself. These Cubans were the bottom of the barrel. Nobody

257

wanted them. Ninety-nine point nine percent had a criminal background." The criminal backgrounds were varied. According to many of the psychological reports, often written by Cuban-American health professionals who had interviewed refugees in the Florida camps, some had "only killed a cow so he could eat," or "stolen a loaf of bread." The caseworkers distrusted these reports, although still admitting that they were useful, and they did a great deal of cross-checking and verification work on their own. Often "a psychiatrist would label someone dangerous but not criminally insane. Then the INS (Immigration and Naturalization Service) would force us to let them go free." During the year in which a final group of forty were resettled in Boston, seven were murdered and two disappeared—who were later reported dead in Florida. Eight or nine are current serving life sentences for murder in the United States. Two were sent back to Atlanta. Responded Roberto, "I wasn't surprised. I knew what we were getting into." Yet among many Cuban-Americans, there was a total denial that "this kind of person" had even existed in the Cuba they had known. In addition to these major problems in resettlement, there were many other occurrences: rapes, attempted rape and murder of agency workers and their families, burglary and theft; and drug dealing.

When speaking of homosexual activity among the refugees, all the caseworkers used the categorization "gay" in contrast to the media, which used the word "homosexual." Those workers with more in-depth contact with the refugees reported contact with the gay communities in other cities right from the start in the resettlement process. The caseworkers felt that, while there was little distinction between gay and criminal in the eyes of most Cuban-Americans, the refugees were represented primarily as "criminals," the gay element being a minor consideration. There was official contact between resettlement agencies and gay groups in at least six cities. The gay groups aided in the resettling of at least 12,500 gay refugees, none of whom were among the last group to be resettled—those with serious felony records. Says one caseworker, "I didn't want to involve anyone with the last group; they were too dangerous. But we sent many earlier refugees to San Francisco, where they set up a private gay shelter."

258

Organizing Scheme

The first section of this chapter set forth the "native categories" used to characterize a specific group of refugees, the Marielitos, during the course of an event with national and international policy implications. These categories were formed by the discourse of three major groups of Americans involved in the making of this event. I have attempted to summarize these characterizations without obscuring the range or multiplicity of representations (perhaps, to the confusion of the reader). This section seeks to explain the conditions that allow for its intelligibility.

A classification system is a system of meaning: a symbolic representation of some aspect of the world and its immanent order. It is an organizing scheme into which individual motivations (how people *want* to see the world) are infused. Yet these individual motivations are not derived from unstructured dispositions. "Man acts as a function of what he thinks," says Louis Dumont, "and while he has up to a certain point the ability to arrange his categories in his own way, to construct new categories, he does so starting with the categories which are given by society."[34] Whereas the first part of this chapter sought to outline three functionally related realms of action (speech-acts) as they pertain to the constitution of a particular event, the second half attempts to situate this action in its "culture-as-constituted" context.[35] To uncover the often unconscious, beneath-the-surface structures that allow for a particular mode of representation, I now turn to basic American perceptual codes.[36]

Two sets of codes, one relating to American kinship or family relations and the other relating to American national identification, when superimposed, begin to reveal something about the classification of the Marielitos. It will be argued that these two domains, of kin and country, are related to one another in the American context through the mediation of the key symbol "conjugal sexual intercourse." In his work on American kinship David Schneider argues that sexual intercourse is the mediating symbol of American kinship relations, meaning it is the most frequently employed metaphor used to establish homologies between kinship relations

259

and other domains, such as the geographical, zoological, technical, philosophical, or political. After an analysis of the basic components—nature and law—of American kinship, Schneider concludes that sexual intercourse is the form that most meaningfully expresses this opposition.[37]

In the kinship domain, the law/nature code, mediated by the symbol of sexual intercourse, refers to and continually aids in the reproduction of other basic dichotomies: top/bottom; male/female; public/domestic; official/unofficial; law abiding-making/criminal; rational/hysterical.[38] These codes are related metaphorically to each other as part of a semiotic system. Their utility derives from their logical relation to one another, by how they facilitate the conceptualization of interrelationships among phenomena, not from their abstract truth-value.

In their perceptions of themselves, Americans clearly use the insider/outsider dichotomy as a basic spatial metaphor. One can establish homologies between terms in this sphere such as insider/outsider; we/they; law abiding/criminal; capitalist/communist.

While the binary codes as codes are metaphorically related to one another, one can also link each half of the code to the corresponding upper or lower halves and relate the terms metonymically to one another. This means that they are related not by analogy, but serially, as contiguous elements of a whole; much as, for example, the following pieces of furniture, sofa, end-table, and reclining chair, are related to one another as "'living room furniture." Organized in this fashion (bottom, female, domestic, unofficial, criminal, hysterical, outsider, they, communist) and (top, male, public, official, law abiding-making, rational, insider, we, capitalist), one finds the characteristics, listed in a serial description, of the American stereotypical categorization of homosexual and heterosexual males, respectively.[39]

What is most perverse about classification of the Marielitos is that we have an odd actual convergence "in practice" of three major American demons—"communists," "criminals," and "homosexuals"—which usually converge only in the mind. One need only recall the Palmer raids of the late teens and twenties and the McCarthy era of the fifties to understand the powerful images provoked in many American minds by and the irrational responses to the juxtaposition of these categories. Today, in many circles the ontological status of these three demon categories, as individual classifications and as a serialized assignation, are called into question. Yet they are still in use, as either descriptions of actions or, alternately, as descriptions of "beings" who derive their self from the behaviors and notions associated with the categories. The interesting question is, given this organizing scheme, why the muted response?

In his discussion of infantile neurosis Freud explores how individuals "gain a conviction of reality," and alludes to the fact that it need not be based on actual behavior or "real occurrences," but might rather be "products of the imagination . . . (a) kind of symbolic representation of real wishes and interests."[40] The characterization of the Marielitos, or any asylum-seeking group for that matter, then, need not be based on some "objective account" of their actual composition (and, one might argue, rarely is), but is always a matter of adjusting abstract representations and codified norms with actual personal interactions. Erving Goffman makes a similar but stronger claim in his work on stigma and labelling, maintaining that a representation is obtained in a process whereby the strange or "deviant individual" is forced to conform to a set of categories by which the "normals" seek to characterize him/her.[41] Actually, this process is rarely so simple, for the image of any social group is, in the end, a crystallization of several interactions between subjective actors and objective processes occurring over time. While the representational models (organizing schemes) can account for a multiplicity of situations, and indeed in this case they conceptually subsume the "problematic elements" of the Marielitos, the normative models—inscribed in legal and media codes—are situationally specific and involved in legitimating a *particular* conceptualization.

One of the major sources of confusion in the Cuban boatlift was in the disjuncture between different culturally-constructed symbolic systems: a particular reality (the Marielitos) whose self-definition was at odds with the normatively-sanctioned legal and cultural categories available to policymakers and media people. In addition, as the event unfolded, some of the immigrants refused to adjust to the preferred American categories available to them (in both refusing to denounce communism and refusing to represent themselves as "non-

261

criminals" and as "heterosexuals"), making for continued ambivalence on the part of the receiving nation.

Each of the American categorizations—single men, homosexuals, criminals, mentally deranged, regular people—is associated with a specific culturally constructed *body hexis*, a way of sitting, standing, speaking, greeting, walking, talking.[42] These body schemas, or signs of the self, have no permanent reality, but are part of a cultivated disposition, and they allow for cultural recognition of gender, social class, ethnicity—for empirical referents of social differentiation and discrimination. As Michael Jackson has recently argued, instrumental uses of the body have "metaphorical correspondences which link personal, social and natural *bodies*."[43] In the American context the most salient Marielitos were those who most conformed to these cultivated dispositions. Media accounts of the Marielitos often sought to justify their characterizations with oblique references to perceived elements of these body schemas.

Of significance is the contradiction between some media attempts to portray all the Marielitos as innocents, while other accounts centered on the "si-sis" or the fact that so many were "covered with tatoos."[44] UPI in early June ran a story showing how four refugees with criminal records were really not "criminals in American categories. To land in jail in Cuba, one need only dress differently, read a Bible, make your own shoes, or walk by the U.S. Interest Section in Havana."[45] These stories ran alongside other commentary claiming that the system had run amok, that we no longer had control over our borders. The content of the Marielitos is sanitized, while the reaction is one of "Whoa boy, stop!"

Immigration and Incorporation

In the following pages, I shall explain how a seemingly political threat is actually perceived as if it were a sexual one, where political boundaries are perceived as if—i.e., felt like—they are boundaries of the body. This analysis follows one put forth by Neil Hertz in an examination of accounts of the 1848 French Revolution. He argues that when "questions of sexual difference, of perception and of politics are rapidly brought into relation . . . (the threat prompts) powerfully rendered Medusa-fantasies . . . (which) are offered as substitutes for a more patient inclusive account of political conflict."[47] He begins his discussion of "male hysteria under political pressure" with some comments from Freud in an article on fetishism, where Freud concludes, "In later life grown men may experience a similar panic, perhaps when the cry goes up that throne and altar are in danger."[48] It is here where the 1848 Revolution and the 1980 boatlift intersect: male commentary on a political event where the "integrity of the . . . system"[49] at its very core—national borders and sexual boundaries—is seen as threatened.

Schneider suggests that in America "what is called 'nationality' . . . [is] . . . defined and structured in . . . (terms identical to those of kinship), namely, in terms of the dual aspects of relationship as natural substance and relationship as code for conduct, and that most if not all of the major diacritical marks which are found in kinship are also found in nationality."[50] The way in which the mediating symbol of sexual intercourse (in the American context) is used to link questions brought about by the convergence of national and kinship categorization is then crucial for an understanding of the manner in which the Marielitos are perceived.

Dolgin and Magdoff, in an article elaborating how the ethnic model in America works, maintain that the incorporation of immigrants into America takes place through a generalization of this ethnic model, whereby successive ethnic groups as groups substitutable for each other are metaphorically related to one another.[51] This is contrasted with the metonymical process of incorporation which Dumont has suggested for the Indian caste system. Metonymy is stressed when "substance (such as blood) is not the primary locus of identity"; rather, groups are incorporated as parts into a hierarchical whole by being differentially ranked. Metaphor is stressed where "the individual remains the metaphoric substitutable referent of identity so that, like individuals, larger groups are substitutable for one another."[52] Dolgin and Magdoff use the notion of "the individual as part of an ethnic group" as the essential metaphor for the American Other. Despite the ideology surrounding the solipsistic individual in America, these authors find the individual always situated in a group.

The "ethnic group model" of incorporation docs not help to explain the American reception of the Marielitos. The notion of the Cuban ethnic group was rarely mentioned in the official public discourse on the Marielitos. It follows that today signifiers other than ethnicity have more definitional import in this American context. The "native categories" used to label the Marielitos may now serve the same purposes as did "the code of substance" formerly found in ethnicity. This new "substance" of the Marielitos is now found in the three constructed "personal" identities: homosexual, heterosexual, and criminal.

Furthermore, Dolgin and Magdoff understate the importance of metonymical incorporation ("metonymization," in their words), which, I suspect, takes place in America at a local level. Either resident ethnic groups must eventually absorb other newly-arrived ethnic groups *of the same kind* (this seems to be less of an option as ethnic identity loses its signification), or this metonymization takes place in the kinship domain through the notion of "the family." Both thought processes—the use of metaphor and metonymy—are simultaneously at work in any situation of incorporation; they simply work processually at different levels and different times.

Having sketched the process by which an event is categorized, let us examine more closely the categories used to classify the Marielitos. The category "criminal" is interesting because of its ambiguity. The "outlaw" image has served as a condensing symbol in innumerable films and fictional accounts of America's mythical past, while simultaneously the "law and order" issue in politics works to glorify the police and authority. The ambivalence surrounding the outlaw—the desire to "crack down on criminals" mixed with the affirmation of the "rights of the individual to protect what he sees as correct"—is expressed in representational ambiguity so that how "the criminal" will be perceived at any time depends upon situation-specific norms. Political refugees, one of America's favored categories, are by definition "criminals" in their mother countries. And, by definition, political criminals in communist countries become capitalist heroes in America. This was also the official governmental approach until two months before the Mariel boatlift, when Congress passed the 1980 Refugee Act removing the automaticity of application of "political criminal" to refugees from communist countries. Yet it is safe to say that there remains sufficient ambiguity and flexibility in the "criminal" classification that, without linkage with other representations, it would not create categorical confusion.

264

Given the odd metonymical alignment of the perceptual categories outlined in the previous section, where one is led to a concentration on the homosexual/heterosexual dichotomy, one might expect the discourse to explicate this, or to use it as a mediating code. Instead, there is relative fear and silence, and when the category "homosexual" is addressed at all, it is done so with embarrassment. In an examination of mind and madness in ancient Greece, Bennett Simon indicates that "in both family and cultural style . . . an official suppression of sexuality (and repression of the knowledge of sexuality)"[53] would often result in behavior that "can properly be called the disease of motivated ignorance."[54] He is specifically referring to female hysteria in Greece as "a way of expressing and redressing serious social and psychological imbalance between the sexes."[55] Without wishing to enter into a debate about the possibility of male hysteria, I will nonetheless suggest that the response to the Marielitos, marked by a refusal (or inability) to deal directly with the underlying sexual issue, was a means of expressing the conflicted self-images associated with the representation of criminals and homosexuals.

This response can be characterized as a form of defensively motivated ignorance. Its dynamics might best be explained by addressing how, specifically with reference to American immigration policy, the domain of sex is encompassed by the kinship categories. And ultimately, wherever sex appears it serves simultaneously as indexical signs of "self," kinship categories, and notions of "the family." Despite the variety of categorizations discussed in this chapter, an initial bifurcation of the refugees is made by all actors: some refugees are connected with "family" and some are not. This is in accord with U.S. immigration law, which is both shaped by and aids in the structuring of basic representations and norms.[56]

In the alien preference classification effective at the time of the Marielitos (*Title 22*, FCR 42.12.), eighteen categories if immigration are listed, the eighteenth being "non-preference immigrants." Of the other seventeen categories subdivided into six preferences levels, fifteen relate to reuniting families. The categories used are "son," "daughter," "child," and "spouse"—essentially the nuclear family. Only two categories, "professional or highly-skilled immigrant" and "needed skilled or unskilled worker," do not make

265

family ties a priority. *Title 22.41.91* retains two provisions that are still used to deny homosexuals visas to the United States, one classification [a(9)] of "crimes of moral turpitude" and a second [a(13)] involving an "immoral sexual act." In applying immigration laws to the Marielitos, the distinctions made were threefold: heterosexual/homosexual/criminal. The criminals still institutionalized were denied any resident status. The Advocate reports, "While heterosexual refugees will become eligible for permanent resident status after two years, and later for citizenship, the Cubans who admitted their homosexuality to INS will remain on indefinite parole."[57]

Often, the assumption is made that the "family" category is primarily intended to prevent the immigration of those likely to become public wards. There are two provisions to this effect, listed in Regulations Relating to *VISAS 41.91.* (#7 and #15). Without a doubt, this has been and remains a major concern in immigration policy. Yet the conceptualization of this concern is psychosexual and topographical, not economic, in origin, and is derived from America's masculine image of itself as a tough and projecting presence in the world and from the meaning infused in the concept "family." In an article advocating the use of a "psycho-geographical perspective" for explicating symbolic group-boundaries, Howard F. Stein emphasizes that "Fantasies about the body and the family are transmuted into descriptions of one's own group, other groups, shapes and features of the world. Projected outward, the fate of the body becomes the fate of the world."[58]

American attitudes toward immigration and immigration laws are linked to a projected psychosexual self-image, which structures who is to be admitted, under what conditions, and how they are to be classified. Immigrants must be reclassified once admitted to the American fold; they must be conceived of in a proper conceptual form. A family entering America, or an individual as part of a family, is the most readily incorporated group because it is seen as a substitutable group in an already existing universe of families. Single, unattached men with no acceptable group referent, unless reclassified, are seen as penetrating, therefore as threats. Single women, on the other hand, have long been seen as exchange products, and are nearly universally trafficked by men. "Exchange of women," argues Gayle Rubin, "is a shorthand for expressing that

266

the social relations of a kinship system specify that men have certain rights in their female kin, and that women do not have the same rights either to themselves or to their male kin."[59] Unlike the exchange of men, the exchange of women presents no threat. Or rather, the threat tends to have an economic, not a sexual base. Seen from this perspective, modern immigration policies are nothing more than culturally elaborated forms of gift exchange.

Men are trafficked also, but not simply as individual men. They must be redefined and metaphorically incorporated. The two most common ways in which this is effected is to define them as kin—thus they are already we/official/law-abiding/reproductive units—or to define them as a particular kind of needed commodity, at least temporarily. This second categorization is the argument of Michael J. Piore in *Birds of Passage,* about the absorption of migrant labor in industrial societies.[60] Defining men as needed labor commodities effectively makes them an object of exchange, much like women, but the temporary status renders migrant males harmless. Often, the label "political refugee" has been used to escape this conundrum, but at the time of the 1980 boatlift, this categorization has been limited in its applicability.

Because of the overwhelming number of single men among the Marielitos, they were perceived as a male threat, an invading horde, "penetrating like bullets," rather than as workers or kin; they were incapable of being properly metaphorized. Furthermore, a large subcategory of the Marielitos were homosexual men, most of whom were self-defined as such, meaning consciously representing the structurally perceived antithesis of the model heterosexual male.

A third factor enters here: that these men were linked with communism. Many had been forced to leave Cuba, and did not engage in the anti-communist rhetoric often expected of refugees. There is a long history of linking gay men and communists in America. This topographical configuration persists as a popular form of mental association. One finds this link made explicitly mostly in right-wing circles today. Witness the evangelist James Robison in a born-again "Christians for Reagan" rally of 15,000, which Reagan attended, in October 1980, "I am sick and tired of hearing about all the radicals and the perverts and the liberals and the

267

leftists and the Communists coming out of the closet. It's time for God's people to come out of the closet."[61]

Political Event, Sexual Attack, Structure

It should be apparent how, through the convergence of questions concerning kinship, sexuality, and national boundaries, a political event will be perceived in symbolic terms as a sexual attack. Given the limited repertoire of normative responses available to the American male, a hysteric-like response should not be unexpected. One can understand the Carter administration's confusion in how to classify "Castro's refuse." It seems likely that the whole Executive branch, preoccupied with the abortive Iranian rescue mission which had occurred simultaneously with the Cuban boatlift, was predisposed to see the political and sexual metaphors as fused, or even the former transformed into the latter, through the mediating symbol of sexual intercourse.

The resettlement workers are exempt from this critique. Because they had to deal directly with the Marielitos rather than with "policy" in the abstract, as the government and media do, they were forced to consider the definitions the refugees gave to themselves, and thus negotiate a reality—a classification—with the immigrants. Therefore, the caseworkers talked openly of the different elements of the event and the kinds of people with whom they were dealing. There was no confusion of sexual and political realms in their minds.

American attitudes on these matters are more complex and differentiated than I have given them credit for in this discussion. What I have hoped to explicate is the underlying structure that shapes these conceptions and a situation in which this structure is subject to change. In practice, structured dispositions confront concrete situations and are often renegotiated, expanded, or even transformed. I would argue that the perceptual categories such as homosexual/heterosexual, criminal/law-abiding, and communist-they/American-us were indeed challenged by the Marielitos, precisely because there was no fit between structure and event. Considering the confusion of categories, the quasi-hysterical reaction of "defensively motivated

268

ignorance" was not an ineffective response. It is out of events such as this that social transformations are effected.

NOTES

1. Normal L. Zucker, "Refugee Resettlement in the United States: Policy and Problems," *The Annals,* May 1983 (Beverly Hills, Cal.: Sage Publications), p. 174.

2. I wish to thank Professor Sally Falk Moore, Paul Brodwin, and Terry O'Neil for their most helpful readings and criticisms of earlier drafts of this paper.

3. Ronald Copeland, "The Cuban Boatlift of 1980: Strategies in Federal Crisis Management," *The Annals,* May 1983, pp. 143–144.

4. *Ibid.,* pp. 143D4.

5. Arnold H. Liebowitz, "The Refugee Act of 1980: Problems and Congressional concerns," *The Annals,* May 1983, p. 167.

6. *Ibid.,* p. 167.

7. *U.S. Dept. State Bulletin 80,* "May 14, 1980," p. 74.

8. *Change 13,* July/August 1981, "A New Community Role," p. 29.

9. *Ibid.,* p. 29.

10. D.M. Alpern *et al.,* "Carter and the Cuban Influx," *Newsweek 95,* May 26, 1980, p. 22.

11. *U.S. Dept. State Bulletin 80,* "White House Statement, June 7, 1980," p. 75.

12. Lance Morrow, "Guarding the Door: Time Essay," *Time,* June 2, 1980, p. 80.

13. *The New Republic 182,* May 24, 1980. "A Half Opened Door," p. 5.

14. Emmanuel Geltman, "The Cuban Exodus—A taste of freedom," *Dissent 27,* Summer 1980: p. 263.

15. E. Howard Hunt, "Castro's Worms," *National Review 32,* June 13, 1980, pp. 722–724.

16. Alpern *et al.*, p. 22.

17. J. Nielsen, J. *et al.*, "The Flight From Havana," *Newsweek* 95, April 28, 1980, p. 38.

18. Richard Harbron, *Macleans* 93:32; Morrow, p. 80.

19. Alpern, p. 22.

20. Morrow, p. 80.

21. James Conway, "Unwanted Immigrants: Cuban prisoners in America," *Atlantic* 247, February 1981, p. 75; Morrow, p. 80.

22. Elizabeth Holzman, "Cuban Refugee Policy," *The New Republic,* June 14, 1980, p. 4.

23. Habron, p. 32.

24. Conway, p. 75.

25. J.S. Fuerst, "Images of Emigres: the U.S. is never far away," *Commonweal* 108, July 3, 1981, pp. 30–31.

26. Michael Massing, "The invisible Cubans: press treatment of homosexual refugees," *Columbia Journalism Review* 19, September/October 1980: p. 49.

27. Hunt, p. 724.

28. R.Y. Tomlinson, August 1980. "Fleeing Cuba for Freedom." *Reader's Digest* 117, August 1980, pp. 92–96.

29. *Time* 116, September 8, 1980, "Camp of Fear in Wisconsin," p. 28.

30. T. Morgenthau and R. Henkoff, June 16, 1980. "The Refugees: Rebels with a Cause," *Newsweek* 95, June 16, 1980, p. 28.

31. *The Economist* 275, April 12, 1980. "Smoke in whose eyes?" pp. 8–9.

32. Milton Mayer, "Massaging the News: UPI interviews the huddled masses," *Progressive* 44, August 1980, pp. 44–45.

33. This interviewing was conducted in March 1984 in Boston, Massachusetts. I was also involved in a minor way with resettlement of a group of Marielitos in Seattle, Washington, during late 1981. Although this "data" is not used directly, the personal experience informs the general line of analysis followed.

34. Louis Dumont, *Homo Hierarchies* (Chicago: University of Chicago Press, 1980 [1970]), p. 6.

35. David M. Schneider, *American Kinship: A Cultural Account* (Englewood Cliffs: Prentice Hall, 1980 [1980]), pp. 126–127.

36. I regret that I cannot provide a historical account of the origin and transformation of these codes, for it would add another important dimension to the analysis. Such a task would take me too far away from what I have set forth as my central project: to explicate the social logic of an event and to examine the relationship between events and the possibilities for transformation of structures (here defined as historically—specific perceptual codes).

37. Schneider. For an account of the centrality of sexuality to conceptions of self in America, see David S. Kemnitzer, "Sexuality as a Social Form: Performance and Anxiety in America," pp. 292–309, in Janet L. Dolgin, David S. Kemnitzer, and David M. Schneider (eds.): *Symbolic Anthropology: A Reader in the Study of Symbols and Meanings* (New York: Columbia University Press, 1977).

38. For an analysis of popular images of the family in America, see Arlene Skolnick, "Public Images, Private Realities; the American Family in Popular Culture and Social Science," pp. 301–304, in Virginia Tufte and Barbara Myerhoff (eds.), *Changing Images of the Family* (New Haven: Yale University Press).

39. For two extended accounts dealing with these categorizations yet with very different approaches to American sexual stereotypes, see John D'Emilio, *Sexual Politics, Sexual Communities* (Chicago: University of Chicago Press, 1983) and Erving Goffman, *Stigma* (Englewood Cliffs, N.J.: Prentice Hall, Inc. 1963).

40. Sigmund Freud, *Three Case Histories* (New York: Collier Books, 1963), pp. 236–237.

41. Goffman.

42. Pierre Bourdieu, *Outline of a Theory of Practice* (New York: Cambridge University Press, 1982 [1977]), p. 52.

43. Michael Jackson, "Thinking Through the Body: An Essay on Understanding Metaphor." *Social Analysis* 14 (1983): pp. 127–148.

44. Conway, p. 75.

45. Mayer, p. 45.

46. *Ibid.,* p. 44.

47. Neil Hertz, "Medusa's Head: Hysteria under Political Pressure," *Representations* 4 (1983): pp. 27–54.

48. *Ibid.,* p. 27.

49. Alpern *et al.,* p. 22.

50. David M. Schneider, "Kinship, Nationality, and Religion in American Culture: Toward a Definition of kinship," pp. 70–71, in Dolgin *et al.* (eds.).

51. Janet L., Dolgin and JoAnn Magdoff, "The Invisible Event," pp. 351–363, in Dolgin *et al.,* (eds.).

52. *Ibid.,* p. 362.

53. Bennett Simon, *Mind and Madness in Ancient Greece: The Classical Roots of Modern Psychiatry.* (Ithaca: Cornell University Press, 1978), p. 241.

54. *Ibid.,* p. 260.

55. *Ibid.,* p. 257.

56. The appropriate Federal Codes on immigration and refugee status referred to in this analysis are *Title 22.* FCR 41:91. (a) (9) & (13), *Administrative Regulations* Regulations relating to VISAS. 17 Federal Register 1565 as amended, and *Refugee Act of 1980.* PL 96–212. 94 Stat. 102 (1980).

57. *The Advocate,* October 16, 1980, "Immigration Softens its Antigay Policy." p. 3.

58. Howard F. Stein, "The Scope of Psycho-Geography: The Psychoanalytic Study of Spatial Representation," *The Journal of Psychoanalytic Anthropology,* 7 (1) (1984): p. 24.

59. Gayle Rubin, "The traffic in women: notes toward a political economy of sex," p. 177, in Rayna Reiter (ed.): *Toward an Anthropology of Women.* (New York: Monthly Review Press, 1975).

60. Michael J. Piore, *Birds of Passage.* (New York: Cambridge University Press, 1979).

61. *The Advocate,* October 2, 1980, p. 11.

10

Toward a Theory of Ethnic Cleansing: Territorial Sovereignty, Heterosexuality, and Europe

As we near the end of the twentieth century, it has become apparent that genocides and atrocities directed against groups of people are not unique events limited to particular cultures or regions but in fact pan-human responses found throughout the globe. How does one account for the particular type of violence—systematic use of rape and humiliation—perpetrated in the five-year war (1991–1995) in Bosnia-Herzegovina? This war and the violent dissolution of Yugoslavia have been subjected to multiple and varied explanations at the level of political economy, state and international politics, propaganda, animalistic sentiment, and modernist ideology. In contrast to the complexity of explanations for the war, the reasons most frequently offered for the ethnic cleasing of Muslims by Serbian and Croatian nationalists, including the systematic raping and sexual abuse of men and women as a method of cleansing, are surprisingly simplistic. Most of the rape and sexual assaults occurred in a two-year period, between 1991 and 1993. The world's ethical authorities seem to be in nearly unanimous agreement that the ethnic cleansing—territorial displacement, terror, and murder—

of Bosnia's Muslim population is an attempt to "bring about its physical destruction in whole or in part," the definition of genocide under Article II of the United Nations convention. In fact, on April 8, 1993, the International Court of Justice in The Hague, the world's highest institutional moral authority, belatedly declared this ethnic cleansing to be a genocide. Yet this declaration does not solve our problems of explanation, for genocides vary, particularly in motivations and in methods—gas chambers, bodily mutilation, sterilization, work camps, starvation, execution. Each of these methods demands a particular historical and cultural explanation in terms of motivations. A major question concerning how the Bosnian genocide was imagined has yet to be systematically explored: Why exactly did the perpetrators focus on humiliation and rape as methods of ethnic cleansing in order to bring about the "physical destruction in whole or in part" of Bosnia's Muslims? What motivated them to "cleanse" in this particular way?

The first part of my discussion will concern the context of ethnic cleansing within Europe and the relation of Yugoslavia's dissolution to Western European order. Although the events of 1989, specifically the dissolution of antagonistic East and West blocs, provided an opportunity for a resignifying of European order, why instead has the established principle of a culturally homogeneous nation—meaning a numerically constituted "normality"—within a sovereign, territorial state been reaffirmed? Is it that because the former Yugoslavia was never able to organize itself according to this principle, it was never properly European?[1] To imagine people as culturally homogeneous and territorially distinct was perhaps a necessary (though not sufficient) condition for admittance of these peoples into the Western European order *as presently conceived.* Ethnic cleansing was a primary means used to realize the principle "separation and partition," to divide Yugoslavia into separate states with distinct peoples.

Second, I will argue that the practice of ethnic cleansing is a conceptual and practical extension of the interplay of two institutionalized modes of perception and behavior—"territorial sovereignty" and "heterosexuality." For now, I will defer a definition of territorial sovereignty. I will be using heterosexuality, following Adrienne Rich (1981), to refer to a political institution, a program

274

for the construction and institutionalization of a particular kind of gendered and sexed human. It references more a habitus (institutions, processes, practices) than an ideology (heterosexism) or a sexual preference that might be opposed to, for example, homosexuality. Heterosexuality is also a historical habitus, as Thomas Laqueur (1990) has written, which, in its contemporary form, from the mid-eighteenth century to the present, has defined humans in terms of a "two-sex model" of "sexual incommensurability," who imagine themselves as incomplete unless paired with a member of the opposite sex. European heterosexuality, I will maintain, in tandem with territorial sovereignty generated the categories and inter-national forms that both motivated and made sense of ethnic cleansing in Bosnia, including rape as its most violent expression.[2]

Finally, I will briefly compare contemporary violence in Bosnia to parallel forms in pre-1945 Germany and to the conditions that led to a redefinition of these practices in postwar Germany. This comparison suggests that these institutions are historical, hence subject to change. Their change, I maintain, is a precondition for the refiguring of Europe. When I talk about Germany, where I have been working since 1986 (Borneman 1991; 1992), my discussion will be based on evidence from both documentary research and ethnographic fieldwork. Although I have visited different parts of the former Yugoslavia three times, my discussion of Bosnia will be based solely on a reading of documentary literature.

The Significance of Ethnic Cleansing to Europe

By the end of World War II, Europe had become, for the larger world and even for the residents of the continent itself, a descriptive category without moral authority. The various national governments in Europe had surrendered, if somewhat reluctantly, this moral high ground to the Americans, and, in some cases, to the Soviets. This surrender facilitated the Cold War division of Europe into an East and a West, with the West claiming centrality for itself as the most European of the Europeans. The idea of Europe was slowly and with great effort resurrected, mostly by those in the West, so that by 1987, Mikhail Gorbachev, the leader of the East,

275

could proclaim a "common European home" from the Atlantic to the Urals, in effect appropriating for himself and extending the geographical, political, and cultural frontiers of the reconstituted Western European universalist tradition (1987: 195).[3] The optimism that accompanied this mid-eighties thaw in the Cold War was followed by the opening of the Wall, the collapse of the authoritarian regimes in the East, along with enactment of the Maastricht Accords which were to accelerate the pace of the European Community's unification. This optimism has since all but dissolved into a hardening and strengthening, if not creation, of national demarcations and interests, and a pessimism about Europe as a whole. Above all, the inability of Europeans and their governments to deal with the slaughter in Bosnia struck a severe blow to the self-confidence and new moral authority that was emergent in 1989. For the time being, it has brought to a halt a brief period in the re-imagining of a more inclusive, free, peaceful Europe.

At stake in the dissolution of Yugoslavia and the war in Bosnia have been the two core principles of modern Western European order: the creation of sovereign peoples conceived as culturally homogeneous, self-constituting majorities within a nation form, and the assertion of this sovereignty through territorial control in a state.[4] These principles have for a long time been not merely "European" but part of a global dogma about political and cultural organization. From 1945 to 1992, the number of sovereign states recognized internationally grew from 51 to 184. The end of the Cold War and breakup of the Soviet Union opened up the possibility for new demands for territorial-based states in Europe. Most of these new states are still busy creating the nation form, which entails constituting both new majorities (often called "ethnic majorities" or "majoritarian interests") and minorities—which, in turn, are frequently suppressed or expelled. Even if these new states are successful at creating a moment in which "the people"—that scandalous rallying cry of the French Revolution—perceive themselves to be ethnically homogeneous nations representable as culturally united wholes, their economic and territorial viability as states remains questionable. In other words, however one may want to evaluate territorially sovereign states, this form of world order is extremely fragile. If this kind of fragmentation occurs in Africa,

276

some observers estimate that the number of states in the world could reach 450.

What kind of process has led to the institutionalization of the European nation-state model? The concept of a state's territorial sovereignty is usually attributed to Jean Bodin (1576), though it actually had a long gestation, formulated in response to the breakup of absolutism and in conjunction with the doctrine of the "king's two bodies" (Kantorowicz 1957). After the discovery of the New World at the end of the fifteenth century, Spain and Portugal literally "played" with this concept, as did the other European powers shortly thereafter, but more in the New World than in the Old. Clebsch writes that "in the epoch between the abdication of Charles V from imperial office (in 1556) and the rise of Napoleon Bonaparte (in 1804) as self-crowned emperor" territorial sovereignty became the principle that mapped "the human endeavor" (1979: 21). It received its major gestalt with the signing of the Treaty of Westphalia in 1648.

In turning to the principle of the territorial sovereignty of discrete states, signers of the Treaty of Westphalia ostensibly thought they were ending religiously motivated war by territorially separating the disputing parties. This "separation and partition" solution falsely assumed that religious or ideological dogma were geographically confinable, and that territorial separation would produce toleration. Clebsch points out that after the Peace of Westphalia, "'territorialism' more accurately than 'toleration' describes most attempts . . . to disinfect religion's divisive virulence" (1979: 185). Barely two decades after the end of the Thirty Year War, Louis XIV initiated a series of conflicts—expansionist wars—that lasted for nearly a half-century. This conflict-ridden pattern is not a side effect of "territorialism" but its telos; it has been institutionalized and is now self-reproducing. States, whose "peoples" and "religions" are never in fact discrete and bounded, have strong interests in generating, exacerbating, and institutionalizing differences with neighbors or neighboring ideas so that the justification for standing armies and the pretext for intervention is always at hand. Hence, what was initially merely a top-down strategic solution became a form of bottom-up self-identification and a political entity supported by a conglomeration of interested parties.

The concept of statehood remains the central principle asserted in much international law, and it generates most of the categories used by scholars of international relations. The 1933 Montevideo Convention defined the criteria for statehood as having: 1) a permanent population; 2) a defined territory; 3) government; and 4) the capacity to enter into relations with other states (Article 1, League of Nations Treaty Series No. 881). In practice, however, only criteria 1 and 2 have been consistently upheld by the United Nations and already existing nation-states. This concept of statehood politicizes ethnically mixed and territorially dispersed populations by combining the two criteria in such categories as "national sovereignty" and "national integrity," which are then appealed to in justifying war against external or internal enemies.

The nation form has another, parallel but separate, history. Initially taken up as a political program in the French Revolution and subsequently written into the United Nations Charter (Balibar 1991; Brubaker 1992; Israel 1967), the nation form grew out of transformed empires and tribes during the process of European state formation. This transformation of diverse peoples into unified nations was rarely accomplished without intermittent purges, cleansings, or other kinds of homogenizing processees. From the late fifteenth to the early seventeenth centuries, all modern Western European states have engaged in various forms and degrees of ethnic cleansing, in what Zollberg calls "the generic process leading to the formation of victim groups" (Zollberg 1983: 35). Spain was the first, expelling unconverted Jews in 1492, perennially persecuting and finally expelling residents of identifiable Muslim descent in 1609, and between 1577 and 1630 expelling its Protestants, who at that time comprised fourteen percent of the overall population. For the "purifiers," the economic consequences of these "cleansings" were disastrous (Zollberg 1983: 31–32). Human sacrifice was practiced in the service of group unity and not motivated primarily by individual economic gain.

In the twentieth century, the process of creating victim groups has reached new heights. Writing in 1951, Hannah Arendt perspicaciously pointed to "the stateless and the minorities"—the two groups being globally reconstituted (sic) after 1989—as making a mockery of national sovereignty "except for giant states." She writes

278

that the peace treaties concluding World War I "lumped together many peoples in single states, called some of them 'state people' and entrusted them with the government, silently assumed that others (such as the Slovaks in Czechoslovakia, or the Croats and Slovenes in Yugoslavia) were equal partners in the government, which they of course were not, and with equal arbitrariness created out of the remnant a third group of nationalities called 'minorities.'" The result, she concludes, was to make it seem to the stateless and the minorities that the treaties were "an arbitrary game which handed out rule to some and servitude to others"; the newly created states regarded the treaties "as an open breach of promise and discrimination" and subsequently ignored them. She singled out for criticism the importation of the two conditions of West European nation-states—"homogeneity of population and rootedness in the soil"—into Eastern and Southern Europe (1951: 149–150). Following World War I, the League of Nations solution to one Balkan conflict was to transfer 380,000 Muslims from Greece to Turkey and move 1.3 million Orthodox Christians in the other direction.

East-Central Europe has certainly had more than its share of pogroms and cleansing but it has never undergone the same kind of homogeneous nation-building processes, nor in this period did it produce the strong, central states that characterize Western Europe. Whereas the breakup of the Holy Roman Empire in Western Europe was followed by the Reformation, nation building, and the construction of central states with parliamentary democracies, in East-Central Europe it was followed by autocratic federal systems with multi-ethnic populations. In a brilliant article on the inheritance and future of the European nation-state, M. Rainer Lepsius (1988: 256–269) argues that despite the wars, revolutions, and massive repressions that the nation-state has created, the particular advantages it has offered to West European states include the institutionalization of peaceful conflict solving through the rule of law, guarantees of individual freedom, the organization of interests through parliamentary democracies, and the integration of economic development in the world economy. In each of these measures East-Central European states have been at a permanent disadvatage vis-à-vis their West European counterparts. Religious

279

and territorial fragmentation and the inability to centralize decisions and organize power have been the major factors in their
relative backwardness. Hence, it should come as no surprise that
most East Europeans, including peoples in the former Yugoslavia,
seek to build nation-states along what they understand as the
Western European model.

Much as the events in Bosnia and its status as an entity are
being shaped by a Western European ideal, the status of Europe as
an entity is being reshaped by events in Bosnia. When speaking of
the entity Europe, I am referring to a stategy of self-representation
and device of power, not to a stable, sovereign, autonomous object
(Geyer 1993). Such a strategy has always been dependent on the
externalization or creation of negative others. As Geyer writes,
European "identities become visible in efforts to map the divide
between Europe and the world. The boundaries of Europe and its
negative identities were persistently negotiated in the inscription
of otherness on 'strangers'" (1989: 336). This strategy of self-representation, of achieving consciousness of itself and the parameters
of its powers through the creation of negative identities, was already operative in the fourteenth and fifteenth centuries, long before
it appeared as a strategy in "Africa," "Asia," or any of the other
continents. European coherence has always been tied to some ex-
ternality, some hypostasized other—for example, the infidel, the
Orient, or the East. During the Cold War partition of the continent,
this other was Communism. Western Europe united against an
externally placed (East European and Soviet) Communism, while
Eastern Europe, the site of that external, came to see itself as part
of Europe only insofar as it could imagine exorcizing Communism
from its body. The collapse of Communism as an externally and
internally hypostasized enemy dissolves Europe's most recent ex-
trinsic other. Whereas before 1989 this shared goal of exorcism
provided the grounds to unite East and West, now the reasons for
unity rest solely within the West European principles of nation-
state order.

"1989" still awaits its signification within Europe. It is pulled in
two not necessarily contradictory directions. For one, Western
Europe is undergoing supranational, unifying processes, driven by
the (Western) European Union. These supranational processes do

not replace the nation-state, which for now remains a superior form of organizing democratic participation and a territorial form of group identification. But the result will be that territorial states yield some questions of sovereignty—above all, military and economic—to the EU or other transnational bodies. The other direction is the reaffirmation of national state sovereignty and group differences among EU members. Along these lines, Eastern Europe is engaged in a catching-up process to the West, creating relatively homogeneous nation-states as a precondition for entrance into the EU.

Sex and Territoriality in Anglo-American Anthropology of Europe

Anglo-American anthropologists of Europe have produced a substantial body of literature on the meanings of sex and land in the Mediterranean area, but they have not theorized this in a way that links meanings to the institutions of statehood. They have consistently identified for study two objects—the "people" and its "history"—without linking both to the development of territorial states. This approach to the study of Europe is an exercise in what Carl Schmitt in 1919, more than forty years before such studies began, associated with "political romanticism": a replacement of the metaphysics of "God" with that of either "the people" or "history." Schmitt's critique was aimed at liberalism and what he called "subjectified occasionalism," a perspective that aestheticizes politics by prioritizing the exotic and alien over the political and by reinforcing a public/private distinction. Setting the subjective and private in opposition to (and to be protected from) the political, political romanticism effectively removes the possibility of critique of "commonplace reality" and therefore legitimates the exercise of power and the status quo (Schmitt 1919: 99–100). Schmitt's critique of political romanticism applies equally to the anthropological studies of the Mediterranean that operated with the folk model of "the people," and to conventional historical studies that employed a model of autonomous national "history."

Anthropologists doing village studies constructed the Mediterranean as a cultural unity, with an "honor and shame" complex characterized by a cult of masculinity as its central organizing meta-phor or trope. Julian Pitt-Rivers's first Mediterranean study, *People of the Sierra*, published in 1954, was about an Andalusian village under Franco's rule. He took up a "community of 3000 souls" and focused on social organization and structure (1971: 208). He was concerned with the "closed" nature of the community, revealed in the title of his first chapter, "El Pueblo: the boundaries of the com-munity." Toward the middle of the book, he began developing the theme of honor and shame, with honor attached to the male, the legal structure, and the state, shame to the female, the private, and social relations. He defined masculinity as "the conquest of prestige and individual glory, the pursuit of pleasure, a predatory attitude toward the female sex and a challenging one towards the male" (1971: 118). In his subsequent work in Spain and in Cyprus, Pitt-Rivers continued to develop the theme of honor and shame, mapped onto a theory of gender as a system of oppositional and complementary roles that produce a harmonious whole (1966; 1968). Many other anthropologists have subsequently followed Pitt-Rivers's lead in developing the theme of honor and shame and creating the Mediterranean as a unity.

My aim here is not to reinforce the idea of the cultural unity of the Mediterranean, but to point out the possible significance of village studies of masculinity for understanding territorial sover-eignty, heterosexuality, and Europe. The significance of heterosexual masculinity is to be found neither in its regional specificity, nor by situating it in its relation to the domain of politics, but rather by understanding masculinity itself, or gender and sexuality more generally, as a generative source of the political. In other words, heterosexual masculinity of the sort discussed by Pitt-Rivers is not merely a separate domain of discursive practices that at times interacts with the political, but itself generates the political do-main along with the illusion that this domain is semi-autonomous. In the discussion that follows, my comparisons are not meant to establish a unitary field around heterosexuality in the Mediterra-nean or elsewhere, but rather to isolate specific heterosexual prac-tices as they articulate with territorial sovereignty and to understand the stakes in this articulation and mutual constitution for defini-tions of the political.

Critiques of the anthropology of the Mediterranean have tended to focus on the relation of cultural constructs of masculinity and femininity to proper political, or politicized, research contexts without specifying what is generating either set of practices. Michael Herzfeld, for example, does not argue against an assumption of "Mediterranean society," nor against village studies, but instead for a new trope, a displacement of research away from "honor and shame" and toward "hospitality" (Herzfeld 1987b). From another position, João de Pina-Cabral has criticized the use of stereotypes of Mediterranean cultural unity "as tools for the legitimation of academic authority," proposing instead sub-regional studies (1989: 401). Both critiques fail to address the actual truth-claims and the wider significance of the postulates about masculinity set forth in earlier studies.

We might draw out the theoretical significance of these studies by reexamining the findings. Two examples. Michael Herzfeld's *The Poetics of Manhood* (1985) seems to engage in what Schmitt identified as "political romanticism." Taking a folk of 1,425 people on the island of Crete as its object, it focused on the "variety of rhetorical poses" men assume in displaying their (masculine) selves. But for Herzfeld, poetics and power did not exclude each other. Rather, male rhetoric was an articulation of power plays situated in local, village, island, and national contexts. In a rich analysis of card playing, he demonstrated how "positive contests of generosity merge conceptually with negative contests of violence." The rhetoric of the card game is entirely sexualized by cards being talked about as either "immoral women" or "passive homosexuals," except in the case of the ace, which is glossed as "penis" (1985: 123)—a neat and frightening triangulation, with the self (penis) as phallus—the ideal identification or sole referent—denied a sexual relationship based on respect with either women or men. Throughout the study, Herzfeld represented village men as engaged in agonistic patterns of male interaction, above all performed in ritualized theft of animals. A constant tension between latent violence and the possibility of alliance is always at hand. "Although [these contests] may occasionally lead to violence," Herzfeld stressed that the games convert "uncertainty into truce," that they "are ultimately the best foundations for alliance" (1985: 162). These self-representations need not be read in such a generous fashion.

Indeed, Herzfeld offered some sobering findings that lend themselves to another interpretation. For example, the villagers associate all female sexuality with pollution. Therefore freedom from sexual contact is associated with success in battle, except, men remember, in the case of raping Turkish women, which "was less serious because it was essentially an attack on their husbands" (1985: 159). In other words, sex—in a world where this appears to be the exemplary metaphor for all relations—is okay, even commendable, if tied to violence, sadism, or the humiliation of one's enemy. Any expression of sex tainted by forms of mutual affirmation or respect is denigrated. Are we really to assume that the "best foundations for alliance" rest in the reproduction of this particular agonistic structure? It just so happens that the poetics of masculinity in this village, as outlined by Herzfeld, is structured quite similarly to that of the Andalusian villagers studied by Pitt-Rivers: status achieved by a denigration of the woman and a fear/distancing from homoerotic/homosexual desire. In fact, in *Anthropology Through the Looking-Glass*, Herzfeld made some of these connections analytically explicit. There, he argued that "control over intimacy is not only the basis of political control, but it also becomes the means whereby nations protect their inner flaws from outside intruders" (1987a: 180). Moreover, a "human being" or "a Greek"— the terms are interchangeable—was defined as one who does not "passively surrender the right to resist." This counter-concept of the human is, in turn, "contemptuously attributed to the pous[h]tis, the passive homosexual" (1987a: 34, 208; see also Faubion 1993: 216–241).

We find a further specification of this masculine trope in Stanley Brandes's *Metaphors of Masculinity* (1980), a study of sex and status in Andalusian folklore. Brandes argued that the men of Monteros "are concerned above all with two problems of identity: their place in the social hierarchy and their relation to women" (1980: 6). He was in fact restating the more general thesis we encountered in Pitt-Rivers's and Herzfeld's work. Men in this small town were concerned about women because they were regarded as "seductresses who use their inordinately great sexual powers or desires toward male destruction"; they were "emasculating creatures" and produced a fear of "symbolic castration"(1980: 105). Because women were also regarded as "sexual insatiables," men could never adequately satisfy them.

As in Herzfeld's research, Brandes found that the sexual metaphor extended to both opposite- and same-sex relations. Masculine metaphors about the penis and testicles abound. Even "the human will is somehow related to the male genitalia" (1980: 92). In male-male interactions, it was not the fear of penetration that is foregrounded, but the fear that desire for such penetration will arise (and increase?) if one becomes accustomed to it. In that case, men would become feminized, asserts Brandes, for "masculine behavior is conceptually located in the male genital region, feminine behavior is concentrated linguistically on the anus" (1980: 95). In other words, gender has little to do with the biological sex of the person but is a matter of symbolic location. Men can be both male and female, depending on their position. What Brandes and Herzfeld are describing is a "jealousy-competition" system between males, based, as Guy Hocquenhem explains, on making the phallus "the universal reference point for all activity" and on sublimating anal desire. Only later in life is this anal desire gendered (as female, in Brandes' example); initially it is identified with male-male interaction. "Homosexual sublimation," Hocquenhem (1972: 81, 91) concludes in a major early theoretical work on the topic, "provides the solid ideological basis for a constantly threatened social unity."

Men, wrote Brandes, "are unafraid to joke about playing the phallic, 'male' part in homosexual intercourse. . . It is . . . the dread of assuming a feminine posture—of being the victim of sexual attack, instead of the perpetrator—that preoccupies the men of our town." This dread was indeed a pre-occupation with the anus, rooted in a fear of becoming "accustomed to having objects placed [in the anus, after which] he may begin to derive pleasure from it and will be transformed into a homosexual, and worse, one who is relegated to the female, passive role" (1980: 96).[5] Let me emphasize here that this fear of deriving pleasure from penetration is the wish-fantasy of the penetrator, not of the man who is penetrated. In this sense, it is not a modern gay male fantasy (which propagates an ideal of reciprocity between men), but a heterosexual desire: it assumes two unequal and ranked genders, male and female, active and passive, being mapped out onto two anatomical males.[6] This same

285

point is reaffirmed in a detailed description of the meaning of machismo and homosexuality for "real men" in Seville by Haller (1992: 27–35).

Male fears of sexual inadequacy in satisfying women and of awakened sexual desire to be penetrated by men are further revealed in Brandes's analysis of jokes about Gypsies. These jokes focused on "the larger size of male Gypsy organs, their sexual potency, and the unwillingness to submit to anal penetration" as the "essential ingredients of the rebellious, insubordinate spirit" (1980: 72). The means most frequently employed to control this threatening sexual power were extreme sadistic pain or repression of the self, and/or, by extension, political repression by the state. Thus, male fears of the desire for penetration, of sexual inadequacy, of anarchic sexual desire, are linked together and metaphorically extended onto a state apparatus that functions within and as paradigm for this phallic complex.

Let me summarize. I have assumed the truth of the empirical ethnographic claims of Mediterranean studies but reinterpreted them. My reinterpretation has sought to avoid aestheticizing honor and shame, or, more specifically, gender and sexuality. I took the domestic domain to be the generative site of politics and situated it in the larger context of the institution of heterosexuality. This anthropology moves away from political romanticism and avoids what Schmitt identified as "a kind of lyrical paraphrase of experience," a desire "to be productive without becoming active" (1986:159).

Ethnic Cleansing and Heterosexuality in Bosnia

Are acts of humiliation or annihilation of the other in Bosnia understood as legitimate self-assertions, as personal realizations of the principle of territorial sovereignty? My explication will be limited primarily to the perspectives of Serbian and Croatian nationalists, since they have been the major perpetrators of the attempted genocide.

In early accounts of perpetrators' motivations for engaging in ethnic cleansing, explanations rarely revolved around issues of military or economic gain. Rather, thick descriptions of the conflict invariably returned to expressions of a heterosexual masculinity as it played into the constitution of a numerically defined majority alongside minorities (identified as external ethnic others) and the assertion of sovereignty through territorial control under a homogeneous nation—the two foundational principles for post-Westphalian European order. It is generally agreed that all of the post-Tito political leaders in Yugoslavia had considerable interest in territorial expansion, for in order to establish economically viable and autonomous nation-states, each national-religious-ethnic group required some land from the others. But my interest here is not in the obvious culpability of the leaders but to explain how these principles manifest themselves in the actions of local perpetrators in the Bosnian genocide. Could ethnic cleansing be the expression of a specific form of heterosexuality motivated by two anxieties: anxiety about women's sexuality and about homosexuality?

Journalistic accounts of the violence and murder in Bosnia and its aftermath often simply repeat two "causes" offered by participants themselves. These causes correspond roughly to the two units anthropologists have also constructed and studied, namely "history" and "folk".[7] Serbian nationalists, for example, conveniently use "history" as an explanation for the acting-out of "ancient hatreds." They select events several hundred years apart, such as the defeat by the Turks in Kosovo in 1389, Ottoman occupation during the Middle Ages, the massacre of Serbs by the Croatian Ustashe at the end of World War II, and Croatian legal discrimination against Serbs in 1991/92, to construct a narrative as if one person had experienced all these events sequentially, from the fourteenth century to present. (Croatian nationalists have a similar story.) Then this "history-as-process-of-continuous-suffering" is mapped onto essentialized and distinct ethnic groups ("the people" or "the nation"), creating a causal explanation for the present human subject in terms of its past histories unfolding teleologically according to primordial sentiments (see Kaldor 1993: 24–34).[8] Conveniently ignored in this kind of story are events that disturb the trajectory of the narrative, such as "Cetnik" crimes against Croats, or the period of Communist rule under Tito when peoples lived together peacefully, and "unclean" categories of people, such as offspring of mixed-marriage Croats, Muslims, and Serbs, who by 1989 numbered close

287

to twenty-five percent in some parts of Bosnia, with much larger percentages in big cities (Denitch 1993: 287).[9]

One cannot fault people for not remembering accurately events about which an officially enforced quasi-silence had been maintained during the entire period of Tito's rule. Those who experienced the events earlier in this century as either victims or perpetrators had never engaged in an actual confrontation or working through of this past with their counterparts. For both victims and perpetrators, to remember massacres and other acts of such extreme brutality some sixty years after an event is to confront a trauma of tremendous psychological and sociological depth (see Parin 1993). This remembering was especially difficult, if not impossible, during the recent genocide, for memory work can not begin while engaged in a repetition of the initial event; it is possible only after the trauma is over. A historically accurate memory is not at issue here, for memory under these circumstances can be expected to produce nothing but denial and self-justificatory myth. The attempt by many historians, journalists, and others to get at an exactly remembered truth, to recount past horrors in an accurate chronology, has only fostered the "ancient hatreds" thesis, supporting revenge motives and desires for "ethnic cleansing." Given the histories of extreme violence in the Balkans, each ethnic group predictably found sufficient reason in the past to fear the others and to seek personal revenge.

The question is therefore never just remembering history, but turns around when one is remembering, which memories to select, and what to do with them. If memories are woven into a coherent and linear historical tale of primordial difference and right, then ethnic cleansing is indeed a rational response to this historical memory. But if remembered events are used to tell stories about disjunctive histories, about alternate periods of doing wrong and being wronged, then history might instead indicate alternative persons, communities, and paths—i.e., contingent, non-essential— that were not but could have been realized. But that is not the kind of remembering that has been encouraged by local politicians and most reporters of the conflict, who instead have focused their energies on telling the "true story" of each "people."

Early accounts of soldiers fighting this war describe a culture troped by vast amounts of drinking, indiscriminate murdering, fetishization of weaponry, pornographic magazines, rape, and prostitution (Burns 1992: A12; Glenny 1992; Horwitz 1993: 41–44). That much of this war is being financed, and in some cases even fought, by Serbs and Croats who have repatriated from Canada and the United States does not lessen the responsibility of the soldiers for their behavior, but implicates other national communities and the international order itself in the ways in which ethnic cleansing and murder is accomplished and expressed (Glenny 1992; Phillips 1991: 42–46).[10] One reporter describes his encounter with a leader in the Croatian shock troops (HOS): "Three men who looked like bikers—black leather vests, bulging biceps, lewd tattoos—sat out front, cleaning a bazooka. One of them ushered me inside to meet a man he called 'the Commander.' Jadrenko sat with a revolver on the desk in front of him. Behind him a cleaver had been sunk into the windowsill. On the wall was a portrait of Ante Pavelic, the leader of the Croat fascists; they had formed an alliance with the Nazis in World War II and are believed to have killed more than 500,000 Serbs, Gypsies, and Jews. Beside the portrait was a favorite HOS slogan: MAN MAKES THE HOMELAND AND THE HOMELAND MAKES THE MAN. The thirty-three-year-old commander wore camouflage pants, running shoes, and a tight black T-shirt, which he rolled up to reveal a shrapnel scar on his taut rib cage. 'Killing Serbs is hard work,' he said. 'When we fight, it is an eye for an eye. No compromise.' Jadrenko talked for an hour, chain-smoking Marlboros. He explained that all of Bosnia and parts of Serbia belonged to 'greater Croatia,' historically speaking (history in this case being the eleventh century, when Croatia was last independent). He boasted about the toughness of his men and how they'd cleansed Serbs from many villages. I asked him about the Croat death camps during World War II. 'I wasn't alive then,' he said with a shrug." (Horwitz 1993: 44). Later, Jadrenko revealed to Horwitz that he had been an interior decorator before the war, that he had two kids and a wife whom he visited on the weekends. This passage makes explicit the equation of masculinity with homeland and control over territory. The so-called private domain or familial ideology generates the metaphors necessary to make sense of public war. Through the selective use of historical memory, the other is essentialized and violently externalized in order to legitimate the assertion of cultural differences and the necessity of genocide.

289

Tom Post, reporter for *Newsweek*, described his encounter with two Serb deserters now being held in prison in Bosnia: "They were ordered to rape and murder for the amusement of their commander in Brcko, in northeastern Bosnia, in May 1992. Panic says he balked when two battered women, each about 18, were brought to him in a room in a warehouse where 500 to 600 civilians were imprisoned. Serb soldiers 'said they'd kill me if I didn't' rape them, he recalls, insisting that he "only did a little" to his screaming victims... Three other women were dragged out for the display. During these episodes, Panic says, soldiers stood around in the circle and laughed. Then they hauled two badly beaten Muslim prisoners before Panic and handed him a gun. 'I said, "I can't, they've never done anything to me,"' he remembers. "'You have to or else we'll kill you,'" Panic says he was told. He shot each man in the chest. Two more male prisoners appeared. A soldier handed Panic a knife. 'Butcher them,' he commanded. When Panic protested, the soldier replied, 'I'll show you how it's done.' Then holding Panic's hand around the knife handle, he seized the man by the hair, jerked back his head and cut his throat" (Post 1993: 34–35).

First-hand accounts of participants in the Bosnian war, especially but certainly not exclusively those of Serbs, indicate a kind of violence and "male poetics" that is reminiscent of accounts of Balkan atrocities beginning at the outbreak of World War I and continuing, with interruptions, through 1945 (see Hirschfeld 1946: 254–264). Proof of masculinity through acts of brutality, such as rape of civilians or physical assault on prisoners of war, is often equated with an assertion of self, and understood as a legitimate expression of anger or domination (Benard and Schlaffer 1993: 176–185). Assertions of masculinity through rape (limited to acts involving penile penetration of the anus or vagina) and sexual assault in Bosnia are well-documented and were committed by all sides, although "Muslim women have been the chief victims and the main perpetrators have been members of Serbian armed forces" (Amnesty International 1993: 3). The *Final Report of the United Nations Commission of Experts* (1994: Annex I.C) based on more than 900 pages of testimony, also seeks to "avoid moral equivalency," citing the Bosnian Serbs, who ran "over 60 percent of the nearly 150 detention centers," as "the great majority of alleged perpetrators." This UN *Final Report* (1994: Annex I.A) details 1,100 reported cases of rape and sexual assault, with 800 named victims, 1,800 unnamed or insufficiently identified, with an additional 10,000 victims identified through approximations. Of the alleged perpetrators, 700 are named, 750 identified but not named, 300 approximately identified, with an additional 900 cases referring to classes of perpetrators not specified in numbers.

These abuses are not limited to the rape of females, estimates of which range from 20,000 to 60,000; as well, men have widely raped and sexually abused other men, though we have no numerical estimates (Amnesty International 1993: 5; Butkovic 1993: 7–8; Drakulic 1993: 270; Helsinki Watch 1992; UN Final Report 1994; Seifert 1993: 88). In an article on Serbian mass rapes of Muslim women, Butkovic (1993: 8) cites clinical evidence from the Dean of the Medical Faculty at Zagreb University, concluding, "Just like the raped Muslim women, so too raped men are intentionally eliminated from the reproductive cycle, and that too is a deliberate means of genocide." These violent sexual acts, then, cannot be understood only as "violence against women," for they involve a more general violence against an other-identified people—a genocide.

While it is difficult under any circumstances for the victims of rape to talk about, or even to admit to, what happened, it is doubly difficult to get information on male victims of rape. Yet male rape of men has been widespread and practiced by all sides in the war. In contrast to rape of women, which seems to have occurred equally in detention centers, forests, and homes, most rape and sexual assault of men has occurred in detention centers. Given the stigma attached to being victims of sexual abuse, men have been willing to talk to reporters and investigators only when confronted with accusations that members of their own ethnic group have already been accused of the same thing. The pattern of reporting in such accounts that I have gleaned from reading accounts is first a total denial of all knowledge, then, after long conversations about other topics, some stories were told, though most men reported these as if they neither witnessed nor personally suffered such abuse. Over time, male victims show increasing reticence "to report incidents of rape and sexual assault at an international level" (Final Report 1994: Annex IV.I.A). Therefore, the overwhelming majority of accounts

291

about rape of men have remained second-person. In addition to the UN Final Report, which I will summarize below, I would like to cite several first-person descriptions to illustrate the sexual and territorial idioms in which the war is being conducted.

Pierre Salignon of Medicins sans Frontières, who worked with refugees in the Croatian town of Karlovac, believes that male sexual abuse and mutilation was carried out by "intelligent" torturers who "want to degrade their victims as much as possible. They don't want to kill them, they want to break them." Emir Jakupovic reported to United Nations psychologists that Serb forces forced him "to bite off the genitals of four friends as they screamed in agony. They were already close to death" after being forced, by Serbian guards who used to be their neighbors in Kozarac, to drink tractor oil (Branson 1993: 13).

In the town of Pula, a Serb bricklayer named Rade Drinjaca described "being tied to the wall" with a Muslim man named Goran, where he was "sexually abused and beaten. We were made to perform oral sex on the guards, and Goran was raped a few times even before my arrival. I cannot even describe the other things we were made to do to the guards. It was like the Middle Ages." A reporter describes that one of the favorite games of the guards was apparently to "see which one of them could ease themselves longer in their faces." A young Muslim driver, Dian Menkovic, who was in the Serb-run Omarska camp in the summer of 1992, described being "strung up by his hands to a wall as a guard used a bayonet to attempt to cut off his genitals." The castration attempt was not successful; Menkovic escaped with twenty stitches. A young man named Rasim Mulic told of being "forced to stand with his hands behind his back and legs apart" while beaten in the genitals. His friend told of being forced to lie on his side on the floor while "eight or ten people stepped on his genitals with their heels." Another man told of being forced (with a gun at his head) "to rape another man or woman, often from the same family" (Branson 1993: 13).

In addition to unspecified "sex acts," which frequently means anal intercourse, the *Final Report of the United Nations* contains hundreds of cases describing the specific forms of violent sexuality practiced on male victims in Bosnia, Croatia, and Serbia. The list includes forcing detainees to perform fellatio on fellow prisoners, to fellate the guards, to perform mutual masturbation (Final Report 1994: II.A.31; II.A.42.6; II.B.3); to anally penetrate other prisoners, male and female (Final Report 1994: II.A.10; II.A.38.a); to stick a Coke bottle up one's ass, to perform sex with each other, to rape female prisoners, including one's own daughters, to copulate in each other's mouths; guards cutting off nipples, attaching electrodes to penises, fist-fucking a prisoner (Final Report 1994: II.A.11, II.A.38.c; II.B.7; II.B.14; II.B.13; II.B.16); group sex with a single prisoner of either sex, tying prisoners' genitals together with wire and having them walk around in the room they are held (Final Report 1994: II.A.12); circumcising Bosnian Serb boys (Final Report 1994: II.A.23; II.A.25). Castrations appear in the testimony with great frequency, performed in a variety of ways: by forcing one internee to bite off another's testicles after performing oral sex, biting off the penis, using a Great Dane to bite off the testicles; tying one end of a wire to the testicles and the other to a motorcyle, then using the motorcyle to yank off the testicles; forcing detainees to castrate other prisoners with their bare hands; cutting off the genitals with a knife (Final Report 1994: II.A.7; II.A.24; II.A.37; II.A.38.a; II.A.38.b).

The *UN Final Report* (1994: I.D) concludes that very few of the rapes and sexual assaults were "opportunistic"; most displayed an "ethnic motiviation." Being a total affront on "the victims's dignity," they were particularly "effective means of 'ethnic cleansing.'" Frequently, perpetrators explicitly justified the above sexual acts to their victims in terms of limiting or advancing the reproductive heterosexuality of a particular ethnic group. What is shocking about this brutality is not its uniqueness but its familiarity—from Nazi concentration camps to Stalin's gulags to the most recent genocides in Burundi and Indonesia.

One type of explanation for these acts is that the men are pawns of their leaders in a war fought for statehood, (international) economics, interest group formation, or religion; alternately, the war is an instant replay of ancient tribal feuds or the revenge of barbarian country folk against civilized urbanites. These facts are not to be denied, but they cannot be called "causes." Even if partly correct, they are an incomplete set of facts. They do not adequately explain what *motivates* the culturally specific forms of violence practiced at this point in time. To the extent observers explain these events in terms of culture, they most frequently attribute violence to some generalized Balkan (or male) aggression, or patriarchy, or hatred of women (Parin 1993 and Seifert 1993 are exceptions to this pattern). The popular sociobiological thesis that culture is the result of men's desire to maximize their genes and of women's desire to produce and protect good children is totally circular, positing heterosexuality as both the cause of this (natural) behavior and as the (cultural) result of human nature. Equally important, a sociobiological thesis does not permit any discrimination between different types of masculinity and personhood. If all heterosexuality is the same, then rape is a natural, if extreme, violent sexual response of men to women; murder a natural, if extreme, expression of domination of men over men. In Bosnia, however, aggression directed against both males and females is interpreted in the same sexual-political idiom. This "group" aggression is not the cause of anything, but the effect, or the acting out, of sexual-political categories—of the interimplication of heterosexuality and territorial sovereignty—that are individually internalized, interpreted, and practiced.

The twisted logic of the principle of territorial sovereignty in fact lives off its continual violation and reassertion. As James Faubion argues in his experimental monograph on modern Greece, a point he extends to the Occident more generally, "Sovereigns must perpetually reiterate their superiority over other sovereigns" (1993: 126). In Bosnia, the principle of the sovereignty of states, ethnic groups, economies, religions, or persons is being asserted, while the practical sovereignty obtained in each of these domains is continually relegated to the status of epiphenomena. So long as states are dependent on the principle of territorial sovereignty, they must defend the integrity of a distinct "people," or a nation with a continuous history, an integrity that manifests itself only at the moment of its threatened violation. In providing the reasons for their existence, states must recreate moments of territorial violation.

When state sovereignty is linked to reproductive heterosexuality, a pronatal policy for oneself often entails a genocidal policy for the other. In the twentieth century, the two domains are so intertwined that it is no longer relevant to ask which domain is prior

294

or dominant. The assertion of one set of principles necessarily reinforces the other. From the everyday perspectives of the perpetrators of acts of violence in Bosnia, motivations and excitations for action lie in a melange of hopes of territorial gain, dreams of historical revenge, fantasies of domination and humiliation, general anxieties of manhood and worth, fears of demasculinization, and female pornography. Explanations of the beginning and expansions of the conflict over territoriality, sovereignty, and statehood in Bosnia must include an account of reproductive heterosexuality, for the interimplication of the two are generative of the motivations behind the particular male expressions of self in this war through humiliation, rape, sexual assault, murder, and genocide.

Serb and Croat women were also participants in the war and share no small part as agents in perpetrating "ethnic cleansing." For example, Serbian and Croatian women played a central role in blocking U.N. food convoys and other forms of humanitarian aid to Bosnian Muslims.[11] Nor did many Serb and Croat women show much reluctance to move into expropriated Muslim homes. It is true, of course, that the various local political authorities consciously involved as many individuals as possible in their crimes. This argument has already been rehearsed widely in discussions of responsibility of local Germans for the atrocities of the Third Reich, a more totalistic regime than anything that exists in Bosnia. Even there, though scholars differ on degrees of culpability, few would maintain the total innocence of any part of the population or the lack of alternatives to complicity.

Perhaps women's most important function in the genocidal war in Bosnia was to legitimate the brutal actions of their male relatives, specifically in well-documented cases of condemnation of men who refused to fight. In a story published in *Der Spiegel*, a young Muslim man named Faris told of leaving Sarajevo as the sole man in an evacuation bus with children and pregnant women. His mother, who is sixty-five, gave him her ticket, insisting that she had already led a full life. Faris claimed that he still has a hard time blocking out the screaming of the women on the bus at his refusal to get out as it left Sarajevo. For these women, status as victims is constructed as innocent and feminine in opposition to the perpetrator as evil and masculine. Though I have focused on the motivations generated by heterosexual masculinity in the war, I certainly do not wish to propose femininity as a solution to this conflict, nor do I wish to portray all women as "victims of war," as do most media accounts in the American and Western European press. Rather, it is precisely the use of a rigid gender binary that justifies the dichotomy of people who are victimized and defended (women) versus people who perpetrate and defend (men) (Seifert 1993: 92–94). Without the naturalized gender binary as base metaphor to rely upon in making sense of the conflict, one might be more likely to see heterosexuality as a constructed habitus with links to race (the "people" who reproduce themselves in a "territory" with a continuous "history"). Gender does not generate this habitus but is constructed within and for it.

With this gender/sex framework in mind, I might call attention to the political significance of the rape of Muslim women by Serb and Croat soldiers for the project of "ethnic cleansing," and to the rejection of the children of these rapes by these women (the Bosnian government estimates that some 35,000 Muslim women have been impregnated by rape [Drakulic 1993: 271]). Ethnic Serb and Croat nationalists have always viewed the religious conversion of their compatriots by the Ottoman Turks, after the Turks conquered the current area of Bosnia-Herzegovina in 1463, as an act of betrayal and, most importantly, of submission. In contrast to Serb and Croat resistance, this "betrayal of the Serb or Croat ethnic heritage," wrote Kaldor, "is [taken to be] the only fundamental aspect of the Muslim character" (1993: 30). Indeed, here we see Serbian and Croatian use of a kind of sociobiological thesis to justify the naturalness of rape and ethnic cleansing. As with the more sophisticated versions of sociobiology, there is also a "feedback loop" where, in turn, the resultant culture influences the further evolution of the biological base. Because Serbs and Croats view Muslim "betrayal" (re: 500 years of submission to the aggressive Turks) as having a genetic base and therefore not a historical act (i.e., arbitrary, contingent), it marks the Muslims as non-Europeans forever more, which in turn mandates and validates Serbian action as necessary to protect "Europe." Submission further figures Muslims as feminine, not fully human, and therefore not deserving of respect.

It is widely reported that both perpetrators and victims in Bosnia frequently understand the rape of Muslim women as a way of humiliating Muslim men. In other words, it functioned much as male rape of men, as an interaction between masculine men and feminized men, with the women acting only as vessels of or proxies for their men. Young Muslim women who have been raped often report that they will never be able to marry because other refugees do not believe that they were forced to have sex with Serb men. For example, one Muslim woman who had been raped reported that she was accused of wanting "to sow the seeds of the Serbs in Bosnia" (Zülch 1993: 112).

An alternative understanding of the rapes, which was repeated with incredible regularity by the perpetrators in 1992 and 1993 (Final Report 1994) is that they are a way of getting "foreign" women to carry one's own genetic line or of creating impotence in "foreign" men—an explanation that again invokes a sociobiological understanding of gender-motivated action.[12] This explanation for male behavior, however, assumes total irrationality among the rapists, since they continued to impregnate foreign-identified women even though most of those women refused to carry the children to term. Drakulic reports that *all* of the women she spoke with in her investigation into the mass rapes said they would either "strangle [the child] with my own hands" or abandon it (1993: 271). The fact that many of the rapes have been committed by neighbors who knew the women personally suggests that the attribution of both foreignness and nativeness was made on the basis of ethnicity alone. Moreover, the value of a fetus was thought to derive from semen alone, independent of what the mother or the environment might bring to it. If hostility or friendship between individuals is predetermined by the father's ethnicity, then it cannot be influenced by social interaction, by learning or ascribed traits that can change over time.

Whether all of the women who were raped actually believe this is doubtful and ultimately irrelevant. There was probably no other socially sanctioned option available to them in the middle of the war than to abort. What I want to emphasize are the consequences of employing a sociobiological theory of culture emically, from the native's point of view, to make sense of and frame what is going on.

For the raped women, that kind of explanation required aborting babies produced by the semen of foreign men; for the raped and sexually abused men, it provoked impotence; for the men who perpetrated these acts of humiliation, it legitimated the fantasies and pragmatics of raping foreign-identified women and men.

Pre-1945 German Heterosexuality, Territoriality, and Genocide

Anthropological work in the Mediterranean could be extremely important in understanding the genocidal war in Bosnia if one avoids its tendency to political romanticism and to aetheticize masculinity. An alternative would be to understand the cultural conceptions and practices themselves as the generative site of the political, of governance, authority, and order.[13] If the production of and then externalization of minorities and a fetishization of territorial sovereignty (ultimately institutionalized in male self-assertion and statehood) are principles not simply of "European order" but also, both more universal and closer to home, so to speak, of certain forms of heterosexual masculinity, then it is incumbent on us to account for the relation between European order and heterosexuality and for the importance of specific modes of domesticity in generating and reproducing particular international orders.[14] To assume that supra- and international order is or can be constructed and reproduced independent of local cultural practices is anti-anthropological thinking; it contradicts everything anthropologists have described since the foundation of the modern discipline by Malinowski, Radcliffe-Brown, and Boas.

Changing expressions of German masculinity, and of notions of majority/minority relations and territorial sovereignty, serve as an illuminating comparison to the same set of relations in contemporary Bosnia. German heterosexuality in the early part of this century was not totally different, particularly in certain forms of masculine expression, from forms of expression in contemporary Bosnia. Many of the German soldiers in both world wars, in particular the "irregulars" who brutalized much of Germany during the Weimar period and later as members of the SS, shared, I think, the basic principles of the "cult of masculinity" outlined in this chapter. But expressions of German masculinity have changed remarkably since 1945 in both East and West. This change is evidence that constructs of masculinity are not stable metahistorical templates but indeed alterable historical products.[15] We have not studied these conditions of change comparatively, and I hope that the following discussion will be understood as suggestions for further study of the possibility for change of heterosexual expressions and institutions. My purpose in this brief, admittedly overly generalized excursus is not to posit the Germans as a model people who have eliminated the preconditions for thinking war and genocide, but rather to indicate the possibilities for historical change in one determinate factor that continues to generate the terms necessary for thinking territoriality and violence in Europe (on interpreting current right-wing radicalism in Germany, see Chapter 8, this volume).

The best-known of the studies of German masculinity from the early part of this century is Klaus Theweleit's (1987) account of the German Freikorps. The Freikorps originated as largely autonomous militias that were subsequently hired by Chancellor Ebert in 1918 to bring order to revolutionary Germany; they ultimately formed the core of Hitler's SA. Theweleit examined the personal diaries of Freikorps members and found that motivations of rage and revenge ("stabbed in the back" and "betrayed" for World War I) in many ways prefigured the even more grotesque actions of the Third Reich. Their rage was organized around two axes, by now familiar to us: the fear of female sexuality and, in Theweleit's words, the "fantasy of a threatening penis" (1987: 75). Women and homosexuality: is this not the same psychosexual anxiety put to ethno-nationalist use for territorial gain and ethnic cleansing in Bosnia? Theweleit writes, "It is phallic, not a vaginal potency that is fantasized and feared" (1987: 73). These men desired to annihilate because of fear of women as castrating and because of anxieties about anal penetration and a possible loss of self, a "feminization." Their phallocentrism and inability to measure up to fantasies of completeness and invulnerability required a projection onto others—women, homosexuals, racialized others—as hypostasized sources of this fear. Subsequently, these men asserted themselves by negating (annihilating) the perceived (ra-

299

cially and sexually) impure (minority), and by expanding territorial control (*Lebensraum*).

During the Third Reich, a similar set of masculinist self-understandings could be found in the fantasies of many men. The murderous activities of the National Socialists differed from those of irregulars of the Weimar years less in terms of motivations than in how the state participated in institutionalizing these motivations. Nazi policy normalized and thus sanitized genocide as a legitimate expression of the desire for territorial sovereignty.[16] The nationalist imagination was linked to militarism in a very specific way, as Michael Geyer has written, the state was seen as "the means for the regeneration of society," leading to an equation of "warfare as welfare, violence as regeneration, virility as virtue" (1992: 85). Everyday life came to be understood in terms of the attractiveness of war. In an examination of letters of soldiers on the front in World War II, Alf Lüdke has shown that "many individuals perceived their masculinity in military terms and images. To these people, their original claim to perform a 'clean' job at home increasingly became linked to the efficient killing operations of the army. In the end, participation in the extermination of 'others' might appear to many as the ultimate fulfillment of those cherished notions of 'German quality work'" (Lüdke 1993: S66–67).

Women were also involved in the war effort, and Claudia Koonz has drawn our attention to their roles. Nazi ideologues, such as Walter Gross, singled out women in matters related to "blood and race, "arguing that "the German woman participates more fully than the man, [who is busy] with his state, and his fighting units, ever can" (cited in Koonz 1993: S9). Koonz details the practices in which women were most directly involved, in selecting "racially fit" mates, indoctrinating children, reporting on "suspicious" activities of neighbors, boycotting Jewish shops, refusing shelter to friends wanted by the police, aiding in the administration of forced abortions, sterilizations, and euthanasia. For comparisons with the war in Bosnia, particularly revealing are the resonances of Nazi appeals to the concept of protecting the "Erbgut," a term that "refers both to the landed property inherited by offspring and genetic property" (Koonz 1993: S20). Here physical reproduction and land, more simply, "Blut und Boden," are semantically linked to, are the

Erbgut of, heterosexuality, which finds its institutional expression in territorial sovereignty. Although the idea of sovereignty feigns a delimitation of state authority outside the national territory, this doctrine in fact presupposes and establishes the grounds for its constant violation: a latent, natural desire for intervention and territorial expansion.[17] Wasn't European colonial expansion the next historical advancement of the principle of territoriality (i.e., non-intervention within Europe) established at Westphalia? Hannah Arendt goes so far as to argue that at the end of the nineteenth century, the nation-state was organized "for the looting of foreign territories and the permanent degradation of alien peoples" (1951: 35). Where, we must ask, does this desire to loot and degrade come from? Even if the sociobiological thesis were true, those of us who wish for humans to behave otherwise have no choice but to act as if these desires were historically contingent and therefore under certain conditions changeable.

National Socialist expression and reinforcement of heterosexuality, embedded in notions of normality, was, in turn, motivated, in the words of Frank Trommler, by the desire to "normalize the exceptional" (1993: S82–S101). Whereas George Mosse (1985) ties normality to a heterosexual bourgeois respectability in Nazi ideology, Trommler traces the desire for normality from the Nazi period through West Germany of the Cold War and even into the present post-unification years. At this point, I wish to emphasize that there existed certain continuities in heterosexual masculinity and in the function of normality in Germany from 1914 through 1945, and that these expressions have since changed. Elsewhere, I have written about the refiguring of German selfhood in Berlin since the war, how the "Blut und Boden" model was radically transformed in both East and West (Borneman 1992). Based on my own ethnographic work over the last ten years, it is apparent that fantasies and self-conceptions, across the political spectrum and irrespective of gender or sexuality, have indeed changed dramatically among men and women in Germany. That this change is not unidirectional, nor the same for each sub-group or class within Germany, goes without saying. But even many members of radical right-wing groups today try to distance themselves from the more extreme misogyny, homophobia, nationalist xenophobia, and dreams of territorial expansion found in the generation of their fathers and grandfathers.

With respect to the war in Yugoslavia, this change is expressed, for example, in how both German men and women seem to have accepted all of the male refugees from the various groups in Bosnia without accusations of "cowardice" or "effeminacy." Although the debate on the German role in Bosnia generated many different positions, there is a strong private commitment to the belief that men (German and "Yugoslavian") have the right to refuse to fight in war. Without a clearly drawn distinction between (male or masculinized) perpetrator and (female or feminized) victim, the whole logic of heterosexuality that provides an unexamined set of references and that generates the terms to make the war sense-ful is undermined. On the other hand, this commitment to male refugees has been in practice extremely limited. It is not shared, for example, by the German Foreign Office (Ausländerbehörde), which has refused to give asylum to any of the male "deserters" from the war in Bosnia-Herzegovina. In contrast to the deserved public sympathy and institutional support extended to women victims of the war, to my knowledge no group of Germans have organized to support the plight of military deserters, men who have nobly and with great courage refused to partake in the politically administered rape and extermination policies.[18]

If one grants that many Germans have changed in non-trivial ways, the difficult question remains as to why. To be sure, one must first emphasize the peculiarity of postwar German sovereignty following the "unconditional surrender" of the nation. Given pre-1945 German gender codes, this surrender was a radically feminizing and humiliating act. Germany was occupied by four foreign armies; it lost huge amounts of territory; six million ethnic Germans were dispossessed and made into refugees; its borders remained permeable and contested for forty-five years; "the people" were divided into two. I need not go on. Certainly this initial violation of territorial sovereignty and delegitimation of its link to national identity created a window of opportunity for subsequent changes in domestic practices. At the same time, this initial violation should not be seen as a perpetuation of the cycle of rape and violence, as a supranational authority assuming the role of sovereignty formerly occupied by the patriarchal national father who now humiliates his son. Perhaps the penalties inflicted on Germany following World War I could be seen as instances of this sort—and the result was thus predictable: the lifting of penalties was followed by a continuation of violence. But the "solution" imposed on Germany following World War II was one that enabled Germans to regain integrity by redefining themselves as a "people" with regard to their own history and to that of others. The Nuremberg trials not only reaffirmed that Germans had lost the war; they also established the principle of individual responsibility for heinous crimes. Most importantly, the trials along with the Allied occupation delegitimated the link between reproductive heterosexuality and territorial sovereignty. And by creating a public domain, the most pernicious aspects of German and Nazi ideology were open for continual contestation.

In this light, we might rethink the commonly expressed disappointment in the German's "inability to mourn" (Mitscherlich 1967) and the expectation that if they did not accurately remember their pasts they would suffer trauma and engage in some sort of repetition compulsion (cf. Bude 1992; Caruth 1991). Perhaps memory work was only possible after the rupture provided by Allied occupation and postwar reorganization. More significant indices of historical transformations are precisely the changes in German domestic practices in East and West—the refiguring of same- and cross-sex relations—along with changes in the institutional context (especially the educational system, an independent and critical media, and historiography). Certain kinds of remembering have been encouraged and other kinds discouraged, but, most importantly, memories are repeatedly contested and examined with respectful attention to their efficacy in the present. Transformed domestic practices and institutional contexts necessarily go hand in hand. They have enabled many German men to think of themselves as substantially different from past historical male selves in Germany. The same goes for German women, whom I have here addressed only indirectly.

In short, the way in which heterosexuality has been reconstituted in Germany indicates a post-1945 rupture in fantasy and practice. Likewise, historical memory, having been shaken by the

'68 generation's questioning of authority and by historical revisionist work, now offers a plethora of group narratives, some continuous, some discontinuous, from which to understand German history and in which one can situate oneself. Both "the peoples" and their "histories" have been pluralized and non-romantically politicized. In public discourse, the everyday, myths of the autonomy and grandiosity of culture, physical and social reproduction, and questions of aesthetics are also now most often seen not as private, natural, and separate from but as constitutive of present power and politics (for a history of some of these transformations, see Elias 1989).

If, as I assume, the possibilities for a future Europe rest on a transformation in the necessarily linked concepts of heterosexuality and territorial sovereignty, then a critique of the domestic practices and historiography of each of its member nations is our first task as scholars of Europe. This means a deconstruction of "the people" and "its history"—the very objects the disciplines of anthropology and history often proudly take to be their own. These objects are our non-innocent children. The war in Bosnia was being fought in the name of a facticity, an autonomous people with a continuous history, for which we scholars have created the conditions of possibility. "This chase for autonomy and control in the creation of fictions of the integrity of the individual, the purity of the ethné, and the self-reliance of the nation state was," Michael Geyer (1989: 340) wrote shortly before this war, "the most persistent source of disaster in central European life." The sacrifice of Bosnia-Herzegovina and its violent dissolution—one of the new signs of Europe—demands of us scholars a specific ethical responsibility: to indicate possibilities where heterosexuality and territorial sovereignty can be de-linked, and thereby work toward a world order not predicated on ethnic cleansing.

NOTES

This paper is an expanded version of a talk delivered initially at a SSRC conference on the origins of European identity, organized by Michael Herzfeld at Harvard University, May 6–9, 1993, and published in 1994 in the series Working Papers on Transitions from State Socialism #94.4, pp. 1–45, Cornell Project on Comparative Institutional Analysis (Cornell: Center for International Studies). It benefitted from criticisms as a talk given at a conference on sexuality and the public sphere organized by Michael Warner and Lauren Berlant at Cornell University, April 23, 1994, and finally, at the Department of Anthropology, Cambridge University, May 12, 1995. In addition to the SSRC and the conference organizers, I would like to thank the following grant agencies that have supported various parts of the research that was integral: IREX, MacArthur Foundation Grant from Cornell University's Peace Studies Program, Institute for European Studies at Cornell University, National Council on Soviet and East European Research. These agencies and programs bear no responsibility for the arguments expressed. Finally, I am most grateful to conversations with Eric Kaldor with whom I worked closely on this topic, and to Tone Bringa, who began working in a Bosnian village in 1986, for close readings. They not only corrected my most egregious errors, but also made some key suggestions that have led to substantive changes in several of my interpretations. Also, I thank Stefan Senders for great research assistance, and Jim Steakley and Chris Waters for criticisms of an early version.

1. Specialists in the study of Yugoslavia have often maintained that the lack of a clear (ethnic) majority has been the major obstacle to creating a Yugoslav nation (e.g., Djilas 1958; Halpern 1967; Simic 1991), missing the point that a "clear majority" would have made the political entity "Yugoslavia" itself impossible. The creation of a clear majority was the problem posed for the Yugoslavian state which continued working within an Ottoman model that allowed for participation of different groups, neither coercing them to convert confessions nor sending them into exile (see Banac 1994: 128–151). In a 1971 Yugoslavian census, Serbs comprised 40%, Croats 22%, Muslims 8.5%, Slovenians 8.2%, with 13 other groups, along with "undeclareds" making up the rest. Unlike Serbia and Croatia, Bosnia's ethnic groups were comparatively balanced in terms of numbers— 43.7% Muslim Slavs, 31.3% Serbs, 17.3% Croats—and the largest group, the Muslim Slavs, have long been thought of as a secular, cosmopolitan people content to live at ease with others. But "Muslim Slavs" itself is a conglomerate category, even including such an unsual religious identity as Christian Jehovah's Witnesses. Much of the anthropological literature has focused on describing tribal or familial mentality and the segmentary lineage type of kinship found throughout the Balkans as the model for ethnonational identities, and on explaining how kinship-based identities have fostered ethnic hostilities. The link between ideologies of land, patriliny, and home is in fact found throughout the region, if not throughout Europe. To my knowledge, however, none of this literature has examined critically heterosexual masculinity as generative of the principle of territoriality.

305

2. Although this chapter examines European heterosexuality's relation to territorial sovereignty and genocide in only two historical contexts, it is likely that these institutions are dependent on each other and inextricably linked elsewhere. But they are not related to each other in the same way everywhere, nor do they have the same semantic range in all cultures. Specifically, one should pay close attention in other genocides to the way in which victims are murdered (for example, slitting the throat versus crushing the head or genitals), for different kinds of fantasies (some nonsexual) can serve to motivate humiliation and annihilation. To avoid confusion, I should also stress that heterosexuality as a political program is not necessarily the opposite of homosexuality (same-sex relations). In Western ideology they are not always asymmetrical counterconcepts, for European homosexuality has historically been a subset of non-institutionalized practices and identities regulated by heterosexual norms and institutions. Specifically "gay" practices, norms, and identities, for example, are more recent historically—some say even post-Stonewall (post-1969)—and something entirely different from late-nineteenth-century homosexuality (among the more recent theorists, cf. Butler 1993; Halperin 1990; Sedgwick 1990; Warner 1993); they tend toward an institutionalization parallel (and often in opposition) to the process and program of European heterosexuality. Heterosexuality itself is also not a conventionally defined culture—a set of essential, ahistorical characteristics that can be geographically confined —but a set of fluid and variously figured practices, norms, and identifications.

3. Gorbachev's appeal to a "common Europe" is at the level of consciousness. It is still far from realized in any substantive way in political, economic, and cultural practices. It reminds me of Edmund Burke's proclamation in 1796, "No European can be a complete exile in any part of Europe" (cited in Hay 1957: 123)—by which Burke surely meant Western Europe. Hay dates the emergence of "a European self-consciousness" to the fourteenth and fifteenth centuries, in response to a "Christendom weakened by internal contradiction and pressure from without" (1957: 96). This consciousness had little effect on a sense of the political unity of Europe before the second half of the sixteenth century, on a sense of the cultural and economic unity of Europe before the seventeenth century. The development of "Europeanism," tied to Enlightenment values of progress, liberty, and freedom (versus the putative lack of those values on other continents), did not have much impact until the end of the eighteenth century.

4. The exceptions to the principle of the nation form within Western Europe confirm its significance, as the rule always lives from its exception. Belgium and Switzerland, for example, both of which contain ethnic

and linguistically distinct groups, have always been thought of as excep-
tional (e.g., non-typical, non-modular) forms of political sovereignty, and
Belgium remains an essentially contested political entity. The United King-
dom might be seen as an alternative to the nation for at least part of
Europe, as an alternative historical answer to the collapse of the Holy
Roman Empire (as well as its successor). Yet the Glorious Revolution in
England in 1689 was at its time interpreted as a reaffirmation of the
reliability of the nation-state, and not as an alternative to it.

5. A cursory review of clinical and psychoanalytic studies of male
rape of men in France, England, Australia, and the United States supports
Brandes's interpretations: most rapists are attempting to validate a heterosexual masculinity through a demasculinization/feminization of the
victim. The frequency with which the offender gets the victim to ejaculate
indicates that the idea of pleasure at being raped is part of the fantasy of
the rapist, however misplaced this projection may be with respect to the
victim. There is inconclusive evidence for the thesis either that most victims of rape are women, and practically no evidence for the assumption
that rape "reflects a homosexual orientation on the part of the offender"
(Groth and Burgess 1980: 809; see also Anderson 1981–2: 145–162; Mezey
and King 1989: 205–209).

6. Whether institutionalized heterosexuality is universal, as argued
by Adrienne Rich (1981), who initially opened up research into what she
called "compulsory heterosexuality," is irrelevant for my argument here. I
am merely interested in the articulation of these two syndromes of male
heterosexuality—fear of sexual inadequacy in satisfying women and of
awakened anal desire—and in their relationship to territorial sovereignty.

7. The United Nations–initiated Vance-Owen peace plan for Bosnia,
first proposed in 1991, also worked within conventional categories of folk
and history, proposing division of the country into three different ethnic
enclaves. No provision was made for a possible fourth enclave that would
include those individuals who were either themselves mixed or were interested in living in non-ethnically defined enclaves (see the critiques in Ali
and Lifschultz 1993). On anthropology's role in constructing the people in
another massacre situation, Sri Lanka, see Spencer 1990; Tambiah 1986.
On the role of masculinity in Sri Lankan violence, see Kapferer 1988.

8. Indeed, the U.N. role in supporting the Serbian and Croatian
dismemberment of Bosnia-Herzegovina cannot be understood apart from
its official representation as a "humanitarian" mission isolated from and
in opposition to economic or military interests. It is almost as if the U.N.

has to ignore the specifically human conditions and historical contingencies—of kinship, of the economic and political nature of tribal identities, of Cold War subventions of local divisions—in order to justify a world interest in intervention.

9. In a very rich analysis of the Yugoslav national project, Andrei Simic argues that it failed largely because of a "lingering traditionalism." The people were caught because of "narrowly conceived ethnic and chauvinist tendencies . . . and the exigencies of the larger Yugoslav state" (1991: 21). He points to the lack of "larger multinational or supranational political units based on principles transcending the more limited scope of tribalism, regionalism, and ethnicity" (1991: 18). For evidence, he focuses on the Serbs and points to the way in which the moral community of the folk is reduced to the family or lineage, conceived as opposed to other similarly organized groups, with no universalist pretensions of being part of a human community where "the same moral standards should be applied evenhandedly to every one" (1991: 30). Certainly the universalistic standards he wishes for are no guarantee that the moral community will be extended beyond the nation. Nor do I think they are a solution to ethnic particularism. During the Cold War, for example, neither France (in Algeria) nor the United States (in Vietnam), both countries with strong universalist traditions, seemed to have problems applying their own moral standards consistently to other nations. My analysis in this chapter has been more limited, dealing only with an account of ethnic cleansing in terms of the relation of a particular form of heterosexual masculinity to territorial sovereignty. Although I have not tried to account for the failure of Yugoslav nation building, nor for the specific triggers that broadened the conflicts into a genocidal war, such an account would have to go beyond the notion that any universalist ideology would have spared victims the chauvinisms derived from traditionalism.

10. For example, the Defense Minister of Croatia, Gojiko Susak, emigrated from Herzegovina to Canada in 1967, and there headed an émigré organization of 100,000 with 37 cultural schools and 33 folklore groups and with links to the 1,000,000 Croat émigrés in the United States. Using this network and the several million dollars he had earned from his Ottawan pizza empire, he repatriated to Croatia and financed President Tudjman's first campaign because, the New York Times notes, Tudjman's party represented itself as "the most Croat party" (Kifner 1994: 14).

11. Serbian and Croatian voices were not unitary, but most of the oppositional voices to the official nationalist ones were either forced into emigration or silenced at home. It is worth noting that the peace move-

ments in both Serbia and Croatia have been dominated by women who in this region have traditionally had less access to voicing than men.

12. Even reporting sympathetic to rape victims tends to emplot the rapes in a sociobiological story. For example, commenting on the rape of men, the Croat writer Butkovic reports that "raped men suffer life-long bodily and spiritual consequences, of which the most important is the almost usual impotence. So, just like the raped Muslim women, so too raped Muslim men are intentionally eliminated from the reproductive cycle, and that too is a means of fully deliberate genocide" (1993: 8, translation from Croat by Chip Gagnon).

13. Outside the field of anthropology, the problem is not so much aestheticizing masculinity as ignoring it. Even the best academic work on genocide, such as that by Dekmajian 1986, Fein 1993, or Melson 1992, tends to view genocide as caused either by an anthropomorphized state or a "strategy that ruling elites use to resolve real solidarity or legitimacy conflicts or challenges to their interests" (Fein 1993: 813). This explanation is correct as far as it goes, but it reduces the perpetrators (nearly always men defined in opposition to women) to system-effects rather than accounting for their motivations to partake in the massacres and other actions designed to destroy the biological and social reproduction of a group.

14. The historical connection between the international order and a particular form of group and gender/sexual identity deserves further research. For a start, see Wischenbart (1993) who ties the creation of majorities to the exclusion of minorities in the development of Central European states. The connection between genocide and the territorial state is made explicit by Adam Kuper, who writes, "that the sovereign territorial state claims, as an integral part of its sovereignty, the right to commit genocide, or engage in genocidal massacres, against peoples under its rule, and that the United Nations, for all practical purposes, defends this right" (1981: 61).

15. The position I take with regard to culture, in particular German culture, is at odds with the spirit of Alan Dundes's study of German folklore and literature. Dundes sought to establish "the continuity of German national character with respect to anality" (1984: 149). Whether true or false, such theses positing continuities at such a general level tend to be essentialist and conservative in nature; they support the perpetuation of ethnic or national stereotypes. Establishing a continuity of traits in national character is less revealing for the social scientist or the historian than understanding the historically specific conditions and mechanisms

309

that make the continuity or change of specific dispositions and practices possible and probable.

16. It is important to note that Nazi ideology represented the military Männerbund, a comradeship-in-arms, as central to the historical formation of the state and the family, for whose benefit the woman sacrificed herself as a social complement to male solidarity. The male culture of the Männerbund—erotically charged and based on sublimated homosexual desire-was supported and exploited by Heinrich Himmler, the head of the SS, among other top brass, who periodically tried to purge state organizations of homosexual practices (Mosse 1985; for an overview of literature on male bonding, militarism, and German nationalism, see Oosterhuis 1991: 241–259). The Nazi kind of homoeroticism was explicitly anti-female, presupposing and relying for sense upon the same two-gender, heterosexual model that I have outlined as characteristic for the Balkans. In contrast, postwar American or Western European male homosexuality most often explicitly rejects this model of heterosexuality, instead drawing its meaning from a same-sex love not predicated on opposition to and completion with the female (that is, on two genders). Gay male projects overlap considerably with feminist ones where the goals are not organized in terms of heteronormativity.

17. As Sieghart writes, international law has always "demanded substantial protection for the aliens within a State, while demanding none for the State's own citizens" (1983: 12). For an attempt to rethink territoriality within international relations theory, see Ruggie 1993. For an alternative "human rights approach" within international law, see McCorquondale 1994: 857–884.

18. Amnesty International estimates that close to 10,000 deserters from Serbia and Montenegro alone live in Germany. During the war they faced a maximum prison sentence in their home countries of fifteen years for desertion, with ten years if they did not initially appear for their induction (Schneider 1995: 3).

REFERENCES

Ali, Rabia, and Lawrence Lifschultz, eds.
>1993. *Why Bosnia? Writings on the Balkan War.* Stony Creek, Conn.: The Pamphleteer's Press, Inc.

Amnesty International
>1993. *Bosnia-Herzegovina: Rape and Sexual Abuse by Armed Forces.* New York: Amnesty International U.S.A.

1992. *Bosnia-Herzegovina: Gross Abuses of Human Rights.* New York: Amnesty International U.S.A.

Anderson, Craig L.
1981–82. "Males as Sexual Assault Victims: Multiple Levels of Trauma." *Journal of Homosexuality* 7 (2–3): 145–162

Arendt, Hannah
1951 [1968]. *The Origin of Totalitarianism, Part Two: Imperialism.* San Diego: Harcourt Brace Jovanovich

Balibar, Etienne
1991. The Nation Form: History and Ideology. In *Race, Nation, Class: Ambiguous Identities.* E. Balibar and I. Wallerstein, eds. Pp. 622–633. New York: Routledge

Banac, Ivo
1994. Bosnian Muslims: From Religious Community to Socialist Nationhood and Postcommunist Statehood, 1918–1992. In *The Muslims of Bosnia-Herzegovina.* Mark Pinson, ed. Cambridge: Harvard University Press

Benard, Cheryl, and Edit Schlaffer
1993. "Die geborenen Monster?" *Der Spiegel* 14: 176–185

Bodin, Jean
1576 [1955]. *Six Books of the Commonwealth.* New York: MacMillan

Borneman, John
1992. *Belonging in the Two Berlins: Kin, State, Nation.* Cambridge: Cambridge University Press
1991. *After the Wall: East Meets West in the New Berlin.* New York: Basic Books

Brandes, Stanley
1980. *Metaphors of Masculinity: Sex and Status in Andalusian Folklore.* Pittsburgh: University of Pennsylvania Press

Branson, Louise
1993. "Sexual Abuse of POWs Widespread in Yugoslav War." *The Straits Times,* (August 2): 13

Brubaker, Rogers
1992. *Citizenship and Nationhood in France and Germany.* Cambridge: Harvard University Press

Bude, Heinz
1992. *Bilanz der Nachfolge. Die Bundesrepublik und der Nationalsozialismus.* Frankfurt a.M.: Suhrkamp

Burns, John F.
1992. "Ghosts fill nights for Serbian fighter." *The New York Times,* November 27, p. A12

311

Butkovic, Davor
>	1993. "Srbi siluju i muskarce" (Serbs rape men too), *Globus* (Zagreb), January 22, pp. 7–8
Butler, Judith
>	1993. *Bodies That Matter: On the Discursive Limits of "Sex."* New York: Routledge
Caruth, Cathy
>	1991. "Introduction." *American Imago: Studies in Psychoanalysis and Culture* 48 (1): 1–13
Clebsch, William
>	1979. *Christianity in European History.* New York: Oxford University Press
Dekmejian, R. H.
>	1986. Determinants of Genocide: Armenians and Jews as Case Studies. In *The Armenian Genocide in Perspective*. R. Houvannisian, ed. New Brunswick, N.J.: Transaction Press
Denitch, Bogdan
>	1993. A Personal Report: The Last Days of Yugoslavia. In *Why Bosnia?* Rabia Ali and Lawrence Lifschultz, eds. Pp. 286–299. Stony Creek, Conn.: The Pamphleteer's Press
Derrida, Jacques
>	1992. *The Other Heading: Reflections on Today's Europe.* Bloomington: Indiana University Press
Djilas, Milovan
>	1958. *Land Without Justice.* New York: Harcourt, Brace, and World
Drakulic, Slavenka
>	1993. "Women Hide Behind a Wall of Silence." *The Nation* (March 1): 1–272
Dundes, Alan
>	1984. *Life is Like a Chicken Coop Ladder: A Portrait of German Culture Through Folklore.* New York: Columbia University Press
Elias, Norbert
>	1989. *Studien über die Deutschen.* Frankfurt a/M: Suhrkamp
Evans-Pritchard, E.E.
>	1940. *The Nuer: A Description of the Modes of Livelihood and Political Institutions of a Nilotic People.* Oxford: Clarendon Press
Fabian, Johannes
>	1983. *Time and the Other: How Anthropology Makes its Object.* New York: Columbia University Press

Faubion, James
> 1993. *Modern Greek Lessons: A Primer in Historical Construc-tivism*. Princeton: Princeton University Press

Fein, Helen
> 1993. "Revolutionary and Antirevolutionary Genocides: A Com-parison of State Murders in Democratic Kampuchea, 1975 to 1979, and in Indonesia, 1965 to 1966." *Comparative Studies in Society and History* 35 (4): 796–823

Final Report of the United Nations Commission of Experts
> 1994. *Rape and Sexual Assault*, Add. 2 (Vol. V) 28, December. Director M. Cherif Bassiouni, Commission of Experts estab-lished Pursuant to Security Council Resolution 780

Foster, George M.
> 1953. "What is Folk Culture?" *American Anthropologist* 55 (2): 159–173

Geyer, Michael
> 1993. "Resistance as Ongoing Project: Visions of Order, Obliga-tions to Strangers, Struggles for Civil Society." *Journal of Mod-ern History* 64: S217–S241
> 1992. "The Stigma of Violence, Nationalism, and War in Twen-tieth-Century Germany." *German Studies Review* (Special Is-sue, Winter): 75–110
> 1989. "Historical Fictions of Autonomy and the Europeanization of National History." *Central European History* 22 (3/4): 316–342

Glenny, Misha
> 1992. *The Fall of Yugoslavia: The Third Balkan War.* New York: Penguin Books

Gorbachev, Mikhail
> 1987. *Perestroika*. New York: HarperCollins

Groth, Nicholas, and Ann Burgess
> 1980. "Male Rape: Offenders and Victims." *American Journal of Psychiatry* 137 (7): 806–810

Haller, Dieter
> 1992. "Homosexuality in Seville." *SOLGAN* 14 (3): 27–35

Halperin, David
> 1990. *One Hundred Years of Homosexuality*. New York: Routledge

Halpern, Joel
> 1967. *A Serbian Village*. New York: Harper Colophon Books

Hay, Denys
> 1957. *Europe: The Emergence of an Idea*. New York: Harper & Row

Helsinki Watch
> 1992. *War Crimes in Bosnia-Herzegovina.* New York: Human
> Rights Watch

Herzfeld, Michael
> 1987a. *Anthropology Through the Looking Glass.* Cambridge:
> Cambridge University Press
> 1987b. "As in your own house": Hospitality, ethnography, and
> the stereotype of Mediterranean society. In *Honor and Shame
> and the Unity of the Mediterranean.* David Gilmore, ed. Pp. 75–
> 89. Washington, D.C.: American Anthropological Association
> 1985. *The Poetics of Manhood: Contest and Identity in a Cretan
> Mountain Village.* Princeton: Princeton University Press

Hocquenhem, Guy
> 1972. *Homosexual Desire.* London: Allison & Busby

Horwitz, Tony
> 1993. "Balkan Death Trip: Scenes from a futile war." *Harper's*
> 1714: 35–36

Israel, Fred L., ed.
> 1967. *Major Peace Treaties of Modern History, 1648–1967,* Vol.
> 1. Pp. 7–49. New York: Chelsea Moose

Kaldor, Eric
> 1993. The War in Yugoslavia: As seen by a spectator. Senior
> Honor's Thesis, Cornell University

Kamm, Henry
> 1993. "End of Communism Worsens Anti-Gypsy Racism." *The
> New York Times* (November 17), p. 3

Kantorowicz, Ernst
> 1957. *The King's Two Bodies: A Study in Mediaeval Political
> Theology.* Princeton: Princeton University Press

Kapferer, Bruce
> 1988. *Legends of People, Myths of State: Violence, Intolerance,
> and Political Culture in Sri Lanka and Australia.* Washington,
> D.C.: Smithsonian Institution Press

Kifner, John
> 1994. "From Pizza Man in Canada to Croatian Kingmaker."
> *The New York Times* (January 16), p. 14

Koonz, Claudia
> 1993. "Ethical Dilemmas and Nazi Eugenics: Single-Issue Dis-
> sent in Religious Contexts." *Journal of Modern History* 64:
> S8–S31

Kuper, Adam
    1981. *Genocide: Its Political Use in the Twentieth Century.* New Haven: Yale University Press

Laqueur, Thomas
    1990. *Making Sex: Body and Gender from the Greeks to Freud.* Cambridge: Harvard University Press

Lepsius, M. Rainer
    1988. Das Der europäische Nationalstaat: Erbe und Zukunft. In *Interessen, Ideen und Institutionen.* Pp. 256–269. Opladen: Westdeutscher Verlag

Lüdke, Alf
    1993. "The Appeal of Exterminating 'Others': German Workers and the Limits of Resistance." *Journal of Modern History* 64: S46–S67

McCorquondale, Robert
    1994. "Self-Determination: A Human Rights Approach." *International and Comparative Law Quarterly* 43 (4): 857–884

Melson, Robert
    1992. *Revolution and Genocide: On the Origins of the Armenian Genocide and the Holocaust.* Chicago: University of Chicago Press

Mezey, Gillian, and Michael King
    1989. "The Effect of Sexual Assault on Men: A Survey of 22 Victims." *Psychological Medicine* 19 (1): 205–209

Mitscherlich, Alexander and Margarete
    1967. *Die Unfähigkeit zu trauern. Grundlagen kollektiven Verhaltens.* Munich: Piper

Mosse, George
    1985. *Nationalism and Sexuality: Respectability and Abnormal Sexuality in Modern Europe.* New York: H. Fertig

Oosterhuis, Harry
    1991. "Male Bonding and Homosexuality in German Nationalism." *Journal of Homosexuality* 22 (1/2): 241–264

Parin, Paul
    1993. Das Bluten aufgerissener Wunden. In *Massenvergewaltigung: Krieg gegen die Frauen.* Alexandra Stiglmayer, ed. Pp. 58–86. Frankfurt a/M: Fischer

Pina-Cabral, Joâo de
    1989. "The Mediterranean as a Category of Regional Comparison." *A Critical View* 30 (1): 399–406

Pitt-Rivers, Julian

> 1971 (1954). *The People of the Sierra*. Chicago: University of Chicago Press
>
> 1968. "Honor." *Encyclopedia of the Social Sciences* 6: 503–511
>
> 1966. Honour and Social Status. In *Honour and Shame: The Values of Mediterranean Society*. J.G. Peristiany, ed. Pg. 7–18. Chicago: University of Chicago Press

Phillips, Andrew

> 1991. Guns of Autumn. *MacLeans*, Vol. 104, No. 40 (October 7): 42–46

Post, Tom, *et al.*

> 1993. "A Pattern of Rape." *Newsweek* (January 4): 34–35

Redfield, Robert

> 1953 (1969). *The Primitive World and its Transformations*. Ithaca: Cornell University Press

Rich, Adrienne

> 1981. *Compulsory Heterosexuality and Lesbian Existence*. London: Onlywomen Press

Ruggie, John

> 1993. "Territoriality and Beyond: Problematizing Modernity in International Relations." *International Organization* 47 (Winter): 151–152

Schmitt, Carl

> 1991 (1932). *Der Begriff des Politischen: Text von 1932 mit einem Vorwort und drei Corollarien*. Berlin: Duncker und Humblot
>
> 1986 (1919). *Political Romanticism*, transl. Guy Oakes. Cambridge: MIT Press
>
> 1985 (1923). *The Crisis of Parliamentary Democracy*. Cambridge: MIT Press

Schneider, Jens

> 1995. "Kanonenfutter mit deutschem Gütessiegel." *Süddeutsche Zeitung* (January 24): 3

Sedgwick, Eve Kosofsky

> 1990. *Epistemology of the Closet*. Berkeley: University of California Press

Seifert, Ruth

> 1993. Krieg und Vergewaltigung. In *Massenvergewaltigung: Krieg gegen die Frauen*. Alexandra Stiglmayer, ed. Pp. 87–112. Frankfurt a/M: Fischer

Sieghart, Paul
    1983. *The International Law of Human Rights*. Oxford: Clarendon Press
Simic, Andrei
    1991. "Obstacles to the Development of a Yugoslav National Consciousness: Ethnic Identity and Folk Culture in the Balkans." *Journal of Mediterranean Studies* 1 (1): 18–36
Spencer, Jonathan
    1990. "Writing Within: Anthropology, Nationalism, and Culture in Sri Lanka." *Current Anthropology* 31 (3) (June 1990): 283–300
Tambiah, Stanley
    1986. *Sri Lanka: Ethnic Fratricide and the Dismantling of Democracy*. Chicago: University of Chicago Press
Trommler, Frank
    1993. "Between Normality and Resistance: Catastrophic Gradualism in Nazi Germany." *Journal of Modern History* 64: S82–S101
Warner, Michael, ed.
    1993. *Fear of a Queer Planet*. Minneapolis: University of Minnesota Press
Wischenbart, Rüdiger
    1993. *Karpaten. Die dunkle Seite Europas*. Wien: Kremayr & Scherlau
Wolf, Eric
    1982. *Europe and The People Without History*. Berkeley: University of California Press
Zolberg, Aristide
    1983. "The Formation of New States as a Refugee-Generating Process." *The Annals* 467: 24–38
Zülch, Tilman, ed.
    "Ethnische Säuberung"—Völkermord für "Großserbien." Hamburg: Luchterhand

INDEX

Dolgin, J. L., 263
domestic policy, 30–31
domestic sphere, 15
domination, 119, 170
  and discourse, 206
  first world, 3
  legitimation of, 213n. 7
domino effect, 158–159
Dotterweich, V., 149n. 8
Doyle, B. W., 80
Drakulic, S., 291, 296–297
Drinnon, R., 35, 46
dual organization, 16, 157, 171–172, 224
Dumont, L., 200, 202, 215n. 13, 259, 263
Dundes, A., 309n. 15
Durkheim, E., 57, 81, 201

East bloc, 178, 180, 235
East Germany. *See* GDR
  (German Democratic
  Republic)
Eckermann, J. P., 204
Education, 18
  after Auschwitz, 221–232, 234
  antifascist, 18, 223, 234
  authoritarian, 113
  Cold War, 226
    and after, 221, 224, 238
  and domestic social relations, 32
  evaluation of, 18, 223
  formal, 235
  general, 32, 34
  German, 222, 224
    FRG system of
      reforms in, 197
    GDR system of, 153–154, 163, 234
      reforms in, 196
  literary, 31
  of masses, 231
  postwar achievements of, 235
  and responsibility, 239

elections, pan-German, 108–109, 199
Elias, N., 87, 111, 304
elites, FRG, 110
emigration, accounts of Cuban, 256
England. *See* Britain
enlightenment
  project, 33
  tradition, 10
Enzensberger, H. M., 7
eroticization, in German unification, 15, 114
ethnic cleansing, 19–21, 222–275, 278, 286–287, 304
  as natural, 296
  role of women in, 295
ethnicity, 11–12, 14, 57–58, 79–80, 139, 263–264, 287–288, 291, 293, 297, 308n. 9
  resurgence of, 38
  and identity, 47
  See also identity, ethnic;
    identification, ethnic
Europe, 12, 21 23, 130, 273, 276, 296
  common, 306n. 3
  ethnic cleansing in, 274
  future, 304
  idea of, 275
  refiguring of, 275
  regions of
    East-Central, 13
    Eastern, 110, 144, 177, 233
    Northern, 21
    Western, 110, 116, 176
  as self-representation, 280
  without borders, 153
European
  categories of
    East, 111
    West, 13, 111
  category of, 12
    in Germany, 12
    in France, 12

inscription of, 15
intergroup, 57
intragroup, 57
Jewish, 141
  and Israel, 143
and metaphor, 263
and narrative, 129
national, 1, 58, 78, 239
  in Berlin, 14
nationalist, 176
negative, 280
recovery, 38
regional, 80
sexual, 19
  homosexual, 161, 264
  heterosexual, 264
and state authority, 2
and territoriality, 2
tribal, 1
ideology, 2, 14, 17, 192, 194
  communist, 193, 215n. 14
  and distancing, 225
  and education, 31
  German, 200, 303
  liberal democratic, 238
  Nazi, 201, 215n. 14, 301, 303,
      310n. 16. *See also* Nazi;
      Third Reich
  political, 138
  supranational
    and Cold War, 224
imaginary, 104
immigration, 20, 31, 35, 48, 175,
    253–258, 262–263, 267
  American, 250, 266
  law, 250, 265
  policy, 265
  and family, 265–266
  and homosexuality, 266
  as penetration, 249
incest, 114
India, 3
intellectuals, 14, 18, 182, 226–
    227, 231, 240
  critical, 230

German
  FRG, 241n. 3
  GDR, 228, 233–235, 238
    generation I, 234
    generation II, 229, 234,
    generation III, 232
  responsibility of, 239
  role of, 221
  Western, 232
  responsibility of, 19
interdisciplinarity, 15
international order, 2, 4–5, 12,
    14, 16, 43, 129, 190,
    193, 309n. 14
  and anthropology, 30, 48
  disorder, 6
  and domesticity, 298
  and ethnic cleansing, 289
  local practice and, 12
  and technology, 7
Israel, 134, 140–141, 143, 278

Jackson, M., 262
Jaimes, M. A., 40
Jakupovic, E., 292
Jameson, F., 8
Japan, 133
Jefferson, T., 35
Jews in Germany, 132
  See also assimilation; identifi-
    cation, German Jewish
JFK, 179
Judaism, 132, 137, 139
June Cleaver, 195, 198–199, 207
  as genre, 190
  romance, 190
  satire, 192
Jus Sanguinis, 165

Kaldor, E., 287, 296
Kantorowicz, E., 277
Kaplan, R. D., 7, 50n. 6
Kays, J., 83
Keesing, R., 30, 39, 48
Kellock, E. M., 87